T0222110

Lecture Notes in Computer Science　　10754

Commenced Publication in 1973
Founding and Former Series Editors:
Gerhard Goos, Juris Hartmanis, and Jan van Leeuwen

More information about this series at http://www.springer.com/series/7409

Marinos Ioannides · João Martins
Roko Žarnić · Veranika Lim (Eds.)

Advances in Digital Cultural Heritage

International Workshop
Funchal, Madeira, Portugal, June 28, 2017
Revised Selected Papers

 Springer

Editors
Marinos Ioannides
Cyprus University of Technology
Limassol
Cyprus

João Martins
Universidade Nova de Lisboa
Caparica
Portugal

Roko Žarnić
University of Ljubljana
Ljubljana
Slovenia

Veranika Lim
Imperial College London
London
UK

ISSN 0302-9743   ISSN 1611-3349   (electronic)
Lecture Notes in Computer Science
ISBN 978-3-319-75788-9   ISBN 978-3-319-75789-6   (eBook)
https://doi.org/10.1007/978-3-319-75789-6

Library of Congress Control Number: 2018934320

LNCS Sublibrary: SL3 – Information Systems and Applications, incl. Internet/Web, and HCI

Cover illustration: Historical image and the resulting 3D model of the City Hall of Calw. Created by Anastasios Doulamis et al., 4D Modelling in Cultural Heritage. LNCS 10754, p. 190. Used with permission.

Printed on acid-free paper

This Springer imprint is published by the registered company Springer International Publishing AG part of Springer Nature
The registered company address is: Gewerbestrasse 11, 6330 Cham, Switzerland

Preface

The rich cultural heritage of Europe permanently challenges researchers and professionals to be active in its preservation and integration in contemporary life. The knowledge gained from research and preventive conservation activities is a basis for sustainable use of heritage assets which significantly contributes to the European economy and well-being of its citizens. European knowledge about heritage management has global value because it can be well applied in other, non-European cultural environments.

The fast development of IT technologies in recent decades offers new tools, protocols, and procedures. They rapidly change traditional approaches to heritage preservation bringing high precision and cost-effective documentation methodologies, efficient preventive conservation techniques, and new tools for partial or full reconstruction of assets. This is of particular importance when heritage is exposed to man-made, technological, and/or environmental hazards.

European countries and the European Commission invest a large amount of research funds in the cultural heritage domain because it bears historic evidence of cultural development of regions and nations and fosters sustainable economic growth. In the current EU research program Horizon 2020, one of the important research topics addresses resilience of cultural heritage assets because cultural heritage is under continuous pressure of change, deterioration, and destruction. Research outcomes should contribute to a more accurate identification and risk monitoring along with the development of appropriate measures to increase cultural heritage resilience. Activities toward the establishment of a European system of data collection and its application in the field of preventive conservation are an on-going process where the issue of risks and resilience is well addressed. The European Commission and its member states are fully aware of the importance of developing IT technologies and the possibilities that they are offering to researchers engaged in heritage preservation.

A good example is COST Action TD 1406 entitled "Innovation in Intelligent Management of Heritage Buildings (i2MHB)." The objective of this Action is to create a pan-European open network, to promote synergies between heritage science specialists, industrial stakeholders, and research/education players, so as to achieve a unified common understanding and operation in the heritage buildings domain, integrating multidisciplinary expertise, technology, and know-how through a novel and independent global framework.

Researchers taking part in this Action organized the "Workshop on Advances in Digital Cultural Heritage" as a multidisciplinary, interdisciplinary, and intersectorial event during the IEEE International Conference on Engineering, Technology, and Innovation, held during June 27–29, 2017, on Madeira, Portugal. The workshop was organized in cooperation with the Digital Research Infrastructure for the Arts and Humanities (DARIAH-CY, EU DARIAH-EU) and key EU-financed projects: FP7 Marie Curie ITN-DCH, FP7 Marie-Curie 4D-CH-WORLD, H2020 INCEPTION, H2020 ViMM, and INTERREG V SUDOE SHCity.

The main objective of the workshop was to present recent developments and applications of IT technologies for cultural heritage preservation, namely:

- Demonstration of the advantages of new-generation equipment for mapping, digital survey, and documentation of heritage assets and sites
- Presentation of technologies for digitalization, optimal documentation, and information sharing on cultural heritage
- Tools and procedures for social interaction enhancing, fostering awareness, and participation
- Rising of the knowledge level in the domain of IT applications for cultural heritage preservation
- Usage of virtual reality for better understanding and learning on cultural heritage

The aim of this book is to contribute to the knowledge concerning the usage of IT technologies in cultural heritage preservation and management, through proper documentation as well in fostering citizens' engagement. The book is a valuable state-of-the art source for future studies, empowering further research and professional activities, supported by the presented digital cultural heritage experiences of the contributing authors.

A final word of appreciation to the ICE/IEEE ITMC Conference organizers and Madeira's Regional Government for their strong support that contributed to the success of the Workshop on Advances in Digital Cultural Heritage.

June 2017

Marinos Ioannides
João Martins
Roko Žarnić
Veranika Lim

Acknowledgments and Disclaimer. The Workshop on Advances on Digital Heritage was part of the activities of the EU COST Action TD1406 supported by the EU COST Programme. The event was in cooperation with the EU projects FP7 PEOPLE ITN2013 ITN-DCH and IAPP2012 4D-CH-WORLD, the DARIAH-EU ERIC, the EU DARIAH-CY, the EU H2020 INCEPTION, the EU H2020 CSA ViMM, the CIP ICT-PSP Europeana-Space, and the CIP ICT-PSP LoCloud.

However, the content of this publication reflects only the authors' views; the European Commission, the CIPA, ICOMOS, Cyprus University of Technology, all the ITN-DCH partners/institutions, supervisors, and associated partners/institutions, and the EU COST Action TD1406 partners and institutions as well as the EU projects FP7 PEOPLE ITN2013 ITN-DCH and IAPP2012 4D-CH-WORLD, the DARIAH-EU ERIC, the EU DARIAH-CY, the EU H2020 INCEPTION, the EU H2020 CSA ViMM, the CIP ICT-PSP Europeana-Space, and the CIP ICT-PSP LoCloud are not liable for any use that may be made of the information contained herein.

Contents

Unmanned Aerial Vehicles and the Multi Temporal Mapping Results of the Dispilio Lakeside Prehistoric Settlement

Dimitris Kaimaris, Charalampos Georgiadis, Olga Georgoula,
and Petros Patias(✉)

Aristotle University of Thessaloniki, 54124 Thessaloniki, Greece
{kaimaris,harrisg,olge,patias}@auth.gr

Abstract. In this paper the authors present the evolution of the Unmanned Aerial Vehicles (UAV) and photogrammetric processing software technology through the multi temporal mapping of the lakeside Palaeolithic settlement of Dispilio (Kastoria, Greece). The study of the settlement initiated in 2006 using a Remote Control (RC) Helicopter, which was not equipped with an automated navigation and image acquisition system. Currently a multi-copter drone is used that can demonstrate flight stability, is capable of hovering in small heights and is equipped with an automated navigation and image acquisition system. With respect to the photogrammetric processing software at the start of the study specialized single image processing software like Bentley IRAS/c® were used for the production of rectified images, followed by the use of stereo image processing software like LPS® (Erdas) that have the ability to produce B/W Digital Terrain Models (DTM) and ortho rectified images. Currently specialized multi photo processing software is used like Agisoft Photoscan® or Imagine UAV® (Erdas) that the ability to produce dense coloured point clouds and ortho rectified images.

Keywords: UAV · Photo processing software · Laser scanner
DSM · DTM · Orthophotos

1 Introduction

According to the definition which was given by the association UVS International - an international non - profit association registered with the Chamber Commercial of Hague, unmanned aerial vehicles (UAV) (or Remotely Piloted Vehicle (RPV), Remotely Operated Aircraft (ROA), Remotely Piloted Aircraft (RPA) and Unmanned Vehicle Systems (UVS) are aircrafts designed to operate without the presence of pilot [1].

The documentation of Cultural Heritage has been one of the earliest application areas of UAVs. There are several reasons for this [2–21]:

- The archaeological sites require a very detailed and a large-scale mapping (normally 1:50–1:500). This requirement cannot be met by regular aerial photography, due to high flying height, small scale and relatively low image resolution.

© Springer International Publishing AG, part of Springer Nature 2018
M. Ioannides et al. (Eds.): Digital Cultural Heritage 2017, LNCS 10754, pp. 1–14, 2018.
https://doi.org/10.1007/978-3-319-75789-6_1

- Additional, UAV overcomes difficulties of ground surveys, as terrain restrictions, country restrictions, high costs and most importantly due to limited amount of ground detail that can be mapped.
- Documentation speed and timely mapping are additional important factors of advantages of UAVs.

The first experiment was a 3 m long airplane (fixed wing UAV), with a flying height of 150 m [19], which was followed by the first model helicopter (rotary wing UAV), with a flying height up to 100 m, equipped with a medium format Rolleiflex camera in 1980.

During the course of time, UAV technology is established as a preferred solution to CH aerial documentation, since additional benefits have been proved [2–21]:

- Decrease of technology costs with the use of low cost and low weight gyroscopes, GPS, INS, etc.
- Estimation of the orientation elements of the camera, thus decrease of the time of the photogrammetric procession of data due to higher accuracy sensors.
- Potential increase of the payload which permits the use of a variety of multispectral sensors and Lidars.
- Capacity of immediate flight and friendly navigation tools, even in areas that - mainly for military reasons- the flights are prohibited.

In this paper the authors present the evolution of the Unmanned Aerial Vehicles (UAV) and photogrammetric processing software technology through the multi temporal mapping of the lakeside Palaeolithic settlement of Dispilio (Kastoria, Greece, Fig. 1).

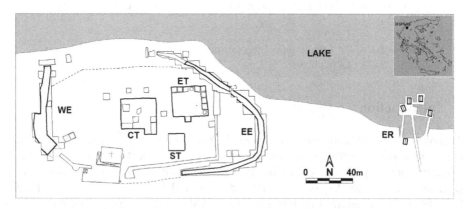

Fig. 1. The archaeological site of the prehistoric Dispilio settlement with the sites: West wall-WE, Central trench-CT, East trench-ET, East wall-EE, South trench-ST, and the modern day representation of the huts-ER.

2 Study Area

The Prehistoric settlement of Dispilio is located north of the modern Dispilio settlement at the south shore of Lake Orestiada. The settlement was discovered in 1932. It was inhabited between 5,500 and 3,500 B.C and covered an area of approximately 20,000 m^2. The pitched roof huts were constructed using wooden structural elements (coniferous trees). They were seated in platforms located above the lake's water surface. The stone wall which embraced the buildings and mainly protected them against the water is dated back to the last years of Bronze Age or at the begging of Iron Age (13–10 century B.C.). Up to date 5,000 m^2 have been excavated (left part of Fig. 1) from an area of approximately 17,000 m^2. Among the retrieved artefacts the wooden inscription which resembles Linear A scripture occupies the top place. It is the older writing sample in Europe as it is dated, based on radio timing, back to 5,250 B.C. Close to the settlement in the east of the archaeological site there is a modern time representation of the Neolithic huts (right part of Fig. 1, ER) [22, 23].

The authors have realized numerous surveys of selected parts of the archaeological site form 2006 and onward using various documentation equipment like total stations, terrestrial laser scanners, RC Helicopter (Fig. 2a). Currently they are equipped with a modern multi copter drone (Fig. 2b). During the testing of the new equipment the full extent of the archaeological site of Dispilio was 3D modelled along with the modern representation of the Neolithic huts (Fig. 1).

3 Multi Temporal Survey of the Site of Dispilio Using Various Digital Sensors and Photogrammetric Processing Software

In 2006 the acquisition of aerial imagery and the production of orthophotos of the west wall (Fig. 1, WE), and the central trench (Fig. 1, CT) of the Dispilio prehistoric settlement was assigned to the AUT (Aristotle University of Thessaloniki) team. The west wall part had a length of 60 m and a width of approximately 15 cm (Fig. 1, WE), while the central trench covered a 30 by 30 m area (Fig. 1, CT). The RC Helicopter equipped with an Olympus C-50 5Mp camera (Fig. 2a) was used for the aerial imagery acquisition. Due to the absence of an automated navigation and image acquisition system the images were acquired manually.

A total of 194 images were acquired. 124 covered the west wall (Fig. 1, WE) and 71 covered the central trench (Fig. 1, CT). The flight height was between 6 and 50 m (in some extreme cases it reached 2 m) leading to a spatial resolution of 2–17 mm, respectively. The ground control points were using the Greek Coordinate reference system (GGRS) 87. Natural elements and artefacts were used as control points. Following the image acquisition well defined points were selected in the images and measured in the field using a total station. For the photogrammetric processing of single images and the creation of mosaics the Erdas Imagine® software was used. The processing resulted in an accuracy of 4–5 cm for the west wall rectified images, leading to the production of 1:200 scale orthophotos (Fig. 2c). Respectively the rectified images

Fig. 2. a. The RC Helicopter. It has a Lifting capacity of 8 Kgr and it is not equipped with an automated flight control and image acquisition. Length 1.39 m., width 0.15 m., Propeller length 1,53 m., weight 5.10 Kgr. The camera mounting is located in the bottom part of the helicopter. b. The new multi copter drone. c. The 2006 orthophoto (5 × 5 m grid) map of the west wall (Fig. 1, WE).

of the central trench demonstrated an accuracy of 1–2 cm, leading to the production of 1:50 scale orthophotos (Fig. 3).

In 2007 the production of orthophoto maps of the east and central trenches (Fig. 1, EE and CT) was assigned to the AUT team. The images were acquired using the RC Helicopter with a flight height of 5 to 50 m., resulting in images with spatial resolution of 2 to 17 mm respectively. In total 410 images were acquired using the Canon 400D 10.1 Mb camera. 250 covering the central trench (Fig. 1, CT) and 160 covering the east trench (Fig. 1, EE). Pre-defined ground control points (tennis balls) measured in GGRS87 were used for the photogrammetric processing. The single photo processing was realized using Bentley IRAS/C. The accuracy of the produced ortho rectified images was 1 to 2 cm for both trenches, leading to the production of 1:50 scale maps (Figs. 3 and 4).

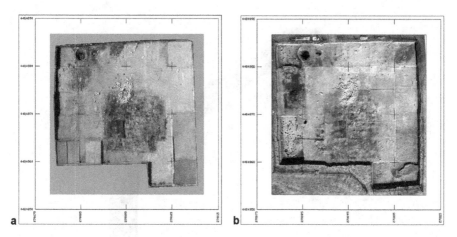

Fig. 3. a. The 2006 orthophoto map (10 × 10 m grid) of the central trench (Fig. 1, CT). b. The 2007 orthophoto map (10 × 10 m grid) of the same position.

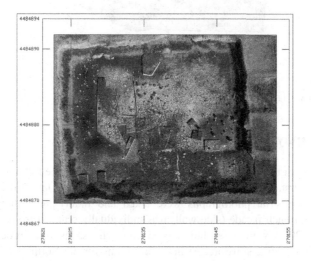

Fig. 4. The 2007 orthophoto map (10 × 10 m grid) of the east trench (Fig. 1, ET).

In 2009 the surveying of the east wall was assigned to the AUT team (Fig. 1, EE). In total 77 ground control points were measured using the GGRS87 reference system. In addition 20 images were acquired (from an average height of 8 m) using the RC Helicopter equipped with the Canon EOS 400D 10.1 Mp camera. The stereo photogrammetric processing of the acquired images for the production of the B/W Digital Terrain Model (DTM), the orthophotos, and the orthophoto mosaics was realized using the Erdas Imagine® LPS software. The accuracy of the produced orthophotos was 1–2 cm leading to the production of 1:50 scale orthophoto map (Fig. 5).

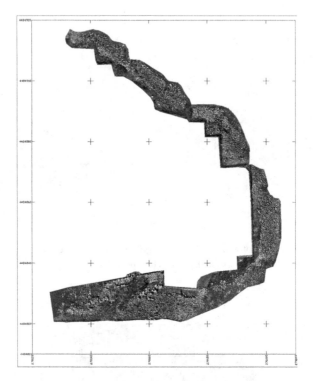

Fig. 5. The 2009 orthophoto map (20 × 20 m grid) of the east wall (Fig. 1, EE).

4 Stratigraphy Mapping Using Laser Scanner

For the mapping of the stratigraphy of the trench (ST) in 2009, the following procedure was applied: at first, the trench facades were scanned using the Optech ILRIS 3D laser scanner, then terrestrial photographs were taken and finally the orthophotos were produced. Each trench façade (side wall) was individually scanned from a distance of approximately 20 m with a resolution of 5 mm. The scans were processed using Innovemetric Polyworks software. At first the 2 scans for the North and South trench facade were merged and then all the scans were merged to a final point cloud. Finally the 3D model (TIN model) of the trench was created and processed in order to fill any holes in the model. After the scanning, terrestrial photographs were also taken. For the creation of the orthorectified images of the side walls of the two trenches, Erdas Imagine software used the calibration archive and the final cloud of the 3D points. The accuracies of the resection solutions were from 0.1 to 0.2 mm and the pixel size of all the orthorectified images of the faces (for example Fig. 6) was 0.2 mm.

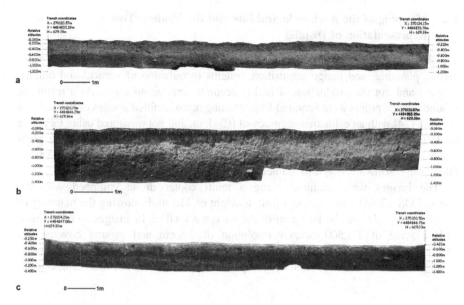

Fig. 6. 3 stratigraphies of the north trench-ST. a. Result of two scans with a spatial resolution of 5 mm and a total of 3,382,495 3D points. b. Result of one scans with a spatial resolution of 6 mm and a total of 840,400 3D points. c. Result of two scans with a spatial resolution of 6 mm and a total of 1,782,669 3D points.

5 The 3D Mapping of Dispilio Using a Multi-copter Drone and Image Processing Using Agisoft Photoscan®

5.1 Multi-copter Drone

The multi-copter drone (Fig. 2b) is equipped with 6 electric motors. It can be navigated either using the remote control or the ground station control software. It can lift off and/or land vertical and has the ability to hover at any height. Its on board equipment and control software allows for automated lift off/landing, planning and realization of a predefined flight and image acquisition. The camera gimbal is capable of 180° vertical rotation (±90° from nadir) during flight. It is also equipped with a live video transmitter that allows the ground control station to receive video in real time during the flight. Its lifting capacity (not taking into account the system's weight) is 2.5 Kgr. That capability allows the mounting of different kind of sensors. Its operational flight time is 15 min.

5.2   Mapping of the Archaeological Site and the Modern Time Representation of Dispilio

The main focus of this study was to test in real time conditions the automated navigation, planning, and image acquisition systems (acquisition of vertical and oblique images) and not the production of highly accurate orthophoto maps. As a result the ground control points were acquired from existing ortho rectified images of the national cadastre [24] with an estimated accuracy of 0.5–1 m, and not measured using GPS or a total station. Furthermore during this mission the creation of coloured dense point clouds, and the creation of very high spatial resolution orthophotos using the Agisoft Photoscan® software was also studied.

The images were acquired using a multi copter drone equipped with the Canon EOS 1200D 18Mp camera from a height of 110 m. Following the planning of the flight (Fig. 7) and the initiation of the survey a total of 19 images were acquired with a scale of 1:6,500, spatial resolution of 2.8 cm and ground coverage of 145 × 97 m per image. The photogrammetric processing (stereo, coloured dense point cloud generation, and production of orthophotos (Figs. 8, 9 and 10) was realized using

Fig. 7. The image acquisition positions.

Fig. 8. Orthophoto map (50 × 50 m grid) of the archaeological site and the modern time representation of the huts.

Fig. 9. Part of the Fig. 8 orthophoto map displaying the central and east trenches (Fig. 1, CT and ET).

Fig. 10. Part of the orthophoto map of Fig. 8 displaying the site of the modern time representation of the huts.

Agisoft PhotoScan®. The accuracy of the ortho rectified image covering the archaeo-logical site and the modern time representation of the Dispilio was 0.5 m. The pro-duced digital surface model and the 3D photo realistic textured model are presented in Figs. 11 and 12.

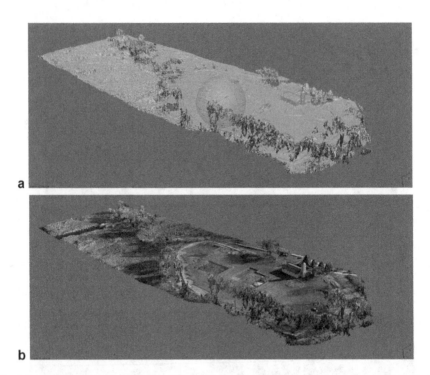

Fig. 11. a. Digital Surface Model (DSM). b. The 3D photorealistic textured model of the archaeological site and the modern time representation of the huts.

Fig. 12. a. Digital Surface Model (DSM). b. 3D photorealistic textured model of part of the archaeological site.

5.3 Mapping of a Part of the West Wall

For the high resolution mapping of a part of the west wall (Fig. 1, WE) oblique images were acquired using the multi copter drone with a flying height of 4 to 25 m. Equipped with the Canon EOS 1200D 18Mp Camera. In total 13 oblique images with a scale varying between 1:1,000 and 1:600 were acquired (Fig. 13). The images covered areas between 26 × 17 m and 13 × 9 m, with a spatial resolution of 0.5 to 0.25 cm. The processing was realized using Agisoft PhotoScan® (Figs. 14 and 15).

Fig. 13. Image acquisition positions.

Fig. 14. a. Digital Surface Model. b. 3D photorealistic texture model of a part of the west wall.

Fig. 15. a. Digital Surface Model. b. 3D photorealistic texture model of a part of the west wall.

6 Conclusions

UAV, digital sensors and photogrammetric processing software technology is constantly evolving presenting new opportunities for the utilization of, earth's surface and its objects, images. Currently easily navigated UAV's with flight stability and automated navigation and image acquisition systems are easily available. Furthermore the capability of hovering and acquisition of vertical, oblique, and horizontal images are some of their present advantages. In addition they also have the capability to mount LIDAR, thermal, multi spectral, and other sensors. In cases that UAV's cannot be used for photogrammetric modelling of objects, other sensors like terrestrial laser scanners are utilized to document them. Finally low cost processing software allows multi photo image processing for the production of coloured dense point clouds, very high resolution orthophotos and creation of optimal presentation results like 3D photo realistic textured models.

References

1. Kaimaris, D., Patias, P., Sifnaiou, M.: UAV and the comparison of image processing software. Int. J. Intell. Unmanned Syst. **5**(1), 18–27 (2017)
2. Bendea, H.F., Chiabrando, F., Tonolo, F.G., Marenchino, D.: Mapping of archaeological areas using a low-cost UAV the Augusta Bagiennorum Test site. In: XXI International CIPA Symposium on CDROM, Athens, Greece (2007)
3. Çabuk, A., Deveci, A., Ergincan, F.: Improving heritage documentation. GIM Int. **21**(9) (2007)

4. Chiabrando, F., Nex, F., Piatti, D., Rinaudo, F.: UAVand RPV systems for photogrammetric surveys in archeological areas: two tests in the Piedmont region (Italy). J. Archaeol. Sci. **38** (3), 697–710 (2011)
5. Cowley, D.C.: Remote sensing for archaeological heritage management. In: Occasional Publication of the Aerial Archaeology Research Group No. 3, p. 307. Europae Archaeologiae Consilium, Budapest (2011)
6. Eisenbeiss, H., Lambers, K., Sauerbier, M., Zhang, L.: Photogrammetric documentation of an archaeological site (Palpa, Peru) using an autonomous model helicopter. Int. Arch. Photogramm. Remote Sens. Spat. Inf. Sci. **34**(5/C34), 238–243 (2005)
7. Eisenbeiss, H., Lambers, K., Sauerbier, M.: Photogrammetric recording of the archaeological site of Pinchango Alto (Palpa, Peru) using a mini helicopter (UAV). In: 33rd CAA Conference, Tomar, Portugal, pp. 175–184 (2005)
8. Eisenbeiss, H., Sauerbier, M., Zhang, L., Gruen, A.: Mit dem Modell helikopter ueber Pinchango Alto. Geomatik Schweiz **9**, 510–515 (2005)
9. Eisenbeiss, H., Zhang, L.: Comparison of DSMs generated from mini UAV imagery and terrestrial Laser Scanner in a cultural heritage application. In: ISPRS Commission V Symposium 'Image Engineering and Vision Metrology', Part 5, Dresden. IAPRS, vol. XXXVI, pp. 90–96 (2006)
10. Eisenbeiss, H.: UAV photogrammetry. Dissertation ETH No. 18515, Institute of Geodesy and Photogrammetry, ETH Zurich, Switzerland, Mitteilungen Nr. 105 (2009)
11. Hendrickx, M., Gheyle, W., Bonne, J., Bourgeois, J., De Wulf, A., Goossens, R.: The use of stereoscopic images taken from a microdrone for the documentation of heritage - an example from the Tuekta burial mounds in the Russian Altay. J. Archaeol. Sci. **38**(11), 2968–2978 (2011)
12. Kaimaris, D., Patias, P.: A low-cost image acquisition system for the systematic observation of traces of buried archaeological structures. Geomatica **68**(4), 299–308 (2014)
13. Lambers, K., Eisenbeiss, H., Sauerbier, M., Kupferschmidt, D., Gaisecker, T., Sotoodeh, S., Hanusch, T.: Combining photogrammetry and laser scanning for the recording and modeling of the late intermediate period site of Pinchango Alto, Palpa. Peru. J. Archaeol. Sci. **34**(10), 1702–1712 (2007)
14. Oczipka, M., Bemman, J., Piezonka, H., Munkabayar, J., Ahrens, B., Achtelik, M., Lehmann, F.: Small drones for geo-archeology in the steppes: locating and documenting the archeological heritage of the Orkhon Valley in Mongolia. In: Remote Sensing for Environmental Monitoring, GIS Applications, and Geology IX, pp. 201–212 (2009)
15. Patias, P., Georgoula, O., Kaimaris, D., Georgiadis, C., Stylianidis, S., Stamnas, A.: 3D mapping using model helicopter and laser scanning: case study activities of the Laboratory of Photogrammetry and Remote sensing, AUT. In: VSMM 2008: Digital Heritage, 14th International Conference on Virtual Systems and Multimedia, Limassol, Cyprus, pp. 1–5 (2008)
16. Patias, P., Geogoula, O., Kaimaris, D.: The chronicle of photogrammetric documentation of the Neolithic limnetic settlement of Dispilio-Kastoria. J. Anaskamma **2**, 81–86 (2009)
17. Patias, P., Georgoula, O., Georgiadis, Ch., Stamnas, A., Tassopoulou, M.: Photogrammetric documentation and digital representation of excavations at Keros island in the Cyclades. In: CIPA XXII Symposium, CIPA Archives for Documentation of Cultural Heritage, Kyoto, Japan (2009)

18. Patias, P., Georgoula, O., Georgiadis, C.: Photogrammetric documentation and digital representation, Chap. 5. In: Renfrew, C., Philaniotou, O., Brodie, N., Gavalas, G., Boyd, M. (eds.) The Dhaskalio and Kavos Terrain: Topographic Survey, Aerial Photography and Photogrammetry: The Settlements at Dhaskalio - The Sanctuary of Keros and the Origins of Aegean Ritual Practice, vol. I, pp. 59–60. McDonald Institute for Archaeological Research Monographs, University of Cambridge (2013)
19. Przybilla, H.J., Wester-Ebbinghaus, W.: Bildflug mit ferngelenktem Kleinflugzeug. In: Bildmessung und Luftbildwesen, Zeitschrift fuer Photogrammetrie und Fernerkudung, vol. 47, no. 5, pp. 137–142. Herbert Wichman Verlag, Karlsruhe (1979)
20. Rinaudo, F., Chiabrando, F., Lingua, A., Spanò, A.: Archaeological site monitoring: UAV photogrammetry could be an answer. Int. Arch. Photogramm. Remote Sens. Spat. Inf. Sci. 39(5), 583–588 (2012)
21. Wester-Ebbinghaus, W.: Aerial Photography by radio controlled model helicopter. Photogramm. Rec. 10(55), 85–92 (1980)
22. Hourmouziadis, G.: Dispilio 7500 Years After. University Studio Press, Thessaloniki (2002)
23. Sofronidou, M.: The prehistoric lakeside settlement of Dispilio Kastoria - a first introduction. Anaskamma 1, 9–26 (2008)
24. National Cadastre and Mapping Agency S.A. http://gis.ktimanet.gr/wms/ktbasemap/default.aspx

Digital Survey and Documentation of La Habana Vieja in Cuba

Caterina Morganti[1(✉)] and Cristiana Bartolomei[2(✉)]

[1] School of Engineering and Architecture,
Alma Mater Studiorum University of Bologna, Bologna, Italy
cate_morganti@hotmail.it
[2] Department of Architecture, Alma Mater Studiorum University of Bologna,
Bologna, Italy
cristiana.bartolomei@unibo.it

Abstract. This article deepens the subject of photo-modelling applied to architecture, on a medium and large scale. It in detail deepens the development of the application of a 3D dimensional rendition technology applied to buildings and historical sites that belong to the architectural and cultural heritage of Havana City (Cuba). This article describes the necessary steps to obtain a 3D dimensional textured models from reality through a photographic set. The project aims at providing some new and innovative methods for the Cuban reality. A very interesting topic for the Oficina del Historiador de Ciudad de la Habana, a Cuban public body, that oversees the architectural and cultural heritage of the city. The survey deals with the five squares of Habana Vieja (old town of Havana), through two different ways of working. The first one has a typical technical scientific nature. It elaborates a survey with the combination of various techniques. In this way there is a rendition of a 2D dimensional and 3D dimensional scale model, that includes the urban and architectural information of the squares and their buildings. The second one provides the useful material to create an application just for mobile devices (like smartphone and tablet), for popular, cultural and tourist purposes that can be used offline and online. It is also used as a database in order to create AR (Augmented Reality) applications.

Keywords: Cultural heritage · Photo-modeling · Augmented Reality
La Habana · Cuba

1 Introduction

3D heritage digitization is as a matter of fact something definitely new for many countries including Cuba. Nowadays that kind of photography named "documentary" takes on more and more value thanks to its ability to be used with the help of modern digital processing techniques.

Photo-modelling technique is a useful and quick solution that allows to rebuild real scenes from photographs and also allows to scale them through some basic measurements. It provides solid bases of the representative system, seizing their essence and showing their meanings.

© Springer International Publishing AG, part of Springer Nature 2018
M. Ioannides et al. (Eds.): Digital Cultural Heritage 2017, LNCS 10754, pp. 15–31, 2018.
https://doi.org/10.1007/978-3-319-75789-6_2

If the photo-modelling technique is applied to architecture, it will become an effective solution to document the state of existing buildings. Specialists find therefore the necessary elements to develop their own study and supports for diffusion and valorisation for general public.

The latest software particularly allows a rendition of a 3D dimensional image, starting from the photographs taken with commercial digital cameras and even with mobile phones. So the results achieved compare with those obtained by using a more expensive and sophisticated equipment such as remote sensing with active sensors, and laser scanners.

This article presents the operational procedures that survey and represent the single architectural element of the aggregate in its characteristics and its inclusion as a whole. The potential of this technique is therefore tested not only on a specific building but also on urban spaces which have by nature very different characteristics from the sole building.

This is an operational point of view typical of the architect-engineer. The specialist is therefore able to combine different tools and techniques, and blend the design and photography to represent reality.

This is the development of the application of 3D dimensional rendition technology applied to buildings and historic sites that belong to the architectural and cultural heritage of Havana City. The old town centre of Havana was sampled, because it is wealthy with its valuable architectural heritage and still in need of surveys and operations for its maintenance, recovery and development [1]. First we located the five squares (Fig. 1), that are the most significant and identifying places of the Cuban historical centre, and that characterize the typical urban layout of the place.

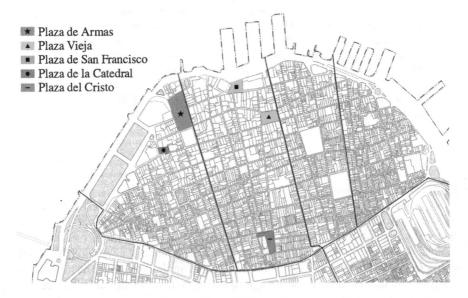

Plaza de Armas
Plaza Vieja
Plaza de San Francisco
Plaza de la Catedral
Plaza del Cristo

Fig. 1. Plan of *Habana Vieja*.

The survey of these squares is the starting point for a more complex work that will later include the main streets that depart from these squares, to later involve the secondary urban fabric. We decided to analyse the survey and the 3D dimensional rendition through traditional measurements tools and the on-site photographic campaign, together with the application of the latest state-of-the-art digital techniques for data processing in order to create 3D models. The context was quite unsuitable to our project because of different and complex reasons. The need to minimize the size of the tools, their weight and cost. Minimize the time of survey and photographic shot on site. To face the difficulties given by the continuing presence of a chaotic influx of people disturbing the work. Not least the difficulty of having a limited number of daily hours available to carry out photographic shots that requires special lighting conditions. This work was supported by a documentary and archival research in order to collect information that gives organic unity to the survey and supports the framing of the context and the historical course. The survey has two aims: the first one produces a database that contains the 2D and 3D rendition of urban environments, as a whole and for each building [2]. The second one uses the data processing to create a popular tool applicable to mobile devices, with the possibility of applications for the augmented reality. The implementation of this replicable in time method also permits to evaluate the changes that took place, in particular the ageing process of the time of the fronts of the buildings into a macroscopic level. This method of rendition and classification of the heritage is entirely new to Cuba and is also useful for the heritage of any other city. Our project was programmed and analysed with the help of the technicians specialized in urban architecture and restoration that work for the major body. It in fact oversees the archaeological, historical, cultural and architectural heritage of Havana: the *Oficina del Historiador de la Ciudad de La Habana*. The Oficina was established in 1938 to protect the old Havana. The restoration of the historic area was developed by Dr. Eusebio Leal Spengler, who was elected as the *Historiador de la Ciudad de La Habana* in 1967 and is currently the highest authority for the complete restoration of the historic centre. Such historic centre was declared a World Heritage Site by UNESCO in 1982. The Oficina is the engine of many initiatives taking place in Havana. It could be called Sovereignty, with the aim of safeguarding the national identity through the research, the promotion and the development of culture [3].

The structure comprises: offices, libraries, archives and laboratories, and also teams up with the University of Havana and other national research organizations. The referring office of this project is *RESTAURA, Empresa de Proyectos de Arquitectura y Urbanismo*. All the Cuban specialists who belong to this institution joined our project. They considered it very useful for the enriching of their archives and the spreading of knowledge of their heritage. There are also aims at both the cultural growth of people and the implementation of tourist offer.

They want to conform to the modern techniques of survey and graphic representation. In that the editing of drawings and surveys till to-day uses traditional hand tools or CAD, prevalently 2D. There is in fact the growing need to digitize the great cultural and architectural heritage of Cuba and in particular of Havana City. Until to-day in the Cuban reality there have not been applied yet the studies of survey and 3D digitalization that are based on photo-modelling or on Heritage/Historical BIM or on AR (Augmented Reality).

2 Relief Methodology

The main aim of the study is the survey and the graphic rendition of the five squares that are part of the Old Town Centre of Old Havana: *Plaza de Armas* (Fig. 2), *Plaza Vieja* (Fig. 3), *Plaza de San Francisco* (Fig. 4), *Plaza de la Catedral* (Fig. 5), and *Plaza del Cristo* (Fig. 6) [4].

Fig. 2. Plaza de Armas.

Fig. 3. Plaza Vieja.

Fig. 4. Plaza de San Francisco.

Fig. 5. Plaza de San Francisco.

The survey was developed with traditional direct methods and a photographic campaign. The graphic rendition was carried out with digital tools and proper software both from computer graphics[1] and computer vision[2] [5]. Photo-modelling was the main technique used for the rendition of scale 3D models, both for scale building and scale urban as well [6].

---

[1] Computer graphics is a discipline aimed at studying techniques and algorithms generated for the display of numerical information produced by a computer.

[2] Computer vision is a discipline that studies techniques and algorithms in order to build systems that can also capture information from images.

Fig. 6. Plaza del Cristo.

The steps of development of our work are now presented in its critical analysis. Surveys on a medium and large scale of parts of cities generate a considerable amount of data and information that are supposed to be processed at a later time and usually in faraway places from where the survey was carried out. Our study in actual fact lays thousands of miles overseas from Cuba. The survey was carried out according to an accurate work program. A precise tool selection was made and data was saved with particular attention. For this last operation, the laptop memory and an external hard disk were used, so that there were at least three supports, including the SD card, where the files were stored at the end of the day. It was also useful to photograph the sheets of paper where we wrote down the notes, in order to have a digital copy of them, too.

The tools that were used for the survey and the photographic campaign were chosen for their practicality, effectiveness, size, weight and cost. They are the ones shown in Fig. 7.

Fig. 7. Tools used for the survey.

The study of the survey needed to take a look at the places for checking which parts of the day had the best light to take the most proper photos. That is why a scouring of the interested sites was carried out at various hours of the day. The results were that the strong shadows disturbed the shot quality and the most suitable hours resulted to be the early morning and the late afternoon ones. They are public places, so it was also estimated the influx of people that complicated the cleaning of the photographic shot. At first the photo-modelling technique seems a simple and automatic method. It yields from a photographic set a 3D dimensional, textured, complete and scale model. Unfortunately this is not the case, although photo-modelling is a method with a high degree of automation, which greatly simplifies the generative process of the 3D model. The whole process needed to be supported by a deep critical interpretation, especially in the shot taking phase, which required the individualization of the architectural shapes of the surveyed squares. As mentioned previously, a Canon EOS 600D reflex digital camera was used with a standard zoom lens EF-S 18-55 IS II. We took photos at the maximum resolution camera of 18 megapixels. The JPEG format was the format used for the images. It is actually the most used format for commercial photo devices to compress the digital image with continuous tone both in grey and in colour. Even if the majority producers of modelling software recommend the RAW format as a method of data storing which shows an image with less recording quality loss.

Most of the photographs were taken with the help of a tripod to get the sharpest images and a 18 mm focal length. Once we decided on the settings for the camera, then we started with the shot taking using the methods analysed in advance in our study. These methods follow the case-by-case rules, that are not always possible to be respected because of objective physical impediments to our view of the five photographed squares (Figs. 8 and 9) [7]. Some of these impediments are common like fixed or mobile obstacles as vegetation, urban furnishing, temporary installations as stages and walking markets, vehicles, people, and auto-occlusions yielded by their own particular shapes (like balconies, porches and other front elements). It was necessary a proper ability to photograph the entire fronts of the buildings, avoiding all those physical impediments. An example is Plaza del Cristo where behind a series of buildings there was a curious parking place used by innumerable "bicycle-taxi".

Fig. 8. Several critical situations.

We classified the five squares according to their era of construction and according to their main aesthetic characteristics: surface, perimeter and number of buildings.

Fig. 9. Several critical situations.

Each square has its own particular elements that determined the survey and conditioned the freedom of movement to choice the right shot taking and to avoid the obstacle present.

Plaza de Armas (Fig. 10) [8] is the first square built and the largest one, with a surface of 9000 m². It lapps against the side of the famous "Malecon", the Havana's waterfront. It is partially paved and partially green with imposing trees that enrich it but limit its overview. It is surrounded by valuable historical buildings, that are the Castillo de la Real Fuerza, the Casa de Correos, the Palacio de Gobierno or the Capitanes Generales. The square is daily occupied by a characteristic "flea market", mainly used books. The market and mostly the thick vegetation made critical the photographic shot because of the lack of a broad point of view. There are two white marble statues in the square, that were photographed using the converging axis technique.

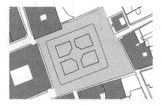

Plaza de Armas
area: 9000 m²
perimeter: 390 m
number of buildings: 7

Fig. 10. Plaza de Armas: surface, perimeter and number of buildings.

The *Plaza Vieja* (Fig. 11) [9] with a surface of 5500 m² is an airy and captivating square thanks to the variety of colours of the 16 prestigious buildings recently restored. It is attended by a lot of people. There are indeed many clubs, bars and commercial activities that occupy the ground floor and the noble floor. A white marble fountain was built in the centre of the square. The critical situations of the survey were the presence of: people, the exterior furnishings of the clubs and bars, some temporary installations, a very tall building and the presence of arcades in each building.

Plaza Vieja
area: 5500 m²
perimeter: 300 m
number of buildings: 16

Fig. 11. Plaza Vieja: surface, perimeter and number of buildings.

Plaza de San Francisco (Fig. 12) [10] is a square with a surface of 4760 m². It can be defined as the square of "commerce" because it is located close to the Havana Bay where there are the customs and seafaring palaces that surround it. This square has also its white marble fountain and an imposing complex comprising the church and the convent of St. Francis from which it is named. The levels of criticality of the survey were the presence of: people, some furnishings and the irregularity of the shape of the square.

Plaza de San Francisco
area: 4760 m²
perimeter: 310 m
number of buildings: 9

Fig. 12. Plaza de San Francisco: surface, perimeter and number of buildings.

Plaza de la Catedral (Fig. 13) [11] is the smallest (1940 m^2) square but not the least impressive. It has a baroque cathedral of the eighteenth century that occupies an entire side of the square and is surrounded by other prestigious buildings.

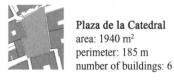

Plaza de la Catedral
area: 1940 m^2
perimeter: 185 m
number of buildings: 6

Fig. 13. Plaza de la Catedral: surface, perimeter and number of buildings.

Plaza del Cristo (Fig. 14) [12] is located on the street connecting Plaza Vieja to Capitolio Nacional. It is a L-shaped square with an area of 5690 m^2. It is the square with the largest number of overlooking buildings, exactly 21. It is partly paved and partly green with trees that partially limit its unitary vision. It is also the only one crossed by a carriageway. Even though it possesses lots of architectural and urban potentials, it is the most neglected and the most in need of recovery interventions. Vegetation and the remarkable vehicular, bicycle and pedestrian traffic made critical the photographic survey. It is also the only square with no tall buildings so that it was difficult to make the photographic set with aerial views.

Plaza del Cristo
area: 5690 m^2
perimeter: 405 m
number of buildings: 21

Fig. 14. Plaza del Cristo: surface, perimeter and number of buildings. (Color figure online)

The necessity to have an aerial view of every building overlooking the square created further problems. We deliberately avoided the use of the aerial photography of drones not to be charged by an economic increase, due to: a place to hold them and the usage permits. So we faced the problem choosing to use the view of the tallest surrounding buildings for the aerial shot taking. Anyway, a critical situation was still the difficulty of obtaining permissions from public bodies or private individuals in order to gain all the accesses to the desired aerial points of view. Always keeping in mind the time limits for a proper lighting. Another difficulty was to photograph complex and large buildings. That is why the shots had to be partially fragmented due to the impossibility of the complete framing of the building.

The photographic shot of each square includes in all: fronts of the buildings and their porches, pavements, monuments and fountains. Different techniques were used in relation to the type of rendition of each different element and to the achievement of analyses and representations. There are three techniques that are used in a combined or integrated way, that are: parallel or multiple axes shot (Fig. 15), convergent axis shot (Fig. 16), and panoramic shot (cylindrical, spherical or partial) (Fig. 17) [13].

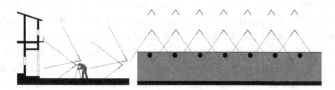

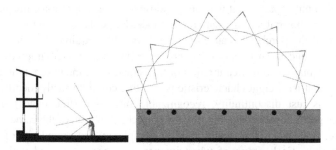

Fig. 15. The parallel axis technique.

Fig. 16. The convergent axis shooting.

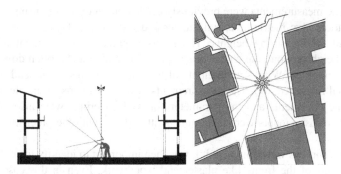

Fig. 17. The technique of cylindrical shooting.

The convergent axis shot, specific for photo-modelling, was used for the shot of the fronts of the building. In this case the camera was placed in portrait (vertical) or landscape (horizontal) position, depending on the size of the object. It consists of turning around the building in a semicircle way, aiming at the centre of gravity of the front. It was not always possible to frame the entire front with one shot as desired, so we ended up by taking photos of portions of the building. The photos were usually taken turning in semicircle at 30° intervals (5 clicks per semicircle). The buildings that have some parts geometrically different required a deeper study, like the columns, the pavements and the ceilings of the arcades which were photographed with the technique of spherical panoramic shots. The fronts of the buildings were photographed using the technique of parallel axis shot as well. This technique involves a multiple photos shot, moving in parallel to the front of the building and taking pictures with a frame that overlaps at least 25% the previous frame (similar to the classic photogrammetry). This method allowed to process the design of the front through the photo-rectifier technique and was actually ideal to determine the weaving of the surfaces. In this case, the shot was taken with the camera in portrait position to take advantage from the maximum resolution of the camera. The technique of cylindrical shot was used for the shot of exterior spaces with a central composition like cloisters, courts and in particular squares. It captures images from a central point, and from that point it starts making with the camera a round angle. The shots we used were selected with an overlapping of the images of about 25%, so that we could choose the most appropriate image between the camera in the portrait and the panoramic mode. Particular attention was also given to the survey of the porches because of their shape, that required the combination of these techniques and the necessity of a very large number of photographic shots.

In order to obtain a correct calibration of the cameras, we made sure that during the shot there were at least eight characteristic points that could be easily identified on the photos. This is just discontinuity, recognizable on shape (like edges) or surface weaving (like pores in materials). Finally, the correct calibration of the cameras was not difficult to verify thanks to the condition of the complexity and irregularity of the fronts and the materials. Each group of taken images was then associated with the measurements of some reference sizes in the three dimensions (widths, heights, depths), that are necessary to scale the model and to control the correctness of the graphic rendition. The measurements were previously carried out in excess by using traditional measuring tools like: metric tape, rigid meter and laser meter. This last one is particularly useful for measuring heights. The fronts required a measurement of general widths and heights among the characteristic points identified and written down on free hand drawn eidotype. Widths and heights of the main openings (doors and windows) were as usual measured, too. The measurements of the main parts of the elements that constitute the pavements and the parameters or wall coverings were also taken into account. All measurements were taken and written down with the precision of half a centimetre.

When the surveys were completed, it was then important to identify the colorimetry of the paintings of the fronts like plaster and woodwork. Even in this case we proceeded with the use of a very simple, quick and effective tool: the bunch of colours. This direct method allowed to detect the colours with a very low error rate, unlike the colours taken with the camera, that are susceptible to so many interferences (Fig. 18).

The error of the model was calculated according to the metric quality and the precision of the result of the data processing with a proper software. It was not important the kind of photographic technique used (convergent, parallel or cylindrical). This calculation took into account the intrinsic errors of the measuring device: camera resolution; a not clear selection in matching points; the correction at cameras

Fig. 18. Metric and colorimetric survey.

calibration and orientation. The scale of the error expressed in pixels corresponds to the error expressed in cm according to the following proportion (1):

$$\text{error (cm)} = \text{error (pixel)} \times \text{real distance (cm)}/\text{image distance (pixel)} . \quad (1)$$

For example. If we measure with a metric tape a front with a real horizontal length of 1748 cm, the error can be estimated in (2):

$$\text{error (6 pixels)} \times \text{real distance (1748 cm)}/\text{image distance (3895 pixels)}$$
$$= 2,7 \, \text{cm (error)}. \quad (2)$$

The error is more than acceptable. The percentage is exactly of 0,16%.

3 The Representation of the Public Space

After the survey and the photographic campaign we proceeded with the data processing through a personal computer with quite good hardware performances. So that if there are many photos it is able to limit the time of loading:

- Processor: AMD Athlon (tm) X4860K Quad Core Processor 3.7 GHz;
- GPU: NVIDIA GeForce GTX 960;
- RAM: 32 Gb;
- SSD: 500 Gb;
- Operating System: Windows 7 (64 bit).

There are various processing programs available on the market about the photo-rectifier, about the photo-modelling and 2D and 3D graphics. The following software was selected for the realization of this study:

- Perspective Rectifier (2D photo rectifier);
- Agisoft PhotoScan Professional (for 3D photo-modelling);
- AutoCAD Autodesk (for graphic re-processing).

The Perspective Rectifier software was applied to create the 2D photoplane. It was used for the photo-rectification and to scale them. To translate the technical drawing sheet in .dwg format, the raster image of the photoplane was imported into the Autocad software. The essential lines were retraced, obtaining the vector technical drawing (Fig. 19).

Fig. 19. 2D photoplane creation (building in *Plaza de San Francisco*).

Agisoft PhotoScan was used for the 3D photo-modelling. This software works through the automatic recognition of homologous characteristic points in all the photographs. These characteristic points are recognized through computer algorithms of artificial vision. The program lines up the photographs with prospective view

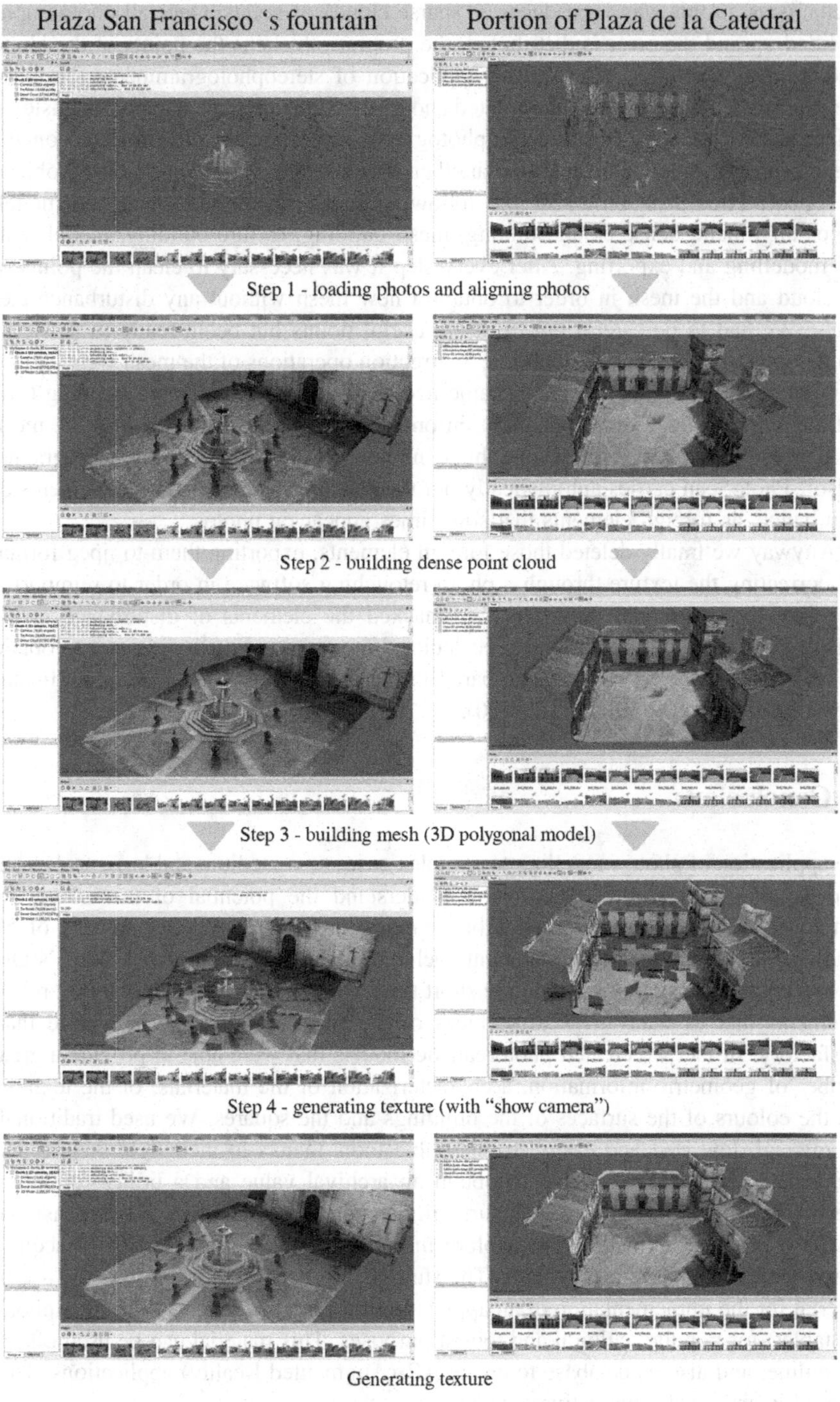

Plaza San Francisco 's fountain	Portion of Plaza de la Catedral

Step 1 - loading photos and aligning photos

Step 2 - building dense point cloud

Step 3 - building mesh (3D polygonal model)

Step 4 - generating texture (with "show camera")

Generating texture

Fig. 20. Photo-modeling 3D (Agisoft PhotoScan).

mechanisms, in this way it produces a "sparse cloud" of points. Once all photographs are lined up and the error is distributed, the program thickens the points of the cloud generating a "dense cloud" with the application of stereophotogrammetry formulas. The "dense cloud" points are interpolated and so then they produce a three-dimensional surface called "mesh". The selected photographs are automatically projected on the "mesh" surface, blend them into one another, creating the entire texture of the object.

Agisoft PhotoScan processes the following steps in order to create the model: photos alignment, dense cloud building, mesh building, texture building, model scaling, modelling and exporting. After every step it was necessary to clean the points of the cloud and the mesh in order to obtain a new mesh without any disturbance elements. We had to be careful not to delete useful points but being ready to delete as many points of disturbance as possible. Correction operations of the mesh were carried out such as holes closing. It also became necessary to work at a single building (one building corresponded to one chunks), in order to join more chunks before the mesh was created. Seeing that there is a huge number of groups of taken photographs. Agisoft PhotoScan carries automatically out the cleaning operation for the elements of disturbance, as foreign elements that sometimes appear on photos.

Anyway we finally deleted those foreign elements, exporting them to .jpeg format and correcting the texture through a photo retouching software in order to reimport it back into the 3D model. Similarly, we masked the elements of disturbance inside Agisoft PhotoScan program and we recalculated the texture. Finally, in order to obtain the scale model, the model was compared to the points where the spatial coordinates were already surveyed on site (Fig. 20).

4   Conclusions

The application of photo-modelling to complex cases on a medium and large scale such as those in question made possible to understand the potential of this surveying technique in the architectural and urban application. The fronts and arcades of 59 buildings, 2 fountains and 2 monuments belonging to the 5 squares of Havana's Old Town Centre were surveyed in a quite short time. In total there are about 30000 m^2 of pavements and as many vertical surfaces of the fronts. The results are more than satisfactory. In fact we created photorealistic models that were able to provide a great number of geometric information, a characterization of the materials, of the textures and the colours of the surfaces of the buildings and the squares. We used traditional, commercial, low cost and easily transportable tools thanks to their light weight and their small size. It was possible to obtain an archival value and a utility for future research. The use of these models furthermore permits to produce 3D dimensional views, to produce animations, to explore through a display software and to acquire data, to create prospects and profiles. The study is also supposed to provide the useful material for the implementation of an application for portable devices (like smartphone and tablet) for popular, cultural and tourist purposes. This material can be used offline and online, and also as database to create AR (Augmented Reality) applications. This material is absolutely innovative for Cuba.

References

1. Weiss, J.E.: La arquitectura colonial cubana. Ediciones de Arte y Sociedad, La Habana (1972)
2. AA.VV.: Manejo y gestiòn de centros històricos. Ed. Boloña, La Habana (2009)
3. AA.VV.: Regulaciones Urbanisticas Ciudad de La Habana - La Habana Vieja - Centro Historico. Ed. Boloña, La Habana (2009)
4. Venegas Fornias, C.: Plazas de intramuro. Ed. Mayra Fernàndez Peròn, La Habana (2003)
5. Garagnani, S.: Architettura in pixel. Elementi di informatica grafica nella rappresentazione architettonica. Patron Editore, Bologna (2009)
6. Foresi, L.: La Fotomodellazione come strumento di comprensione dell'Architettura. Tesi di laurea, Camerino (2008)
7. Foschi, R.: La fotomodellazione per il rilievo architettonico: metodologie, potenzialità e criticità. Rivista ingenio n. 36 (2015). www.ingenio-web.it
8. AA.VV.: Guìa de arquitectura. Ed. consejo editorial, La Habana (1998)
9. AA.VV.: La plaza Vieja de La Habana - proceso de recuperaciòn. Ed. Consejerìa de Obras Pùblicas y Vivienda, Sevilla (2011)
10. Garcia Santana, A.: Urbanismo y arquitectura de la Habana Vieja - siglos XVI al XVIII. Ed. Boloña, La Habana (2009)
11. De las cuevas Toraya, J.: 500 años de construcciones en Cuba. Ed. Chavìn, La Habana (2001)
12. Fernàndez Santalices, M.: Calles de La Habana. Agualarga Editores, Madrid (2000)
13. De Luca, L.: La fotomodellazione architettonica. Rilievo, modellazione, rappresentazione di edifici a partire da fotografie. Ed. Dario Flaccovio, Palermo (2011)

Application of Multisensory Technology for Resolution of Problems in the Field of Research and Preservation of Cultural Heritage

Pilar Merchán[1(✉)], María José Merchán[1], Santiago Salamanca[1], and Antonio Adán[2]

[1] Escuela de Ingenierías Industriales,
Universidad de Extremadura, Badajoz, Spain
{pmerchan,mjmerchan,ssalamanca}@unex.es
[2] Escuela Superior de Informática,
Universidad de Castilla La Mancha, Ciudad Real, Spain
antonio.adan@uclm.es

Abstract. This chapter presents a new line of research that addresses the treatment of data acquired through different sensors to capture reality in order to obtain useful information that can be applied to the generation of knowledge in the field of conservation and restoration of Cultural Heritage. This technology is expected to be used to solve impact problems in this field. The ultimate goal is the generation of work strategies to enhance the quality of the service provided to visitors and, consequently, their satisfaction. The multidisciplinary nature of the tasks to be tackled requires the joint work of specialists from such diverse areas as Computer Vision and Archaeology.

Keywords: 3D modelling · Cultural Heritage · Thermal analysis
Fault detection

1 Introduction

It is undoubtedly true that technology for capturing reality has experienced exceptional progress in the last decade, with the result that huge amounts of data can now be acquired relatively quickly. This means that traditional barriers to acquiring and storing monumental data effectively and efficiently have been significantly lowered. However, this evolution in the techniques of capture of reality has not yet been reflected in a generalization of its use, beyond being considered a tool of digital documentation. So far, most of the contributions made in the field of Heritage have been limited to providing realistic and detailed digital models of archaeological objects and spaces.

A review of the literature and our own experience indicate that analyses of data acquired to provide the information of real use to archaeologists and other Heritage

© Springer International Publishing AG, part of Springer Nature 2018
M. Ioannides et al. (Eds.): Digital Cultural Heritage 2017, LNCS 10754, pp. 32–47, 2018.
https://doi.org/10.1007/978-3-319-75789-6_3

experts continue to be done manually, with a visual assessment of the element to be analysed. This process is often time-consuming, resulting in high economic costs. In addition, concerns frequently arise regarding the subjectivity and variability of the results obtained.

There is, therefore, a growing and undeniable need for methods that automatically extract useful information from the data currently obtained from the technology for capturing reality.

Nowadays, there are numerous groups on an international level working on the generation of digital models of historical-artistic Heritage obtained with 3D scanners and colour cameras; however, there is a minority that has gone one step beyond the mere generation of models and is dedicated to extracting information from these. Amongst others, the Stanford University group in the USA has been a reference in this field since the end of the last century and the beginning of the present (http://graphics.stanford.edu/). This group has developed projects recognized worldwide, such as The Digital Michelangelo Project [1] or the Digital *Forma Urbis Romae* [2]. The group led by Roberto Scopigno of Istituto di Scienza e Tecnologie dell'Informazione in Pisa has also been working for more than 25 years on 3D digitization, surface reconstruction, and visualization and interpretation of Cultural Heritage (http://vcg.isti.cnr.It/) [3–5]. In Spain, several teams have approached the use of the laser scanner with an archaeological objective. Worthy of mention is the Research Group on Photogrammetry and Laser Scanner (GIFLE) of the Universitat Politècnica de València (http://gifle.webs.upv.es), which in recent years has published a number of scientific publications in this regard [6, 7]. The authors of the present chapter also have extensive experience in the application of the techniques and procedures of Computer Vision to the investigation and conservation of Heritage. Also of note is the Restitution of Aeneas's sculptural group, belonging to the collection of the National Museum of Roman Art in Mérida, which has had notable scientific and media impact [8, 9], or the digitization of the *Fori Porticus* and the Temple of Diana of Augusta Emerita (Fig. 1) or the Theatre of Segobriga [10].

The use of thermography applied to the study of pieces of Heritage has already come a long way too, mainly due to its non-invasive nature, which allows inspecting surfaces without contact [11, 12]. In [13], the authors present a proposal for the detection of pathologies in monuments from thermal images taken at different points in time.

Nevertheless, there are currently few groups in the world that have combined both types of sensors, i.e. the 3D laser scanner and thermal cameras, to create a unique model with geometry, colour and temperature information. In recent years, some authors have performed procedures of association between thermal images and point clouds oriented to studies of energy efficiency in modern buildings. Alba et al. [14] have developed a bi-cameral system consisting of an infrared camera, a digital camera and a 3D laser scanner with which they integrate the information and use it to locate, display and analyse anomalies in contemporary architecture. Borrmann et al. [15, 16] have created a 3D thermal modelling system using a light detector, a LIDAR and a low-resolution infrared camera (160 × 120 pixels) mounted on an Irma3D mobile robot commanded to accelerate scanning and recording processes. Due to the fixed position of the camera, its field of view is reduced, so scanning from a distance is necessary for tall buildings, which results in thermal data acquisition of very low resolution. Lagüela et al. [17] also

Fig. 1. Photo and 3D model of the temple of Diana of Augusta Emerita.

introduced a method to project RGB thermal data onto the surface of point cloud meshes of buildings with the aim of carrying out energy efficiency studies on them.

Rather scarce, however, have been approximations made in the field of Heritage. Cabrelles et al. [18] proposed using 3D point clouds and cameras to provide photo-realistic digital models and, in addition, to add thermal images that offer information that allows to infer the current state of preservation of a monument. They show the results obtained in a tomb in Petra (Jordan).

Given our experience in laser sensors and their application to the field of Cultural Heritage, as well as in the use of thermal information in problems solved with Vision techniques, we considered the time was ripe to endeavour to develop a line of research such as the one described in this work.

The rest of the chapter is organized as follows. Section 2 presents some questions we aim to provide answers for as the research progresses. In Sect. 3 we take a look at this new research line, highlighting the originality of the proposal for the two branches of knowledge involved in it, Computer Vision and Archaeology. Section 4 is taken up with some initial results of our work. Finally, Sect. 5 presents the conclusions.

2 Some Questions We Intend to Answer

We propose an investigation from two different but complementary perspectives. On the one hand, we present the point of view of the Conservation and Restoration of Cultural Heritage, which is concerned with what may be termed the practical applications of the research. On the other hand, work in the field of Computer Vision provides tools to be used in basic scientific research in order to identify and correct, as far as possible, impact problems in the field of Archaeology. The ultimate goal is the generation of work strategies to enhance the quality of the service provided to the visitors of Heritage sites and, consequently, their satisfaction.

Regarding the first aspect, detecting humidity, cracks and imperfections in structures (even those hidden from view) with a non-invasive/non-destructive technique is our main aim. To achieve this would allow us to keep the archaeological artefact or monument under control and to proceed to a quick and effective intervention. In this sense, we pose the challenge of developing a basic tool for the detection of the described defects to obtain results that complement, complete or even substitute those that have been obtained and controlled either manually or by using invasive methodologies up to now. Essentially, our work has two purposes: firstly, we would like to demonstrate that it is possible to act on a work of art with the minimum intervention, avoiding the currently used invasive techniques that consist in making tests in several areas in order to detect possible damage. Secondly, we aim to set up a methodology with which, having determined the problems in advance (mainly those that cannot be seen), work on the Heritage Buildings/pieces can be carried out more precisely and effectively, so that the buildings can be accessible to the public again as soon as possible.

To achieve the second objective, we need to develop techniques that combine the information obtained from a laser scanner, a camera and a thermal camera to provide a representation of the acquired object/scenario in which each 3D point has a colour value and a temperature associated with the intention of automatically generating semantically rich thermal models of Heritage Buildings that are useful for working with BIM methodology. Additionally, the information stored in the thermal point cloud would lead to considerable savings in working hours and human resources since all the useful data would be available at the same time. We would focus on different areas such as Architecture, Sculpture or Epigraphy to identify problems that could be solved using this multisensory information.

In the field of Architecture, the importance of having 3D digital models of historical buildings and architectural remains has proven to be extremely necessary in recent times. If we add the data provided by the thermographic camera, we are faced with a model which not only reflects the external reality of the monument but can help us to unveil hidden structures (pipes, drainage systems...) without the need for making excavations and the consequent destruction of the archaeological remains.

Furthermore, we would like to know whether this technology can help us to segment and classify building materials (wood, brick, marble...), especially in those places unperceived by the human eye. If so, and based on the principle that shape, position and the sort of building material used speak to us about ways of working that can define workshops and epochs, we would like to develop software that would help scientists to discern these patterns of work. This way, the archaeological problem of identifying whether two monuments were built by the same itinerant workshop could be solved. In some cases, helping to corroborate what other sources show (e.g. the planimetry of the buildings and the sculptures decorating them lead us to believe that the Roman Theatre of Lisbon (Portugal) and Medellín (Spain) were built by the same workshop [19]. Could the information obtained from the multisensor 3D model help to confirm this supposition?). In other cases, it would be a brand new discovery, as something hitherto unknown. And related to this, could it help to reinforce the supposed chronology of a building?

In other cases, we know that monuments have been restored in antiquity or in recent times but without following the current rules of restoration. So, based on the principle outlined above, would it be possible to know in what zones and when a monument was restored? Continuing with the Roman epoch, it is well known that the *Circus* of *Augusta Emerita* (Mérida, Spain) was restored at the end of the Roman Empire [20]. Would it still be possible for us to detect something of this restoration? Was it done where and with the extension the epigraphy says?

Related to this, we can highlight one other problem in Archaeology, not only in the field of Architecture but in Sculpture and Epigraphy too: knowing whether there are remains of stucco and the polychromy that decorated them. In antiquity, buildings, statues and inscriptions were painted with bright showy colours. From the Renaissance on, we are obliged to see them in white and all of the remains were cleaned of any possible stains. In recent years, some groups from different Universities and Museums [21] have considered that an artefact/building cannot be completely understood if we are unaware of this aspect of it, and they have developed some techniques to detect the invisible remains of pigments. With the application of this technology, we aim to obtain a complete digital replica of the pieces from which we would be able to obtain not only measures, shapes, etc., but even data on colour too. Some authors are already working on this line of research. For example, Poksińska et al. [22] present a method for the detection of polychromy in whitewashed walls using thermography. Doni et al. [23] employ thermographic images for the analysis of surface, subsurface and structural features of several illuminations belonging to a 15th century antiphonary.

Finally, in the detection of building materials, one branch could even be separated to form an independent research line, i.e. identifying ancient white marble, which is a real problem for scientists. Again, we intend to use Computer Vision techniques to be able to discern the different types of *marmi antichi*, avoiding those currently used invasive techniques that include cutting off a little part of the piece [24]. The key may lie in thermography, by studying the reaction of impurities and different types of crystals to changes in temperature.

To conclude, we should point out that the two aspects outlined at the beginning of this section are complementary since knowledge provided by basic research can lead to a better and more effective intervention on works of art. In the same way, the intervention itself can provide us with data to help in the development of scientific research.

3 The Novelty of Our Proposal

In the field of research in Computer Vision, the novelty of this new line focuses on automatically extracting information from a point cloud where each point has associated information on geometry, colour and temperature, which is obtained after incorporating thermal information to the data acquired by 3D laser scanners. New information fusion techniques will have to be developed to combine data acquired with these different types of sensors. So far, few research groups around the world have addressed the fusion of these technologies applied to the study and conservation of Heritage.

With regard to archaeological research, the key question is avoiding, as far as possible, contact with the piece, so as not to produce any type of damage in the interaction. In the area of conservation and restoration of Heritage, we intend to act on concrete and very specific problems that do not alter the remains of the object/monument. Therefore, to be able to use non-invasive/non-destructive techniques that provide at least the same data as the visual-manual studies used so far will be a qualitative leap in archaeological work and a major advance in scientific research.

The results of the research carried out will be embodied in the creation of a software tool that will facilitate and improve the work of specialists in Cultural Heritage. Having a working tool for digitized models from which to obtain accurate data is an important novelty with respect to what has been achieved so far, since this technology has been limited only to the documentation and reproduction of Archaeological objects/spaces. Using the valuable information generated by the proposed fusion of technologies means opening up a new field of action and applications within the research and conservation of Heritage and, consequently, improving its transfer to society.

Aside from results that can be directly applied in the field of Archaeology, Conservation/Preservation of Cultural Heritage or even in the field of Cultural Tourism, we would like to develop a ramification that would involve from Civil to Electrical Engineering, Computer Vision to History, from antiquity to modern techniques of energy efficiency; in short, we aim to raise BIM (Building Information Models) to the higher level of HBIM (Heritage/Historic Building Information Models).

In past decades, BIM has gradually been incorporated by the construction sector due to its many benefits and savings in resources during the design, planning, and construction of new buildings, and is in fact common practice at present. However, for the maintenance, refurbishment or deconstruction of existing buildings this methodology has barely been used [25]. For Heritage Buildings, until now primary data have been 3D geometric models showing physical conditions. But these data alone are neither sufficient nor very useful. Without the possibility of obtaining information in a complete, aggregated and easily accessible way, there remains a lack of knowledge and usability. The importance of semantically enriched 3D models to provide a more comprehensive repository of any architectural Heritage Building has been evidenced by the growing interest of recent research in this field. Nevertheless, applications are still in their early stages due to the multiple challenges of the topic. Recently, Merchán et al. [26] proposed a new subdivision of the dimensions that HBIM should contain that deals with this new line of development in more detail. As a natural continuation of previous works in which

3D points have been used for the creation of BIM models of civil buildings [27], we would like to continue directing our efforts to produce more and more complete HBIM models which are at present at their first stages of development. We aim to make the leap from generating models from 3D dense point clouds with colour and temperature information which is, at present, carried out manually (and is often slow, expensive and, in some cases, incomplete) to developing techniques that permit automation of the process of HBIM generation.

4   Initial Results

As previously stated, we are currently at the initial stages of this new line of research. Concerning our intention to automatically generate semantically rich thermal models of Heritage Buildings, one of the most important milestones achieved so far is the development of a hybrid 3D laser scanner supplied with colour and thermal cameras. This system provides point clouds with both colour and thermal information (i.e. temperature). It consists of a Riegl VZ-400 3D laser scanner that supports a Nikon D90 colour camera and a FLIR AX5 thermal camera (see Fig. 2). The scanner covers an area of 360° × 100° with precision of 3 mm (one sigma 100 m range). The colour and thermal cameras have resolutions of 4288 × 2848 pixels and 640 × 512 pixels, respectively.

Fig. 2. Hybrid 3D scanner. The universal coordinate system used is illustrated.

Calibrating the acquisition systems with each other so that the thermal data can be projected onto the 3D point cloud is the key operation of this process. Several solutions have been proposed up to now in this regard. Ham et al. [28] have a system composed only of a FLIR E60 thermal camera, capable of acquiring thermal and digital images. A 3D model, both thermal and spatial, is generated by extrinsic and intrinsic calibration (made with a panel composed of 42 LED bulbs). Later the models are aligned taking characteristic points chosen by the user. Rangel et al. [29] use a system consisting of a Microsoft Kinect depth camera and a Jenoptik IR-TCM 640 thermal camera.

A calibration panel is used to obtain the geometric relationship between the two cameras. These authors carried out an exhaustive study on the material used in the panel and its geometric distribution, since the reference points must be visible in both the depth and the thermal image. Borrmann et al. in [30] developed a system consisting of a Riegl VZ-400 3D laser scanner and an Optris PI160 thermal camera. A calibration panel is again used to obtain the relation between both reference systems, in this case made up of 30 incandescent bulbs. The acquisition system created by Mader et al. [31] is not a system integrated into a single device like the previous ones, but consists of three drones each equipped with a different sensor. One of the drones, fitted with a laser range Hokuyo UTM-30LX, is responsible for obtaining the 3D point cloud of the stage. The other two drones, equipped with an RGB camera and a FLIR A65 thermal camera respectively, obtain colour data and thermal information. The calibration between the geometric data and the images is achieved by means of a pattern of markers identifiable by all the sensors. On the lines of the methods discussed above, Chao Wang et al. [32] use a chess-board pattern to record the data obtained with a LiDAR and a thermal camera. The pattern contains gaps in the white boxes so that, when placed in front of a hot body, common features can be seen in both the thermal image and the point cloud to perform the registration.

Other authors propose methodologies that allow 3D information to be combined with thermal information acquired through independent systems. Lagüela et al. [17] propose a methodology that records the relation between geometric and thermal data by means of commercial software; points in common between both scenarios are chosen manually and the data is registered. For the acquisition of data, these authors use a laser scanner Riegl LMS-Z390i and a thermal camera NEC TH9260. In this case, the calibration panel (composed of 64 light bulbs) is used for the intrinsic calibration of the thermal camera and the subsequent correction of the distortion. González-Aguilera et al. [33], on the other hand, present a method for automatic registration of information from both sensors by identifying singular points in the 3D point cloud (obtained using a Photon 80 Lighthouse) and the thermal images (obtained by a FLIR ThermaCAM SC640). Finally, López-Fernández et al. [34] also describe a method that records information from two independent systems. First, they acquire thermal images of each wall with a NEC TH9260 thermal camera, and then they acquire point clouds with an indoor mapping system consisting of a laser Hokuyo UTM-30LX 2D scanner, an IMU and two dual-channel encoders. The registration process between both systems is carried out by selecting homologous features in both images manually.

The fundamental differences with the system we have developed lie in three aspects. Firstly, our calibration system is novel since targets (beacons) incorporating both thermal and reflectance discriminants are used, which increases the accuracy and efficiency of the system. Secondly, the position of the targets is not restricted to small regions as in [29, 30, 32] (contained in small boards), frequently active beacons (bulbs) [30, 31], identified in boards [29, 32] or in image characteristics [17, 28, 33, 34]. In fact, our beacons can cover a wide area of the scene, in positions far from the scanner, and where there are no restrictions on its placement. As a consequence, calibration is more reliable and accurate. Third, many of the referenced systems do not address the problem of completeness of the observable space, so they only obtain a partial thermal map of the scene. Our system is prepared to perform a complete 3D thermal map of the space because it performs an integration of views acquired from one or several positions, obtaining a sampled accumulated map that covers the whole scenario.

The system has been designed to operate in two phases (see Fig. 3). Phase 1 consists of the calibration of the elements of the system and is executed only once. The calibration results are used as the basis for the acquisition of 3D-thermal data in phase 2.

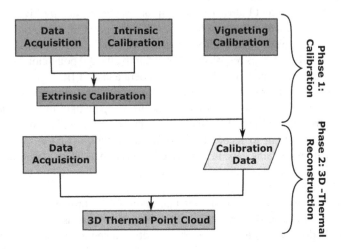

Fig. 3. 3D thermal scanner operation scheme.

In order to achieve the highest quality images, an intrinsic calibration process is performed to obtain the parameters that regulate the distortion present in the images, both for the RGB camera and for the thermal camera, using the method proposed by Heikkilä et al. [35]. The thermal camera, however, has a distortion known as vignetting, which causes a blackening of the edges of the image and which must also be corrected.

Association between pixels of the thermal image with points of the 3D cloud requires calculation of the corresponding projective transformation matrix. This is a transformation that relates the coordinates of the point cloud, (X_p, Y_p, Z_p), to the coordinates of the corresponding projected points in the thermal image, (X_f, Y_f), in pixels. The transformation is modelled in the following equation:

$$\begin{pmatrix} \lambda X_f \\ \lambda Y_f \\ \lambda \end{pmatrix} = \begin{pmatrix} r_{11} & r_{12} & r_{13} & r_{14} \\ r_{21} & r_{22} & r_{23} & r_{24} \\ r_{31} & r_{32} & r_{33} & r_{34} \end{pmatrix} \begin{pmatrix} X_p \\ Y_p \\ Z_p \\ 1 \end{pmatrix} \tag{1}$$

Equation (1) can be expressed as:

$$\begin{pmatrix} X_f \\ Y_f \end{pmatrix} = \begin{pmatrix} X_p & Y_p & Z_p & 1 & 0 & 0 & 0 & 0 & -X_fX_p & -X_fY_p & -X_fZ_p \\ 0 & 0 & 0 & 0 & X_p & Y_p & Z_p & 1 & -Y_fX_p & -Y_fY_p & -Y_fZ_p \end{pmatrix} \begin{pmatrix} r_{11} \\ r_{12} \\ r_{13} \\ r_{14} \\ r_{21} \\ r_{22} \\ r_{23} \\ r_{24} \\ r_{31} \\ r_{32} \\ r_{33} \end{pmatrix} \quad (2)$$

For n pairs of corresponding coordinates, an overdetermined system is formed:

$$\begin{pmatrix} X_{f1} \\ Y_{f1} \\ \vdots \\ X_{fn} \\ y_{fn} \end{pmatrix} = \begin{pmatrix} X_{p1} & Y_{p1} & Z_{p1} & 1 & 0 & 0 & 0 & 0 & -X_{f1}X_{p1} & -X_{f1}Y_{p1} & -X_{f1}Z_{p1} \\ 0 & 0 & 0 & 0 & X_{p1} & Y_{p1} & Z_{p1} & 1 & -Y_{f1}X_{p1} & -Y_{f1}Y_{p1} & -Y_{f1}Z_{p1} \\ & & & & & \vdots & & & & & \\ X_{pn} & Y_{pn} & Z_{pn} & 1 & 0 & 0 & 0 & 0 & -X_{fn}X_{pn} & -X_{fn}Y_{pn} & -X_{fn}Z_{pn} \\ 0 & 0 & 0 & 0 & X_{pn} & Y_{pn} & Z_{pn} & 1 & -Y_{fn}X_{pn} & -Y_{fn}Y_{pn} & -Y_{fn}Z_{pn} \end{pmatrix} \begin{pmatrix} r_{11} \\ r_{12} \\ r_{13} \\ r_{14} \\ r_{21} \\ r_{22} \\ r_{23} \\ r_{24} \\ r_{31} \\ r_{32} \\ r_{33} \end{pmatrix} \quad (3)$$

This can be expressed as $= WP$.

Once the coordinates of pixels (X_f, Y_f), the corresponding 3D coordinates of the associated point are known (X_p, Y_p, Z_p), and on imposing $r_{34} = 1$, Eq. (3) is solved by:

$$P = (W^T W)^{-1} W^T C \quad (4)$$

In practice, in the calibration procedure, reflective targets are glued together in small plastic ice cubes. This facilitates their location in both the reflectance image associated with the 3D point cloud and in the thermal image. Matching of corresponding points is made by means of a search algorithm for positioning of targets in the image and subsequent refinement, and the consistency between the corresponding sets verified.

Data acquisition is performed in three sequential phases:

- First, the 3D scanner captures the 3D coordinates of points reached by the laser in a space defined by the vertical (λ) and horizontal (θ) angle range set by the user. Usually the range of λ is maintained at [30°, 130°], while the range of θ is set at will.
- Secondly, the RGB and thermal cameras perform, starting from $\theta = 0$, the number of captures required to completely cover the range of θ chosen in the session. Depending on the field of view of the cameras, each capture is performed after turning the system at a horizontal angle that guarantees a minimum overlap between consecutive thermal images.

- Third, images are preprocessed and temperature values are assigned to the point cloud taken in the first phase. Preprocessing consists essentially of the elimination of vignetting and distortion correction.

This system has been tested in building indoor environments with very good results. We present here findings obtained in the building that housed the winch of the Nueva Concepción mine in Almadenejos (Spain) as a case study: the so-called Baritel de San Carlos. Considered as a jewel of industrial archaeology worldwide, this curious building dates from the last years of the 18th century and the first of the 19th, and is in a reasonably good state of conservation. It consists of a single piece of polygonal shape on the outside, 16 equal sides, and circular in the interior, 17 m in diameter. It is finished in the interior with a spherical-conical vault and on the outside with a ceramic-tiled 16-sided pitched roof. Moved by animal traction, the lathe of its interior (which is not conserved) was used to introduce and extract men and materials from the mine (see Fig. 4).

Fig. 4. Baritel de San Carlos: exterior and interior views.

To generate the thermal point cloud of this Heritage Building 13 scanner shots were taken from 5 positions, with the following approximate volume of data: 78.3 million spatial points, of which 55% have assigned colour and 3% contain thermal information. In the data collection process, 40 reflective targets were used. The range in θ was [0, 360°], with a scanning step of the scanner of 0.08°. Fifteen photographs were taken for a complete rotation of the scanner. The time for data acquisition was 47 s. for scanner data acquisition (in 360° range) and 80 s. for colour and thermal imaging.

Figure 5 shows the initial results for the thermal model using a pseudocolour code. The complete thermal cloud of the interior building depicted from an external viewpoint is shown at the top. The cones of points that are seen coming out of it correspond with areas of doors and windows. The lower part of the figure is formed by two distinct interior zones. There are no large differences in temperature values, these being around 20 °C, hence the colour homogeneity. The beacons used for calibration appear as red points and the humid areas of the walls are easily identifiable.

(a)

(b)

Fig. 5. (a) Thermal cloud of the interior of Baritel de San Carlos. (b) Details of interior zones of the Heritage Building.

Continuing with the idea of automatic generation of semantically rich thermal models that could be used in HBIM methodology, we have also taken the first steps in a line of research that is currently open: the automatic segmentation of dense 3D point clouds provided by laser scanners.

Segmentation of point clouds is usually solved by region growing methods, which use the similarity between the normal directions of the planes fitted locally at each 3D point [36, 37]. Recently, a procedure that classifies point clouds into architectural elements based on super vector machine (*SVM*) has been proposed [38]. In Fig. 6 some preliminary results, obtained using the method proposed in [36] in the 3D point cloud of Nuestra Señora de la Candelaria church in Fuente del Maestre (Badajoz, Spain), are shown.

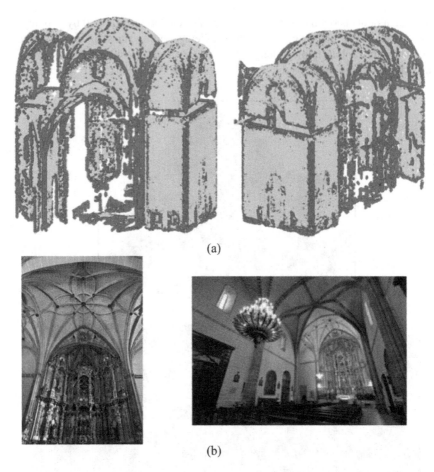

Fig. 6. (a) Segmentation of a partial point cloud of Nuestra Señora de la Candelaria church in Fuente del Maestre (Spain) (b) using the method proposed in [36].

In the near future, we plan to add the information provided by the colour images and the temperatures acquired with the thermal camera to the geometric information contained in the point clouds to enhance the segmentation procedure.

5   Conclusions

In the 21st century, with the growth of digitization and globalized knowledge, the multidisciplinary approach seems to be the most effective way of working. Thus, eminently humanistic subjects need to know how to take advantage of the opportunities that current technology provides. Imbued with that spirit and with the intention of promoting intercultural and interdisciplinary cooperation new lines of research are born.

The incorporation of thermal cameras to the data obtained with laser scanners and colour cameras to generate thermal semantic models of Heritage Buildings is a subject scarcely undertaken until now by research groups worldwide. Using the valuable information generated by the proposed fusion of technologies means opening up a new field of action and applications within research and conservation of Heritage, which will be not only a qualitative leap in archaeological work but a major advance in scientific research.

Acknowledgments. This work has been supported by the projects IB16162 from Junta de Extremadura and Fondo Europeo de Desarrollo Regional "Una manera de hacer Europa" and DPI2016-76380-R, from the Spanish Ministry of Economy, Industry and Competitiveness, and by the FEDER Funds (Programa Operativo FEDER de Extremadura 2014-2020) through the grant "Ayuda a Grupos de Investigación" (ref. GR15178) of Junta de Extremadura.

References

1. Levoy, M., Pulli, K., Curless, B., Rusinkiewicz, S., Koller, D., Pereira, L., Ginzton, M., Anderson, S., Davis, J., Ginsberg, J., Shade, J., Fulk, D.: The digital Michelangelo project: 3D scanning of large statues. In: Proceedings of the 27th Annual Conference on Computer Graphics and Interactive Techniques, pp. 131–144 (2000)
2. Koller, D., Trimble, J., Najbjerg, T., Gelfand, N., Levoy, M.: Fragments of the city: Stanford's digital forma urbis romae project. J. Roman Archaeol. Suppl. **61**, 237–252 (2006)
3. Siotto, E., Dellepiane, M., Callieri, M., Scopigno, R., Gratziu, C., Moscato, A., Burgio, L., Legnaioli, S., Lorenzetti, G., Palleschi, V.: A multidisciplinary approach for the study and the virtual reconstruction of the ancient polychromy of Roman sarcophagi. J. Cult. Heritage **16**, 307–314 (2015)
4. Potenziani, M., Callieri, M., Dellepiane, M., Corsini, M., Ponchio, F., Scopigno, R.: 3DHOP: 3D Heritage online presenter. Comput. Graph. **52**, 129–141 (2015)
5. Scopigno, R., Cignoni, P., Pietroni, N., Callieri, M., Dellepiane, M.: Digital fabrication techniques for Cultural Heritage: a survey. Comput. Graph. Forum 36(1), 6–21 (2016)
6. Lerma, J.L., Cabrelles, M., Navarro, S.: Fusion of range-based data and image-based datasets for efficient documentation of Cultural Heritage objects and sites. In: The International Archives of the Photogrammetry, Remote Sensing and Spatial Information Sciences, XL-5/W7, pp. 277–281 (2015)
7. Domingo, I., Villaverde, V., López-Montalvo, E., Lerma, J.L., Cabrelles, M.: Latest developments in rock art recording: Towards an integral documentation of Levantine rock art sites combining 2D and 3D recording techniques. J. Archaeol. Sci. **40**(4), 1879–1889 (2012)
8. Adán, A., Salamanca, S., Merchán, P.: A hybrid human-computer approach for recovering incomplete Cultural Heritage pieces. Comput. Graph. **36**(1), 1–15 (2012)
9. Merchán, P., Salamanca, S., Adán, A.: Restitution of sculptural groups using 3D scanners. Sensors (MDPI) **11**(9), 8497–8518 (2011)
10. Merchán, P., Adán, A., Salamanca, S., Domínguez, V., Chacón, R.: Geometric and colour data fusion for outdoor 3D models. Sensors (MDPI) **12**(6), 6893–6919 (2012)
11. Grinzato, E.: IR thermography applied to the Cultural Heritage conservation. In: 18th World Conference on Nondestructive Testing (2012)

12. Mercuri, F., Orazi, N., Zammit, U., Paoloni, S., Marinelli, M., Valentini, P.P.: Thermographic analysis of Cultural Heritage: recent applications and perspectives. E-preservation Sci. **9**, 84–89 (2012)

13. Sidiropoulou-Velidou, D., Georgopoulos, A., Lerma, J.L.: Exploitation of thermal imagery for the detection of pathologies in monuments. In: Ioannides, M., Fritsch, D., Leissner, J., Davies, R., Remondino, F., Caffo, R. (eds.) EuroMed 2012. LNCS, vol. 7616, pp. 97–108. Springer, Heidelberg (2012). https://doi.org/10.1007/978-3-642-34234-9_10

14. Alba, M.I., Barazzetti, L., Scaioni, M., Rosina, E., Previtali, M.: Mapping infrared data on terrestrial laser scanning 3D models of buildings. Remote Sens. **3**, 1847–1870 (2011)

15. Borrmann, D., Nüchter, A., Dakulovic, M., Maurovic, I., Petrovic, I., Osmankovic, D., Velagic, J.: The project thermalmapper – thermal 3D mapping of indoor environments for saving energy. In: The 10th International IFAC Symposium on Robot Control (SYROCO 2012), Dubrovnik, Croatia (2012)

16. Borrmann, D., Elseberg, J., Nüchter, A.: Thermal 3D mapping of building façades. In: Lee, S., Cho, H., Yoon, K.J., Lee, J. (eds.) Intelligent Autonomous Systems 12. Advances in Intelligent Systems and Computing, vol. 193, pp. 173–182. Springer, Heidelberg (2013)

17. Lagüela, S., Martínez, J., Armesto, J., Arias, P.: Energy efficiency studies through 3D laser scanning and thermographic technologies. Energy Build. **43**, 1216–1221 (2011)

18. Cabrelles, M., Galcerá, S., Navarro, S., Lerma, J.L., Akasheh, T.: Haddad: N.: Integration of 3D laser scanning, photogrammetry and thermography to record architectural monuments. In: 22nd CIPA Symposium (2009)

19. Fernandes, L., Nogales, T.: Programas decorativos teatrales de Lusitania: teatro romano de Olisipo. In: Escultura romana en Hispania VIII (in press)

20. Velázquez, A.: Placa con inscripción sobre la restauración del circo romano de Mérida. In: Alvarez, J.M., Carvalho, A., Fabiao, C. (eds.) Lusitania Romana. Origen de dos pueblos, pp. 309–310 (2015)

21. Università di Firenze, with Paolo Liverani in the lead, or Ny Carlsberg Glyptotek with its project Tracking Colour (http://www.trackingcolour.com/) among others

22. Poksińska, M., Cupa, A., Socha-Bystroń, S.: Thermography in the investigation of gilding on historical wall paintings. In: 9th International Conference on Quantitative InfraRed Thermography, Krakow – Poland (2008)

23. Donia, G., Orazi, N., Mercuri, F., Cicero, C., Zammit, U., Paoloni, S., Marinelli, M.: Thermographic study of the illuminations of a 15th century antiphonary. J. Cult. Heritage **15** (6), 692–697 (2014)

24. Vide bibliography of G. Borghini, P. Pensabene, P. Lapuente, J. Beltrán, etc.

25. Volk, R., Stengel, J., Schultmann, F.: Building Information Modeling (BIM) for existing buildings—Literature review and future needs. Autom. Constr. **38**, 109–127 (2014)

26. Merchán, P., Rivera, B., Salamanca, S., Merchán, M.J.: From BIM to HBIM: current state and perspectives. In: Cultural Heritage: Perspectives, Challenges and Future Directions. Nova Science Publishers, New York (2017)

27. Adan, A., Huber, D.: Reconstruction of wall surfaces under occlusion and clutter in 3D indoor environments. Robotics Institute, Carnegie Mellon University, Pittsburgh, PA CMU-RI-TR-10-12 (2010)

28. Ham, Y., Golparvar-Fard, M.: An automated vision-based method for rapid 3D energy performance modeling of existing buildings using thermal and digital imagery. Adv. Eng. Inform. **27**, 395–409 (2013)

29. Rangel, J., Soldan, S., Kroll, A.: 3D Thermal imaging: fusion of thermography and depth cameras. In: Quantitative InfraRed Thermography (2014)

30. Borrmann, D., Nüchter, A., Đakulović, M., Maurovic, I., Petrović, I., Osmankovic, D., Velagić, J.: A mobile robot based system for fully automated thermal 3D mapping. Adv. Eng. Inform. **28**(4), 425–440 (2014)

31. Mader, D., Blaskow, R., Westfeld, P., Weller, C.: Potential of UAV-Based laser scanner and multispectral camera data in building inspection. In: International Archives of the Photogrammetry, Remote Sensing and Spatial Information Sciences - ISPRS Archives, pp. 1135–1142 (2016)

32. Wang, C., Cho, Y.K., Gai, M.: As-Is 3D thermal modeling for existing building envelopes using a hybrid LIDAR system. J. Comput. Civil Eng. **27**, 645–656 (2013)

33. González-Aguilera, D., Rodriguez-Gonzalvez, P., Armesto, J., Lagüela, S.: Novel approach to 3D thermography and energy efficiency evaluation. Energy Build. **54**, 436–443 (2012)

34. López-Fernández, L., Lagüela, S., González-Aguilera, D., Lorenzo, H.: Thermographic and mobile indoor mapping for the computation of energy losses in buildings. Indoor Built Environ. **26**(6), 1–14 (2016)

35. Heikkila, J., Silven, O.: A four-step camera calibration procedure with implicit image correction. In: Proceedings of the IEEE Computer Society Conference on Computer Vision and Pattern Recognition, pp. 1106–1112 (1997)

36. Demantké, J., Mallet, C., David, N., Vallet, B.: Dimensionality based scale selection in 3D LIDAR point clouds. In: ISPRS - International Archives of the Photogrammetry Remote Sensing and Spatial Information Sciences, vol. XXXVIII-5/, pp. 97–102 (2012)

37. Nurunnabi, A., Belton, D., West, G.: Robust segmentation for large volumes of laser scanning three-dimensional point cloud data. IEEE Trans. Geosci. Remote Sens. **54**, 4790–4805 (2016)

38. Bassier, M., Vergauwen, M., Van Genechten, B.: Automated classification of Heritage Buildings for as-built BIM using machine learning techniques. In: SPRS Annals of the Photogrammetry, Remote Sensing and Spatial Information Sciences, vol. IV-2/W2 (2017)

Map Portal as a Tool to Share Information on Cultural Heritage Illustrated by the National Heritage Board Geoportal

Anna Fiedukowicz[1(✉)], Andrzej Głażewski[1], Arkadiusz Kołodziej[1],
Krzysztof Koszewski[2], Paweł Kowalski[1], Robert Olszewski[1],
and Leszek Włochyński[2]

[1] Faculty of Geodesy and Cartography,
Warsaw University of Technology, Warsaw, Poland
a.fiedukowicz@gik.pw.edu.pl
[2] Faculty of Architecture, Warsaw University of Technology, Warsaw, Poland

Abstract. The distribution of information has become an element of heritage conservation policy, as well as a tool aiming at sustainable use of historic resources, or even a prerequisite of effective conservation. This aspect is very often underestimated and reduced to simple popularization, which consequently oversimplifies such complex mater, what historic site conservation is. The issues described above are addressed by the authors of this article through the project run on behalf of the National Heritage Board (NHB) attempting to place and publish the information on all historic sites' resources entered in the register of objects of cultural heritage (the heritage register).

Hierarchical classification was prepared within this project in order to sequentially establish: general categories of monuments, separate classes for architectural and archaeological sites, and finally, formal/functional typology for architectural monuments. The signatures for each group were carefully designed and prepared. The efficient visualisation of historical sites was possible due to the common utilisation of advanced information technologies as well as modern cartographical solutions. Authors had shown the importance of spatial reference of historical sites achieved by visualising them jointly with up-to-date spatial topographical and a general database as well as a digital terrain model. Last but not least, the meaning of user interface has been highlighted as the tool of communication and interaction with the final user.

The geoportal developed during this project can be seen as a modern digital tool supporting state heritage conservation policy and popularising knowledge about historical sites among the wide group of users.

Keywords: Geoportal · GIS · Historical sites · Heritage · Map
Geoinformation

© Springer International Publishing AG, part of Springer Nature 2018
M. Ioannides et al. (Eds.): Digital Cultural Heritage 2017, LNCS 10754, pp. 48–64, 2018.
https://doi.org/10.1007/978-3-319-75789-6_4

1 Introduction - The Importance of Information Distribution on Historic Sites from the Perspective of Cultural Heritage Conservation

Contemporary discourse concerning the preservation of historical buildings, in its broad sense, concentrates on the notion of their value. Analogously to the situation over 100 years ago, when in the era of industrialisation and urbanisation, the foundations for the conservation doctrine were developed, such as Alois Riegl's concept of monument value for instance, current phenomena in the social, economic, and cultural sphere have a significant influence on the manner in which we wish to preserve historical buildings and how we intend to define the notion of their protection. Industrial society, being the denominator of the context for the commencement of conservation doctrines, transformed into information society, which in turn converted into knowledge society. The priorities and values altered and became wealthier, including those related to monuments. Apart from their historical, artistic, and scientific value, aspects of usefulness, the possibility to weave such structures into modernity, to actively use and revive them seem to appear more and more frequent. All this may be achieved by the dissemination of knowledge on heritage. This knowledge becomes one of the elements of the historical building's value, a certain added value, the more treasured in the context of the identity and development of modern societies, the more widespread it turns out to be. Thus, disseminating knowledge on historical buildings has transpired to be an immanent element of heritage protection policy and a tool for the sustainable use of monument resources. It is illustrated by numerous references both in doctrine documents as well as in relevant contracts[1].

If a question is posed: how the notion of a historical building should be understood in modern terms, one of the possible answers would state that it is the part of a tangible and intangible acquis of community, at various scales - from local to global, which a given society wishes to inherit from the previous generations and pass on to future generations due to its value in relation to preserving cultural continuity [1]. When assuming such a perspective, increased social awareness of heritage needs to be taken into account.

The results of research [2] conducted prior to the works on the present article concerning the map portal for NHB form a picture of the monument protection system[2] in Poland which lacks effective mechanisms for collecting updates and providing access to panoramic information on heritage subject to legal protection (i.e. resources

---

[1] See for instance: "The Paris Declaration on heritage as a driver of development" adopted at Paris, UNESCO headquarters, on Thursday 1st December 2011; Operational Guidelines for the Implementation of the World Heritage Convention of February 2012 in the part related to education; European Commission Recommendation of 24th August 2006 on digitisation and online accessibility of cultural material and digital preservation (2006/585/EC).

[2] Compare: B. Szmygin, editor, Hertitage Preservation System in Poland - Analysis, Diagnosis, Suggestions, Polish National Committee ICOMOS, Monument Conservator Office for the Capital City of Warsaw, Lublin University of Technology, Warszawa-Lublin, 2011; Jacek Purchla, editor, Report on the functioning of cultural heritage protection system in Poland after 1989, MKiDN, Kraków, 2008.

included in heritage register). One of the alternatives, yet imperfect and far from complete and even more so from the expected professional and official solutions, are services developed by heritage lovers which cover architectural monuments where particular sites are located on maps and briefly characterised.

Therefore, the project conducted by the authors and commissioned by The National Heritage Board of Poland, apart from responding to the formal requirements stipulated in the EU INSPIRE Directive, also addresses factual social and professional needs related to the accessibility of information on location and description of protected heritage sites.

Developing the map portal for the NHB has been preceded by an analysis of other database systems[3] used worldwide which relate to knowledge on heritage as well as theoretical models included in scientific papers [3, 4]. The research allowed for drawing valuable conclusions for the project concerning, in principle, the readability and adequacy of the information and visualisations presented in the systems.

Thus, the information distribution has become a vital element of heritage conservation policy, as well as a tool aiming at the sustainable use of historic resources. This may be seen even as a prerequisite of effective conservation. Such aspects are very often underestimated and reduced to simple popularization, which consequently oversimplifies this complex matter, which is historic site conservation (preservation). To avoid this, conscious utilising of adequate tools, including IT technologies and geoinformation, supported by an appropriately designed visual message has to be adopted. The numerous indications in strategic documents, as well as recommendations concerning heritage conservation serve as evidence [5].

2 Map Portal as Part of Heritage Preservation

The issues described above are addressed by the authors of this article through the project run on behalf of The National Heritage Board of Poland (NHB) in an attempt to place and publish the information on all historic sites' resources entered in the register of objects of cultural heritage (the heritage register). The task was a part of an INSPIRE directive, however, contrary to the basic requirements of the directive, as far as the elaborated portal is concerned, a much broader scope of information on the historical sites was included.

Cartographic representation of protected sites in accordance with INSPIRE Guidelines [6] is limited to basic graphic forms: point symbols presented as grey squares, line symbols and area symbols with grey fill (Fig. 1). Presentation of any qualitative information, above all, including information on the kind or dating of a given site, with the use of such symbols is simply impossible. That is why an original idea of cartographic visualisation of sites on the portal has been developed in order to

---

[3] E.g. English Heritage (http://list.english-heritage.org.uk/mapsearch.aspx, accessed on 18.12.2013); Kulturdenkmaeler in Hessen (http://denkxweb.denkmalpflege-hessen.de, accessed on 18.12.2013); Bayern Atlas (http://geoportal.bayern.de/bayernatlas/, accessed on 18.12.2013); Visualisation of New York buildings according to their age (http://bdon.org/2013/09/12/building-age-nyc/, accessed on 18.12.2013); Buildings in Holland (http://citysdk.waag.org/buildings/, accessed on 18.12.2013).

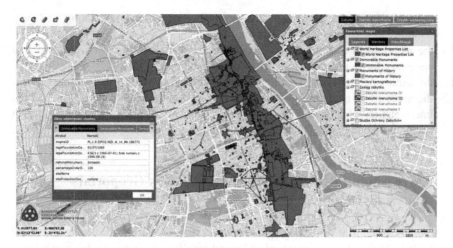

Fig. 1. Cartographic presentation of immovable heritage in accordance with INSPIRE specifications [6]

be able to present on the map data on formal-functional types or dating heritage sites, which are crucial for the issue of heritage protection.

Both the process of symbolisation as well as the preceding stage of source data processing, for instance selection and reclassification of sites, required the use of innovative graphic concepts and geoinformation tools. It resulted from a very complex structure of the source database, as well as from requirements imposed on the final cartographic presentation. The most critical problems included the following:

1. a large number of sites requiring individual presentation: 78 thousand, 70190 of which were immovable, mostly architectural, and 7727 were archeological sites;
2. the need for special treatment, consisting in exclusion form quantitative generalisation, of two site groups: sites from UNESCO World Heritage List (30) and historical monuments (71);
3. irregular density of sites requiring spatial aggregation of clusters which cannot be presented individually in each display scale;
4. collections of sites, especially in historical centres of settlements, which cannot be presented in the medium and small scale require the use of unusual grouping and location of point symbols;
5. multi-representation of site geometry, the range of which is registered in the database as well as lineal sites;
6. a large number of descriptive attributes requiring the indication of a few key classifying characteristics which are significant from the user's perspective and which at the same time, may be represented graphically;
7. a large number of values representing formal-functional characteristics which requires material reduction, re-classification, as well as appropriate graphic representation;
8. presence of uncertain and unspecified values of descriptive attributes, (i.e. dating, which justify the introduction of an additional symbol class);

9. the requirement of multi-scale cohesion of cartographic presentation and map legibility at each declared scale level;
10. the requirement of the use of a geodetic reference base for each scale, which is necessary for the identification of a site's location;
11. the requirement of symbol recognisability and legibility within the Internet service;
12. the necessity to apply the so-called active legend to the map, which allows for the interpretation of the symbols at a given moment displayed on the map area excluding the symbols which are not displayed in the user's browser.

3 Cartographic Representation in the NHB's Geoportal mapy.zabytek.gov.pl

The paramount aim of the cartographic representation of the historical sites in Poland available in National Heritage Board of Poland map Portal (mapy.zabytek.gov.pl) was consistency of the overall visual message. Basic assumptions of cartographic representation are the three following qualities: fidelity, generalisation and symbolisation. However, from the perspective of visual communique, the content classification followed by its visual representation proves to be the key.

The database elaborated by the NHB, which lay at the foundation of the map portals, includes information from the digitised heritage register, both concerning immovable monuments (architectural) as well as archaeological ones and has a very broad chronological and typological scope of objects. It also comprises the information on a number of distinctive features of each object. As the result one of the major challenges proved to be the coinage of simple and clear classification criteria concerning the visual resources, according to which the database shall be converged into finite set of visual representations.

In the process of designing the symbols, the objectives of cartographic symbolisation design needed to be observed, namely: legibility and conciseness. Another criterion implemented was geometric simplicity, while retaining individuality and distinctiveness. The readability of the sign was an utmost priority. As the medium of presentation are electronic devices (geoportal browser) the designed symbols had to meet certain technical requirements. In the course of work on the project a conclusion was reached that in order to retain readability, the visualisation can comprise of a few dozen visually distinctive symbols within a more limited colour range, maximum.

Due to the character of the NHB historical sites' database, both the cartographic representation and the user interface serving as its frame of reference, required novel solutions. To meet the requirements above, such information architecture was assumed which aimed at the simplification of access while providing valid and high quality information. The elaborated system comprises:

- the classification criteria of the historic sites' resources for the purpose of presentation and GIS (responding most of all to problems: 6, 7, 8),
- the rules of information presentation in different scales (along with scale specification with reference to points 9 and 10),
- the rules and mechanisms of spatial data aggregation (1, 2, 3, 4, 5),

- the idea behind the cartographic matrix and it's rules (1, 3, 4),
- the visual communication system including monument symbolisation and map portal graphic specifications (2, 5, 6, 7, 8, 11),
- special user interface functionality (e.g. the dynamic legend mechanisms, thematic data aggregations in answer to points 3 and 12).

3.1 Classification Criteria

It has been decided that the target monument visualisation on the NHB map portals will cover above all typological differentiations represented by the symbol's shape and chronological differentiations by its colour.

New classification introduced for the purpose of the NHB map portal adopted the principal notion of monument which refers to all represented architectural and archaeological phenomena irrespectively of their further classification.

Four general categories have been introduced within the scope of the term 'monument' (i.e. world heritage sites such as; UNESCO, historical monuments, immovable monuments, and archaeological sites).

Further levels of classification within the category of immovable monument includes classes and types constituting a reflection of formal and functional characteristics of the monuments represented. As it has been mentioned above, the number of visual discriminants, both geometrical and by colour, could not be very high. Therefore, the set of visualised characteristics is a limitation of criteria when compared to the information provided by the database developed earlier by the NHB. It is particularly well reflected in the functional discriminants in the group of immovable monuments included within the NHB database, where for instance in the case of the site class 'building' originally over 200 types were found. Due to adopting prerequisites limiting the number of visual discriminants, it has been established that the NHB geoportal will visualise, in the form of icons, all site classes found within the NHB database and only some, the most significant ones, formal-functional types stipulated at further functional levels. The remaining, less significant, types will be assigned to the superior class and represented by the class's relevant icon. The determination of the most significant types of immovable monuments (architectural) was based on the standard rooted in literature on the subject-matter and tradition of cartographic works.

The chronological frame of reference for the data on object's creation was: for the archaeological monuments - division into ages, while for the architectural monuments - into centuries, discarding the style classification. The reason being, that researchers are not unanimous when it comes to the dating of particular historical periods and styles in Polish architecture. To complicate matters even further the area of Poland was under different political and administrative jurisdiction over the last centuries and was subject to different cultural influence, which resulted in diverse dynamics in architectural development. That, consequently, resulted in different times of architectural style changes across Poland.

To illustrate the chronological spectrum the authors resorted to colour. The chromatic scale refers to the established tradition of colour use in stratification illustrations in the architectural and historical research [7]. Additionally, colour was also added to indicate the object with no dating. On the other hand, in cases where specific dating of

Table 1. Chronological frame for architectural monuments and colours assigned to the listed periods

Age	from	to	the centuries included	the colour or discriminant
A- early Middle Ages	901	1250	X - XIII	
B - late Middle Ages	1251	1500	XIII - XV	
(mostly Gothic architecture)	1501	1800	XVI - XVIII	
C- the early modern period (mostly Renaissance + Baroque)	1801	1900	XIX	
D - XIX century	1901		XX -	
no dating				
multi-phase object				

the object was impossible, a cartographic discriminant was used (an affix) in the form of a multicolour bar under the symbol while, the key period for the object was indicated with the colour of the symbol itself (Table 1).

Typological character as well as the chronology of sites belonging to the archaeological sites group and the immovable monuments group (architectural) transpired to be distinct to the extent which makes their simultaneous presentation within common visualisation confusing as far as the map interpretation is concerned. In view of the foregoing, it has been suggested that data visualisation should be presented in two separate and differently configured profiles: an 'archaeological profile' and an 'architectural profile'.

3.2   The Rules of Information

Due to the interactive character of the NHB portal, enabling the user free change of the scale of presentation, 6 scale levels of content permutation were specified. They refer to the following scales: 1:1,000, 1:10,000, 1:50,000, 1:300,000, 1:2 mln., and 1:5 mln.

Each of the levels listed receives appropriate content and visual representation of the reference data by selecting the adequate sources and classes of data, reclassifying and symbolisation. In order to ensure the correct visual perception [8], the authors devised a novel solution in the aggregation of particular historic objects too, the so called, 'cartographic matrix' (Fig. 2). The reference scale in each level defines the level of detail of data (historic objects) and generalisation criteria (including the minimum area and length of an object, represented without resorting to reduction to a point symbol).

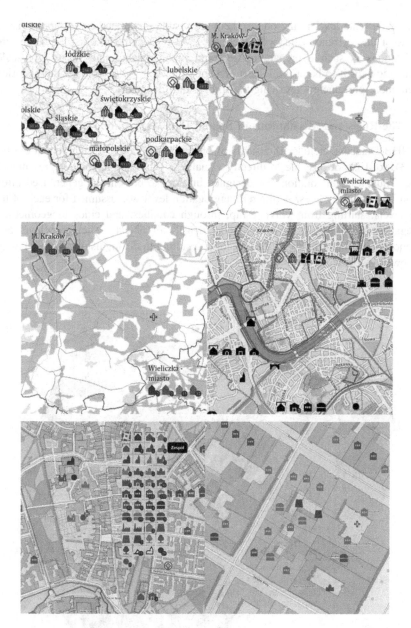

Fig. 2. Different ways of defining the cartographic matrices and aggregation within them, depending on the level of detail of the viewed map: A - the country level - objects for a voivodeship - division into architectural and archaeological sites, with UNESCO, Historic Monument, B - county - division according to monument classes, C - community - division according to chronology, D - an accumulation of object - division according to functional and formal types, E - an accumulation of objects - division according to function and chronology, F - lack of cartographic matrices (large scale) - objects in their real location classified according to function and chronology [source: http://mapy.zabytek.gov.pl/].

On each scale level in the portal, there are visible predefined cartographic visualisations of the reference data, with adequate level of detail. The key idea behind the visualisations is such a preparation of cartographic background (using greyscale, brightening), for it to be at the lowest perceptive level in order to make the historical objects more prominent - reserving the foreground for them.

3.3   The Rules and Mechanisms of Spatial Data Aggregation

The NHB Database includes thousands of objects with relatively high spatial density (Fig. 3), so it is not possible to directly visualise all the data in smaller presentation scales. Thus, a novel solution was designed in order to present the generalised information in particular scales. A different aggregation level was assumed for each of the scale levels: starting from voivodeship, through counties, and cities to geometrical aggregation - resulting from a high local density of objects. The scale level also influenced the generalisation of the typology, resulting in distinguishing from a few up to a few dozen categories.

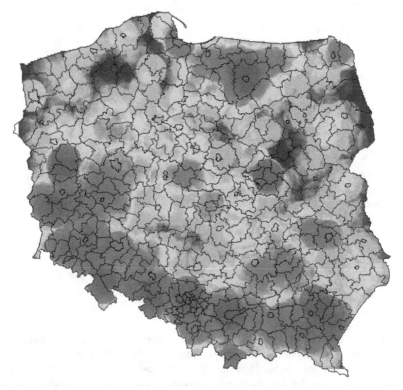

Fig. 3. A map of the density of immovable historic sites in Poland (objects per km^2).

A great number of objects included in the NHB database allows for direct visualisation of the historic sites, both architectural and archaeological in the portal only in the largest scale, namely: 1:500 or 1:1000, where besides a symbol, a dot and area method were used.

3.4   Cartographic Matrix

Visualisation of a large number of sites located on a limited area constituted quite a challenge irrespectively of the technology of map formation. A particular example of that problem is the visualisation of point symbols with a high and frequently uneven density. Analogue maps often address the problem by partially resigning from the preciseness of site location and assigning them to a particular locality, for instance (Fig. 4). Such a solution allowed for more legibility of the map as well as including more information on a greater number of sites when compared to the solution in which their precise location is indicated. In the case of online maps with the possibility of changing the scale, most frequently all icons are displayed, which unfortunately are not legible when smaller scales are used. Another solution is aggregating icons in groups and the most common technology used in such cases is Leaflet Technology. One of the disadvantages of such a solution is displaying solely the number of a given group; until the display is not enlarged to a required scale, there is no information on the types of sites represented.

Fig. 4. A traditional manner of assigning sites to localities on analogous maps; on the right: application of cartographic matrices assigned to localities.

The authors have suggested an innovative solution, namely a cartographic matrix. It is rooted in cartographic tradition as it groups sites either according to particular administrative units or natural settlements using modern geoinformation tools. A cartographic matrix groups sites according to certain criteria, the detailedness of which is

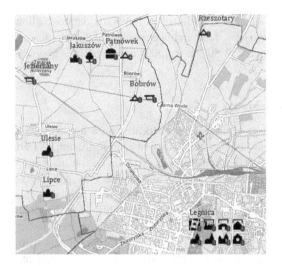

Fig. 5. Application of cartographic matrices assigned to localities.

dependent on the scale, presenting the count of particular groups (Fig. 5). When compared to the solution applied in analogous maps, the presented approach has the advantage that the aggregation criteria may be changed, for instance formal-functional type or dating, and the units to which the matrices are assigned may be altered as well, e.g. voivodeships, poviats, gminas, localities, natural settlements.

3.5   The Visual Communication System

The visual communication system designed for the map portal discussed contains three basic elements correlated to from a coherent whole. These are the following:

- Map compositions selected with special attention paid to legibility which encompasses good icon visibility against the map background
- A set of icons representing hierarchically ordered monument symbolisation: categories, classes, and selected formal-functional types with their variants
- Navigation elements enabling quick access to information (discussed in the previous point)

When designing symbols for sites, special attention has been paid to semiotic issues, Peirce's triad theory in particular: sign-object-interpretant, forming a coherent whole [9]. It has been assumed that the characteristic constituting the sign form (according to the Peirce sign-vehicle), searched for in the object to be marked, is the archetypical form of a given building type and not its ideological connotations. It is a partial migration away from cartographic tradition which, for instance, willingly used the sign of a cross to indicate a Roman Catholic church on a map instead of a sign corresponding to its form [10]. From among the three kinds of signs defined by Pierce: indications, indices and symbols, this approach favours the first one i.e. indications (here: a term used not in the sense of synonym to all signs on maps or computer screens, but in the meaning of a kind of sign reflecting physical similarity to the object). At Times it transpires to be a quite difficult task as formal diversity of monument classes and groups represented is significant, yet such an approach is based on the postulate to achieve cohesion within one semiotic system. Additionally, such a manner of representation which emphasises the physical characteristic of an object is considered to be the most obvious and most efficient in terms of communication [11].

This set of icons has been designed in groups corresponding to the hierarchy categories-classes-types on the one side, and on the other, to the need for generalisation of data displayed on the map.

In the system, there are five general categories (Fig. 6) and corresponding icons, three of which (the monument icon, the so-called 'shield', designed by Jan Zachwatowicz and adopted in 1954 under the Hague Convention; the icon of a UNESCO World Heritage List site, Historical Monument) have been adopted from the existing designations. The remaining two correspond to immovable monuments and archaeological sites. Symbolisation within a category is used at the scale level corresponding to the whole country, voivodeships and poviats (see: Fig. 1).

Classes of monuments are represented by 9 icons used at the scale level corresponding to gminas level (Fig. 5). When the map is enlarged, the classification of monuments becomes more detailed and is represented by 36 icons corresponding to formal-functional types (Fig. 6).

The above-described sets of icons are used for the display of immovable monuments in scales corresponding to gminas (at that scale level, monument typology is visible). The user has the possibility to change the profile of information displayed so that archaeological sites are shown. These are represented by 13 icons corresponding to their formal-functional types (Fig. 6). 9 of the icons reflect the symbols applied in archaeology, the remaining ones are variants of icons used in the symbolisation of architectural monument types which are also found as archaeological sites.

Apart from the variants mentioned above, there have also been colour versions designed corresponding to the chronology of the presented monuments (Table 1 and Fig. 6) as well as versions designating monument complexes (Fig. 7). It is a set of 68 icons, colour versions excluded. From the user's perspective the number is quite vast[4], yet the adopted mechanisms of dynamic presentation of monuments which result from the generalisation corresponding to a given scale and area displayed significantly alleviate the problem. Similarly, the number of icons displayed at a time on the user's screen is limited thanks to cartographic matrices and a dynamic key.

Taking into consideration the importance of icon legibility as well as technical conditions of displaying the icons by the system, they have been designed on a 16 × 16 modular grid so that the size of the smallest element of the sign is at least one module (corresponding to one pixel in the minimum admissible size on the screen).

---

[4] Perception abilities when reading and remembering signs are limited, see: [12].

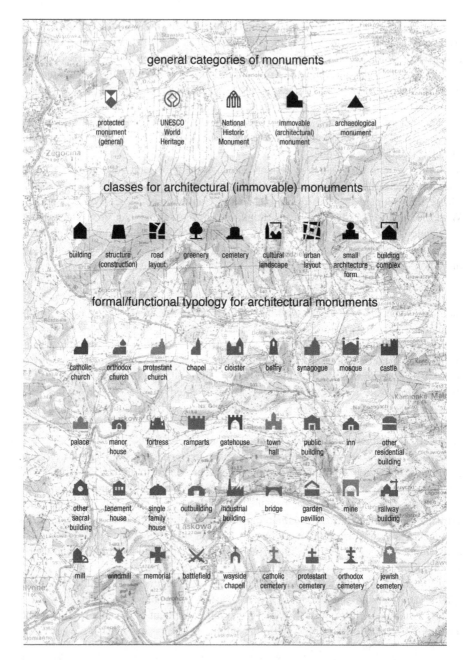

Fig. 6. The symbols on the portal's map divided by categories, classes, and formal/functional typology. The number and type of the designed icons corresponds to the classification elaborated previously. The assumed type of visualisation was illustrated with the map composition in the background.

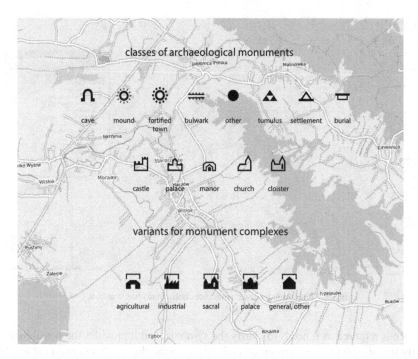

Fig. 7. Graphic representations of archaeological sites with icon variants included in the system.

3.6 Special Functions of the User Interface

Most of the current internet geoinformation portals operate on spatial data resources and mechanisms of their processing and visualisation. The typical scope of such systems, usually called map servers usually comprises of two types of tasks: the choice of the object on the basis of queries and attributes as well as symbolisation of the selected content. The simplest web applications are restricted to the display of predefined maps while more advanced systems give the user more freedom of cartographic presentation.

One of the major advantages of GIS portals is multiscale cartographic representation from big scales depicting the city plan to scales showing the country and the whole globe. Due to such a scale range, the adequate content choice and generalisation of the symbols' form prove to be complicated matters and that is why in case of thematic portals the scope of general geographic content is usually limited for the benefit of the thematic content elements, which are brought to the foreground and depicted with greater detail.

The character of the spatial data on the monuments gathered by the NHB resulted in both the cartographic representation and user interface, which is its functional framework, requiring unconventional solutions. Thus, the web application in the portal, not only allows for map viewing but also modification of the scope of content visible in particular thematic layers, as well as the choice of the layer's elements.

One of the key elements of the interface is the legend panel (Fig. 8). In many geoportals the legend is reduced or absent. However, in the thematic portals its

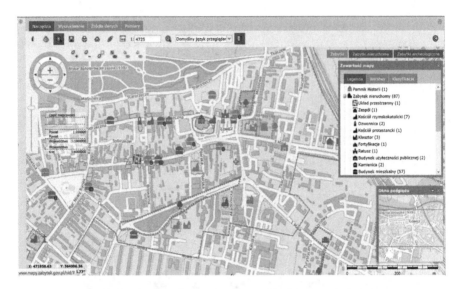

Fig. 8. The portal's user interface with dialogue windows.

presence is required as it needs to clarify the symbols, and it provides the possibility to modify the presentation by turning on and off particular classes of objects. That is why the legend in the Portal comprises of three sections: symbol description (dynamic updating along the scale change), a thematic layer manager, and an object classification panel according to function, chronology or reference to objects in the portal e-zabytek.

An important feature of the legend (in each of the three sections above) is its automatic synchronisation to a current map view. It is of significance for the user, due to the dynamic visualisation of objects on the different scale levels resulting in adjustment of the number of objects, reduction of their geometry to a symbol, change of the topographic mode to matrix mode of object display, and finally map content adjustment and the form of reference background to the adequate scale level.

This is also supplemented by the tools available for logged-in users. They include manager of user-defined combinations: the adding and subtracting of maps, the changing of their order, transparency, and saving and uploading the user's combinations.

4 Conclusions and the Possibility of Further Works

The National Heritage Board map portal designed by the authors of the present article enables not only an effective collection of comprehensive information on heritage subject to legal protection (resources entered in the heritage register), but also rendering information on nearly 100 thousand architectural and archaeological objects subject to legal protection accessible online. Data published on the NHB geoportal (mapy. zabytek.gov.pl) are a source of information on corporeal heritage for a large target group. After the portal's activation in the first half of 2015, the service was visited on average by 5750 unique users a month. The service users of that period browsed the immovable monuments register nearly 5 million times (4 882 322), whereas the archaeological sites register almost 2 million times (1 867 681). The following years show a significant increase of interest in mapy.zabytek.gov.pl, at the beginning of 2016 the number of www.mapy.zabytek.gov.pl website requests reached over 35 000 a month (unique users), which means the interest in the map portal soared by over 600% in only one year of its operation! Therefore, it should be concluded that the original concept of corporeal heritage site visualisation (immovable monuments and archaeological sites), after its implementation by the National Heritage Board, has considerably contributed to the dissemination of knowledge on heritage and manners of heritage protection in society.

The primary (aim of the service creation and elaboration of the rules of presentations of historic resources in the GIS portal is the distribution of information, which raises the awareness of cultural heritage, which in turn increases the efficiency of its conservation. The distribution of knowledge can refer to general issues of awareness raising at both local and country level, and can also mean a fuller and better use of the historic sites' resource, for example for touristic purposes. The consciousness of the value of historic objects in the area can lead to their better and more efficient conservation measures, which is particularly true for archaeological sites, which are less rooted in the public consciousness. Another aim is to make the information available for special purposes, such as spatial planning or architecture design, especially in the case of historic monuments and their vicinity. The use of advanced IT solutions allows for the simulation of a number of phenomena influencing planning on both a local and national scale (e.g. with respect to flood risk). What is more, such information can be used by specialists in their scientific research. And finally, the last aspect worth taking into consideration is the improvement of efficiency of historic sites' resource management, and using the designed system as a tool for conservator-restorer service.

The spatial information system described here offers a wide range of detailed information thus constituting it a unique resource for various kinds of purposes. Complex information sets become readable thanks to the usage of visual means, easily decoded by users. However, the system needs constant development and verification. Representation of such a large amount of data, referring to the fragile matter of heritage protection demands a careful approach and - sometimes - individual treatment in particular cases. On the other hand, due to the scale effect, some generalizations are necessary. Proper relation between these attitudes is crucial to achieve balance between efficiency and accuracy.

References

1. Tomaszewski, A.: Towards New Philosophy of Heritage. International Cultural Centre, Kraków (2012)
2. Włochyński, L.: Revitalisation of the historical residential ensembles in terms of the economy and conservation practice of today's Poland. Master thesis, FA WUT (2013)
3. Kępczyńska-Walczak, A.: Concept of database for Polish architectural heritage in the context of European experience. Herit. Preserv. **4**, 11–22 (2007)

4. Koszewski, K.: Concept of architectural-historical database illustrated by the example of Saska Kępa in Warsaw. Doctoral dissertation, FA WUT (2005)
5. UNESCO: The Paris Declaration on heritage as a driver of development adopted at Paris, UNESCO headquarters, 1 December 2011
6. INSPIRE: D2.8.I.9 INSPIRE Data Specification on Protected Sites – Guidelines (2010). http://inspire.jrc.ec.europa.eu/
7. Brykowska, M.: Methods of Measurement and Research of Architectural Monuments. Publishing House of Warsaw University of Technology, Warsaw (2003)
8. Żyszkowska, W.: Map perception. Theories and research in the second half of the 20th century. Pol. Cartogr. Rev. 1(1) (2016)
9. Peirce, C.S.: The Essential Peirce Selected Philosophical Writings, vol. 2. Indiana University Press, Bloomington (1998)
10. Łoziński, J., Miłobędzki, A.: Atlas of Architectural Monuments in Poland. Polonia, Warszawa (1967)
11. Marcus, A.: Icons, symbols, and signs: visible languages to facilitate communication. Interactions 10(3), 37–43 (2003)
12. Miller, G.A.: The Magical Number Seven, Plus or Minus Two Some Limits on Our Capacity for Processing Information. American Psychological Association, Washington, D.C. (1994)

Knowledge Based Optimal Recommendation of Spatial Technologies for Documentation of Buildings

Ashish Karmacharya$^{(\boxtimes)}$, Stefanie Wefers$^{(\boxtimes)}$, and Frank Boochs$^{(\boxtimes)}$

i3mainz – Institute for Spatial Information and Surveying Technology,
Mainz University of Applied Sciences, Mainz, Germany
{ashish.karmacharya, stefanie.wefers,
frank.boochs}@hs-mainz.de

Abstract. Spatial and spectral recording of material cultural heritage is an interdisciplinary task which requires mutual understanding and agreement for achieving a common goal. This task is often tedious, time consuming and not recorded. COSCH^{KR} captures the core knowledge of these interdisciplinary interactions and logically structures it. COSCH^{KR} is an ontology based knowledge representation that represents the experts' knowledge explicitly so that it can be reasoned to recommend technology(ies) and their technical solutions. In this paper we discuss how technologies are recommended based on their demands from the cultural heritage application especially focusing on large objects. We also demonstrate how other technologies that are suitable for recording smaller objects are ignored while recommending technologies such as photogrammetry and laser scanning suitable for large objects.

Keywords: Knowledge representation · Cultural heritage
Spatial technologies · Laser scanning · Photogrammetry
Structured-light 3D scanning · Ontology · Inference · Recommender system

1 Introduction

A mutual understanding is necessary in order to record and process suitable spectral or spatial data of physical cultural heritage (CH) objects when the outcome has to fit the needs of CH experts who actually work with the data. CH experts have to provide the knowledge about the physical CH objects and the research question which give the trigger for the recording. The research question provides information how the data will be applied and which content is needed. This is the basis for the recording expert to set-up a recording strategy which generates the needed data and information in a suitable resolution, accuracy etc. and for the data processing expert to set-up a workflow which provides optimal data and information for the CH application. Such multi-disciplinary projects focus, e.g., on buildings (e.g., [1, 2]) archaeological sites and artefacts (e.g., [3, 4]), paintings (e.g., [5]), and books (e.g., Sachsenspiegel-online[1]).

---

[1] http://www.sachsenspiegel-online.de/export/index.html.

© Springer International Publishing AG, part of Springer Nature 2018
M. Ioannides et al. (Eds.): Digital Cultural Heritage 2017, LNCS 10754, pp. 65–77, 2018.
https://doi.org/10.1007/978-3-319-75789-6_5

The COST Action TD1201: Colour and Space in Cultural Heritage (COSCH) [6, 7] contributed to the conservation and preservation of CH by enhancing the mutual understanding between experts from various disciplines linked to the spectral and spatial recording of physical CH objects. The Action established a much-required forum for interdisciplinary networking and communication of domain knowledge between experts from technical and humanities domain. Bridging the gap between professionals involved intense interdisciplinary discussions and references to publications such as guides to good practice. The knowledge gained through such discussions and literature can be stored to better allow its reuse. The evolvement of the Semantic Web framework has provided the possibilities to logically structure and store such knowledge for its management, reuse, and reasoning. This machine-readable explicit knowledge involves machines to assist humans in understanding and managing available asserted knowledge. COSCH community draws from the developments in the Semantic Web and structures and encodes the expert knowledge into a knowledge representation ontology, so-called COSCH^{KR}. COSCH Knowledge Representation (COSCH^{KR}) is an ontology-based inference model currently under development that expresses the underlying knowledge from all disciplines involved in CH object recording in logical statements in order to allow machines to make use of the experts' knowledge. The intention is to provide a platform that facilitates CH experts to understand the technicalities in spatial and spectral documentation processes through inferring interactive assertions of the knowledge from the involved disciplines in the recording of physical CH objects. Through COSCH^{KR} the knowledge gap between different experts can be bridged in a flexible and durable way. The complexity and challenge in the development of such an inference model lie in the above described multi-disciplinarity. It is a multi-faceted model developed by humanities and engineering experts involved in CH object recording. Through the knowledge representation, we seek to make these multi-disciplinary dependencies explicit and visible. The purpose and scope of COSCH^{KR} are to guide CH experts by inferring the optimal spatial and spectral technologies for the recording of a specific physical CH object based on facts about the physical CH object and the intended CH application.

CH experts are the primary end user of such a system and their actual requirements define the first direction which the system takes. The heart of the ontology is the fact that a CH application demands specific nature and quality of data and that technical solutions within existing spatial and spectral technologies are capable to generate that specific nature and quality of data. We fondly represent it through the axis "CH Application – Data –Technologies". This axis is influenced to support or restrict right technical solutions by external influencing factors coming from either external sources such as the project limitations and/or from physical/chemical compositions and characteristics of the concerned physical object. COSCH^{KR} is built on classes that are capable to describe these factors semantically and use them for reasoning. The axioms and theorems within the ontology are applied for reasoning the recommendations within the backdrop of CH, but the concept behind COSCH^{KR} is applicable to every other discipline that requires recording physical objects for its concerned application.

2   Relevant Works

Knowledge representation and reasoning in a common established framework has always possessed challenges to the researchers. Ontologies populated with concepts are agreed generally to follow the states of uniform knowledge representation and provide a computational model of a particular domain of interest [10–12]. The main motivation behind ontologies is that they allow for sharing and reuse of knowledge bodies in the computational form [13]. Ontologies existed in the studies of philosophy since the very beginning where it is defined as the theory of objects and their ties and is an integral part in the study of existence [14]. However, their extensive use in computational modeling and structuring gained acceptance in the Semantic Web framework first coined by Sir Tim Berners-Lee [15].

The most prominent ontology for CH disciplines is CIDOC-CRM [16], which is designed as a standard for stakeholders such as museums archiving CH objects. First published in 2000 by ICOM, the CRM achieved ISO Standards in 2006. The aim of the CRM is to provide an explicit conceptualization of key concepts required for interaction between human agents and cultural entities independent of the technical implementations [17]. Terminologies and concepts of CIDOC-CRM are of interest and importance for the research in COSCH and are referenced inside COSCH^{KR}. Nevertheless, the intention and application of COSCH^{KR} differs considerably from CIDOC-CRM and therefore the CRM does not provide the required class structure detailing information about the recording of CH objects. The CARARE 2.0 metadata schema [18] prepared within the framework of the 3D ICONS project provides some parallels to COSCH^{KR}. The schema extends the structure of CRM to include technical para- and metadata of recording strategies. However, it is meant to harvest the content into open knowledge hubs for linking data. It does not have provisions for reasoning towards any choice of optimal para- and metadata from the existing, when new cases arise. The development of CARARE 2.0 metadata schema thus follows a pattern that is necessary for ontologies managing and harvesting contents into Europeana Data Model [19].

COSCH^{KR} defines technologies, their parameters and their situational behaviours explicitly through the logic based taxonomy, relations, and rules. This is in alignment with current semantic technologies research questions within the Semantic Web. They are widely used in modeling behaviours of a domain or an event with the intention to either classify the underlying components for standardizing the interoperability [20] or to decide on the consequences arising from the events [21]. In either case, the primary task is first to identify and model the related entities and their characteristics and second to formulate rules that depict their circumstantial performance. The latter can in many cases help anticipating the possible outcomes of these events.

Recording technologies, their parameters, performance excellences and limitations, and circumstantial behaviour occupy the largest part within COSCH^{KR}. There have been attempts developing ontologies that list the recording technologies, e.g., the so-called Semantic Sensor Network Ontology (SSN Ontology) [22]. However, such ontologies perform as data repositories and provide no or little semantic definitions of concepts for the analysis and/or inference.

3   COSCH^{KR}: The Intention and the Description

Technology and its supportive behaviour against any particular circumstantial situation are keys for its rightful realization on that situation. The first and foremost important task when developing a knowledge representation is to identify, evaluate, and understand the concerned technologies and their underlying parameters and components. This helps seeking out the circumstantial behaviours of their performances. Many studies exist evaluating and recommending optical technologies for spatial and spectral recording applied to, e.g., CH objects [23, 24]. The qualification and description of the available optical systems based on image formation is provided in [25]. The Belgian Federal Scientific Institutions (BELSPO) evaluated spatial recording technologies such as laser scanners, structured-light 3D scanners, close-range photogrammetry (e.g., various mini-domes) and motion sensing within the Agora3D project [26] to recommend their usage based on different limiting factors. A similar study was carried out documenting the so-called "Porta Nigra", a part of the Roman city walls of Trier (Germany). Various spatial data generated by different recording instruments were evaluated: tachymeter, laser scanner, structured-light 3D scanner, and close range photogrammetry using a metric camera [27]. Both works focus on the impact of applied technology on data characteristics and their suitability for the documentation of a specific class of objects. Hence, the same performance of the technologies cannot be assured once the object or the environment changes. However, both works established a basis for further investigations of the mentioned technologies. The above mentioned publications were used during the development of the main concepts of the ontology as they helped to achieve a comprehensive overview. However, for a deep understanding of the various dependencies, these studies could only help to formulate a rather general picture. This is due to the fact that they do not provide a holistic view on the respective technologies in the way we understand this term.

3.1   COSCH^{KR}: The Intention

The primary intention of COSCH^{KR} ontology is to facilitate individual recommendation queries through the encrypted rules. Though not a classical recommender system using machine learning techniques, it can be called an entire knowledge based recommendation tool. A Recommender System (RS) is a software tool and technique providing suggestions for items to be of use to a user [30]. A RS traditionally applies stochastic methods such as machine learning to infer the recommendation and therefore will require a significant amount of data for interpretation and calculation. Although ontologies have started to be used in combination to the traditional methods in recent times, such as works [31, 32] show, they are limited for the profile matching and do not participate actively in inferring the recommendations.

COSCH^{KR} drives on prior experts' knowledge as opposed to classical RS. Taxonomical structure, relational properties, and inference rules describe descriptive semantics of the interdisciplinary knowledge components.

3.2   COSCH^{KR}: The Description

Each class within the top level ontology (Fig. 1) has its own role and importance within COSCH^{KR}. They are additionally interconnected through the relationships that bind them together. Finally, these inter-relationships are formalized through inference rules which are the core for inferring recommendations.

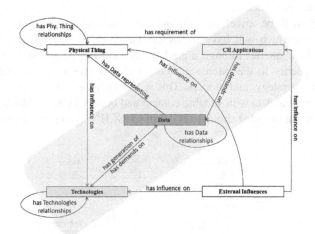

Fig. 1. COSCH^{KR}: Five top-level classes and their dependencies.

The knowledge representation includes five core classes (Fig. 1): (1) Physical Thing – represents the physical objects which should be recorded, (2) CH Applications – lists most common research questions in CH discipline requiring the application of 3D or spectral data, (3) Technologies – involves technologies and their underlying technicalities within spatial and spectral technologies required to record physical CH objects, (4) Data – includes all possible digital/analogue data and document types that are either generated or used for processing to support the CH application and (5) External Influences – includes all external influences that have restrictive/supportive influences on selection of technologies and/or technical strategies.

The axis "CH Application – Data – Technologies" is presented through the grey strip in Fig. 1. The core of the model is the concept "Data" and its semantics that define the requirements and possibilities driving the inference system: spatial or spectral recording technologies generate data with certain characteristics (e.g., type and content of data, accuracy, and resolution) and CH applications demand data with certain characteristics (e.g., type and content of data, resolution). The class "Data" denotes representations of digital and analogue data that are either acquired through data generation processes or required by certain applications. These acquisition processes and/or requirements dictate their requirements on characterizations. For example: the class "Data" contains classes or concepts of 2D or 3D data which are characterized by their dimensions. Their dimensions are defined through how they are generated and contemplate through their requirements. They are defined through the rules within

COSCH^{KR}. This is then supported by two further top-level classes defining semantics of Physical Things (CIDOC-CRM class E18 "physical thing") and External Influences. Each physical CH object (= Physical Thing) has individual surface characteristics (e.g., size, shape, and colour) that limit or support a particular spectral or spatial recording technique. And further restraining semantics for the technologies are defined within "External Influences", e.g., budget, human resource, and available space in the object's surrounding. Details on the class structure of these top level classes and their inter-relations are presented in [8, 9].

The model will be enveloped through an interactive web-based application (COSCH^{KR} App) which will have interactive Graphical User Interfaces (GUIs) for users to assert their queries through a guided mechanism. The application will apply those asserted queries to the inference model and will give recommendations for a recording device, strategy, and process. This will support, e.g., CH experts to receive spectral and/or spatial data with suitable content and quality as needed by the intended data application. An intended simulated GUI of COSCH^{KR} App is illustrated in Fig. 2.

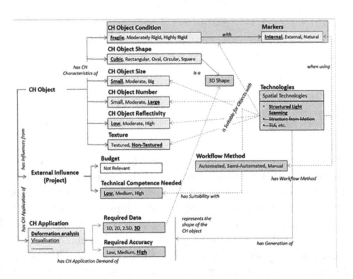

Fig. 2. Intended GUI with simulation of a query of the CH Application "Deformation analysis". The red boxes represent asserted user input knowledge and the grey boxes represent the inferred knowledge. (Color figure online)

The simulation presented in Fig. 2 was exercised to enrich and evaluate COSCH^{KR} and its inference system with the case study and CH application "deformation analysis". The case study included 777 small waterlogged wooden samples that were recorded in 3D before and after conservation treatment to define the influences of various conservation treatments on the shape of the waterlogged wooden samples. The analysis was carried out within the research project "Massenfunde in archäologischen Sammlungen[2]"

---

[2] http://www.rgzm.de/kur/.

of the Römisch-Germanisches Zentralmuseum (RGZM)[3]. The simulation yielded the recommendation of structured-light 3D scanning with the instrument structured-light 3D scanner because of its compliance to a large number of small objects that can be carried to a laboratory and had to be recorded at least twice representing two different condition eras of an object to be able to measure small geometric differences through data comparison (for details, see [8, 9, 28]). Figure 3 shows the inference process for the case study. The process inside COSCH^{KR} for this deformation analysis case study gives the background for the example presented in Sect. 4 focusing on deformation analysis of a large object. For more details and illustrations see [33, 34].

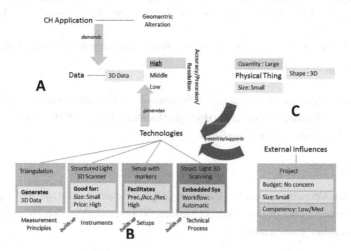

Fig. 3. The inference mechanism (A) demands on data: deformation analysis demand high accuracy 3D data, (B) generation on data at technical level through technologies first through the principle then instruments adapting to the technical process (C) the restrictions provided by CH objects and other external influences on the technologies

4 Case Study (Deformation Analysis Large Objects)

Use cases are necessary to show the capability of such a system which can take knowledge from different expert domains and infer it keeping them in a common single perspective: i.e., requirement on data and the technical capability of technologies to generate the data with those particular situational parameters. The case study "deformation analysis" already presented in the last section is the base for the example presented here: We will focus on large objects and their 3D documentation for dissemination purposes on a website. Extending the deformation analysis-case study focusing on small objects to large objects will demonstrate the strength of COSCH^{KR}. Other technologies such as laser scanning and photogrammetry will be considered as

---

[3] http://web.rgzm.de/.

these are particularly suitable for recording large objects. We have presented the semantic definitions of laser scanning and photogrammetry in [28]. In this paper we will present the description logic rules that are used to infer the selection of photogrammetry and/or laser scanning instead of structured-light 3D scanning.

We will consider the "Analysis of Shape (or Structure)" as the first (of two) exemplary application for large objects such as a building or a ruin. The requirement on data is presented in the given inference rule:

$$\text{has Demand on Data } \textbf{3D} \underline{\text{AND}} \text{ has Requirement on Data Quality } (\textbf{High } \underline{\text{OR}} \textbf{ Medium}) \quad (1)$$

The object of consideration is – as stated above – a large outdoor object (with abundant light) such as a building or a ruin. It can be characterized as a large 3D geometry.

Technologies such as laser scanning or photogrammetry with inference rules:

1. Laser Scanning

$$\text{has Main Operating Instrument } (\textbf{Laser Scanners } \underline{\text{AND}}(\text{has Generation On Data } \textbf{3D} \\ \underline{\text{AND}} \text{ has Generated Data Quality } (\textbf{High } \underline{\text{OR}} \textbf{ Medium } \underline{\text{OR}} \textbf{ Low}) \underline{\text{ AND}} \text{ has Data} \qquad (2) \\ \text{Processing } \textbf{Data Fusion } (\text{Laser Scanning}))$$

2. Photogrammetry

$$\text{has Main Operating Instrument } (\textbf{Cameras } \underline{\text{AND}} (\text{has Generation On Data } \textbf{3D} \underline{\text{AND}} \\ \text{has Generated Data Quality } (\textbf{High } \underline{\text{OR}} \textbf{ Medium } \underline{\text{OR}} \textbf{ Low}) \underline{\text{ AND}} \text{ has Data Processing} \qquad (3) \\ \textbf{Data Fusion } (\text{Photogrammetry}))$$

$$\text{is Suitable for } \textbf{Physical Thing } \underline{\text{AND}} \text{ has Size } (\textbf{Large } \underline{OR} \textbf{ Very Large}) \qquad (4)$$

$$\text{is Suitable for } \textbf{Physical Thing } \underline{\text{AND}} \text{ has Lighting Condition } (\textbf{Bright } \underline{\text{OR}} \textbf{ Very Bright}) \quad (5)$$

are capable of recording such object in such external environment (with bright light) with the required quality. In contrast, the rules defining structured-light 3D scanning:

$$\text{is Suitable for } \textbf{Physical Thing } \underline{\text{AND}} \text{ has Size NOT } (\textbf{Large } \underline{\text{OR}} \textbf{ Very Large}) \qquad (6)$$

and

$$\text{is Suitable for } \textbf{Physical Thing } \underline{\text{AND}} \text{ has Lighting Condition NOT } (\textbf{Bright } \underline{\text{OR}} \textbf{ Very Bright}) \quad (7)$$

ignores the recommendation of structured-light 3D scanning in any application which focuses on (very) large objects with (very) bright lighting condition.

The data are products of instruments these technologies use supported by the data processing steps (see Eqs. 2 and 3). The limiting/supportive constraints of these instruments will be compared through the inference mechanism against external influences (influences coming from both physical objects and other than the physical objects). We used the influences coming from project budget and the technical competence of staff for this use case explanation. Elaborating laser scanning using laser scanner with rules encompassing those influences:

$$\text{has Instrument Cost } \textbf{High} \tag{8}$$

$$\text{has Staff Competency } \textbf{Specialist} \tag{9}$$

and photogrammetry using cameras:
$$\text{has Instrument Cost } \textbf{Low} \tag{10}$$

$$\text{has Staff Competency } \textbf{Layman} \tag{11}$$

recommends technologies based on one's constraints with budget and staff competency in this example. It should be noted that the competency of staff presented in Eq. 4 is related to the operation of instrument and the generation of final data product which would require further processing and hence requires a qualified staff with high technical competence for generating high data quality. There can be more external influencing constraints than listed in this example that have prominent influence in selection of the optimal technology.

We consider second exemplary application: "Dissemination through small scale Web Presentation". The application demands are defined through

$$\text{has Demand On Data } \textbf{3D} \underline{\text{ AND }} \text{has Data Quality } (\textbf{Medium} \text{ OR } \textbf{Low}) \tag{12}$$

$$\text{has Demand On Data } \textbf{3D} \underline{\text{ AND }} \text{has Data Texture } \textbf{Textured} \tag{13}$$

These demands have clear implications on selection of technology. Laser scanners do not generate textured data unless it is combined with photogrammetry. For simplicity we consider the data generated with laser scanning is through this single technology and not through the combination of technologies (see Eq. 14). Photogrammetry, however, generates texture through its instrument camera (with generated images, see Eq. 15). This makes a clear distinction in the selection of photogrammetry over laser scanning for the second application.

$$\textbf{Laser Scanner} \text{ has Generation On Data } \textbf{3D} \underline{\text{ AND }} \text{has Texture } \underline{\text{NOT}} \textbf{ Textured} \tag{14}$$

$$\textbf{Camera} \text{ has Generation On Data } \textbf{2D Data } (\textbf{Images}) \underline{\text{ AND }} \text{has Texture } \textbf{Textured} \tag{15}$$

Photogrammetry, however, needs to process these generated 2D images to generate 3D data. Data fusion (data processing that it applies taking 2D images and generating 3D model of the physical object (see Eq. 16)) can generate lower quality 3D data, if it considers only objects' natural surface information during the fusion (see Eq. 17). The usage of specific targets for the transformation, however, does retain the data quality (see Eq. 18). This is not the same in case of data processing in laser scanning (3D individual scans are used to generate a 3D model of the object (see Eq. 19)). The quality does not change in either case: by using objects' information or by using specific targets (see Eqs. 20 and 21).

$$\text{\textbf{Data Fusion} (Photogrammetry) has Initial \textbf{2D Data} (Images) \underline{AND} has Generation On Data \textbf{3D Data}} \tag{16}$$

$$\text{\textbf{Data Fusion} (Photogrammetry) has Targets \textbf{Natural} \underline{AND} has Generation On Data \textbf{3D Data} \underline{AND} has Data Quality \underline{lower Initial} \textbf{Data}} \tag{17}$$

$$\text{\textbf{Data Fusion} (Photogrammetry) has Targets \textbf{Specific} \underline{AND} has Generation On Data \textbf{3D Data} \underline{AND} has Data Quality \underline{equivalent Initial} \textbf{Data}} \tag{18}$$

$$\text{\textbf{Data Fusion} (Laser Scanning) has Initial \textbf{3D Data} (\textbf{Scans}) \underline{AND} has Generation On Data \textbf{3D Data}} \tag{19}$$

$$\text{\textbf{Data Fusion} (Laser Scanning) has Targets \textbf{Natural} \underline{AND} has Generation On Data \textbf{3D Data} \underline{AND} has Data Quality \underline{equivalent Initial} \textbf{Data}} \tag{20}$$

$$\text{\textbf{Data Fusion} (Laser Scanning) has Targets \textbf{Specific} \underline{AND} has Generation On Data \textbf{3D Data} \underline{AND} has Data Quality \underline{equivalent Initial} \textbf{Data}} \tag{21}$$

The first application case (Analysis of shape/structure) will not consider photogrammetry when the targets are objects' natural surface information. This is due to the fact that it will generate lower data quality. This means, the technology can generate medium quality data at most in such a case. To the contrary, the case is optimal for the second application case (Dissemination through small scale Web Presentation), where 3D data with less quality are required.

5 Conclusion

All elements which set-up spatial recording technologies, CH application requirements on data, data capabilities generated by the technologies, requirements provided by the CH object to be recorded, and all external influences are defined through classes and dependencies and are structured in an ontology. Such an atomized view is needed to represent the knowledge of various experts involved in such a process in a machine-readable format. This provides machines the required understanding that allows them to collaborate in the process of making flexible and adaptable recommendation by taking these various experts' knowledge into account. As exemplarily presented on the basis of photogrammetry and laser scanning applied within the documentation of a building or ruin, relevant elements are identified, split into reasonable units, and are logically structured through classes and dependencies. Through inference rules a qualification of elements based on influencing facts is getting possible. For example, depending on the targeted application different 3D data qualities are needed which influence the selection of a technology due to its capabilities under specific external influences and CH object constraints (such as size and surface characteristics). The overall aim of explicitly describing these dependencies and rules is to infer recommendations from the ontology through an inference mechanism. Through a general view on these recording strategies users of this platform will be able to enter individual parameters to infer individual recommendations adapted to their CH application, CH object, and external influences.

Requirements on data are always application driven and it is not viable to have the same nature and quality of data for every possible application. Through this distinction, technologies are selected which are suitable for applications defined by individual parameters. Technologies are different in terms of their performance, data generation, and circumstantial behaviour. They generate varying nature and quality of data depending on the condition during recording. Those conditions are a bi-product of influences from outside, be it from physical objects' characteristics or other external ones. They have impact on technologies and their generated data. Therefore, the axis "CH Applications – Data – Technologies" is always driven by data and their nature and quality as demanded by the intended application and as generated by the respective technology.

An interactive Graphical User Interface (GUI) will be developed that will provide the functionalities to assert the end users' knowledge. The interface will then provide the recommendation(s) from the asserted knowledge. The interface will be designed and developed to fit the end users need and henceforth will be developed through iterative and interactive discussions with the end users. Such iterative and interactive discussion were also carried out to develop the current structure of COSCH^{KR}.

References

1. De Luca, L., Busayarat, C., Stefani, C., Veron, P., Florenzano, M.: A semantic-based platform for the digital analysis of architectural heritage. Comput. Graph. **35**(2), 227–241 (2011)
2. Kersten, T.P., Hinrichsen, N., Lindstaedt, M., Weber, C., Schreyer, K., Tschirschwitz, F.: Baugeschichtliche 3D-Dokumentation des Alt-Segeberger Bürgerhauses durch Photogrammetrie und terrestrisches Laserscanning. In: Przybilla, H.-J., Kersten, T.P., Boochs, F. (eds) Von low-cost bis high-tech. 3D-Dokumentation in Archäologie & Denkmalpflege. LWL Industriemuseum Zeche Zollern. Dortmund 16–18 Oktober 2013, pp. 30–37. Mainz: Denkmäler3.de, Bochum, Hamburg (2015). http://dx.doi.org/10.13140/RG.2.1.1896.5927
3. MacDonald, L., Guerra, M.F., Pillay, R., Hess, M., Quirke, S., Robson, S., Hosseininaveh Ahmadabadian, A.: Practice-based comparison of imaging methods for visualization of toolmarks on an Egyptian scarab. In: Elmoataz, A., Lezoray, O., Nouboud, F., Mammass, D. (eds.) ICISP 2014. LNCS, vol. 8509, pp. 239–246. Springer, Cham (2014). https://doi.org/10.1007/978-3-319-07998-1_27
4. Wefers, S., Atorf, P., Klonowski, J.: UAV photogrammetry and 3D analysis of CH sites. The millstone quarry district of Mayen (DE) as a case study. In: Proceedings of the 20th International Conference on Cultural Heritage and New Technologies 2015 (CHNT 20, 2015) Vienna 2016 (2016). ISBN 978-3-200-04698-6
5. Cucci, C., Picollo, M., Chiarantini, L., Sereni, B.: Hyperspectral remote sensing techniques applied to the non-invasive investigation of mural paintings: a feasibility study carried out on a wall painting by Beato Angelico in Florence. In: Pezzati, L., Targowski, P. (eds.) Optics for Arts, Architecture, and Archaeology V. Proceedings of SPIE, vol. 9527, pp. 95270P–95270P-9 (2015). http://dx.doi.org/10.1117/12.2184743

6. Boochs, F.: COSCH – colour and space in cultural heritage, a new COST action starts. In: Ioannides, M., Fritsch, D., Leissner, J., Davies, R., Remondino, F., Caffo, R. (eds.) EuroMed 2012. LNCS, vol. 7616, pp. 865–873. Springer, Heidelberg (2012). https://doi.org/10.1007/978-3-642-34234-9_93

7. Boochs, F., Bentkowska-Kafel, A., Degrigny, C., Hauta-Kasari, M., Rizvic, S., Trémeau, A.: Towards optimal spectral and spatial documentation of cultural heritage. COSCH – An interdisciplinary action in the COST framework. In: Proceedings of XXIV International CIPA Symposium. Strasbourg: International Archives of the Photogrammetry, Remote Sensing and Spatial Information Sciences, pp. 109–113 (2013)

8. Wefers, S., Karmacharya, A., Boochs, F.: Development of a platform recommending 3D and spectral digitisation strategies. Virtual Archaeol. Rev. **7**(15), 18–27 (2016)

9. Karmacharya, A., Wefers, S., Boochs, F.: Knowledge Based Recommendation on Optimal Spectral and Spatial Recording Strategy of Physical Cultural Heritage Objects. Semapro 2016, IARIA, Venice, Italy, pp. 49–58 (2016)

10. Brewster, C., O'Hara, K.: Knowledge representation with ontologies: Present challenges - Future possibilities. Int. J. Hum Comput Stud. **65**, 563–568 (2007)

11. Jakus, G., Milutinovic, V., Omerovic, S., Tomazic, S.: Concepts, Ontologies and Knowledge Representation. Springer Briefs in Computer Science. Springer, New York (2013). https://doi.org/10.1007/978-1-4614-7822-5

12. Grimm, S., Hitzler, P., Abecker, A.: Knowledge representation and ontologies: logic, ontologies and semantic web languages. In: Studer, R., Grimm, S., Abecker, A. (eds.) Semantic Web Services, pp. 51–105. Springer, Heidelberg (2007). https://doi.org/10.1007/3-540-70894-4_3

13. Studer, R., Benjamins, V., Fensel, D.: Knowledge engineering: principles and methods. Data Knowl. Eng. **25**(1–2), 161–197 (1998)

14. Corazzon, R.: Theory and history of ontology. A Resource Guide for Philosophers. http://www.formalontology.it/. Accessed 18 May 2017

15. Berners-Lee, T., Hendler, J., Lassila, O.: The semantic web. Sci. Am. **284**(5), 28–37 (2001)

16. Boeuf, P.L., Doerr, M., Ore, C.E., Stead, S.: Definition of the CIDOC Conceptual Reference Model, ICOM/CIDOC CRM Special Interest Group (2013)

17. Crofts, N., Doerr, M., Gill, T., Stead, S., Stiff, M.: Definition of the CIDOC conceptual reference model. ICOM/CIDOC Documentation Standards Group. CIDOC CRM Special Interest Group 5 (2008)

18. Fernie, K., Gaverilis, D., Angeli, S.: The CARARE meta data schema v2.0. In: Europeana Carare project (2013)

19. Doerr, M., Gradmann, S., Hennicke, S., Isaac, A., Meghini, C., van de Sompel, H.: The europeana data model (edm). In: World Library and Information Congress: 76th IFLA General Conference and Assembly, pp. 10–15 (2010)

20. Mayerhofer, T., Wimmer, M., Berardinelli, L., Maetzler, E., Schmidt, N.: Towards semantic integration of plant behavior models with automation ML's intermediate modeling layer. In: GEMOC Workshop (2016)

21. Patino, L., Ferryman, J.: Semantic modelling for behaviour characterisation and threat detection. In: Proceedings of the IEEE Conference on Computer Vision and Pattern Recognition Workshops, pp. 43–49 (2016)

22. Compton, M., Barnaghi, P., Bermudez, L., García-Castro, R., Corcho, O., Cox, S., Huang, V.: The SSN ontology of the W3C semantic sensor network incubator group. Web Seman. Sci. Serv. Agents World Wide Web **17**, 25–32 (2012)

23. Barazzetti, L., Binda, L., Scaioni, M., Taranto, P.: Photogrammetric survey of complex geometries with low-cost software: application to the 'G1' temple in Myson, Vietnam. J. Cult. Heritage **12**(3), 253–262 (2011)

24. Bettio, F., Gobbetti, E., Merella, E., Pintus, R.: Improving the digitization of shape and color of 3D artworks in a cluttered environment. In: Proceedings Digital Heritage, pp. 23–30. IEEE (2013)
25. Gross, H., Blechinger, F., Achtner, B.: Handbook of optical systems, volume 4, Survey of Optical Instruments, Wiley-VCH, Weinheim, Germany (2008)
26. Mathys, A., Brecko, J., Semal, P.: Comparing 3D digitizing technologies: what are the differences? In: Digital Heritage International Congress (DigitalHeritage), vol. 1, pp. 201–204. IEEE (2013)
27. Boochs, F., Hoffmann, A., Huxhagen, U., Welter, D.: Digital reconstruction of archaeo-logical objects using hybrid sensing techniques-the example Porta Nigra at Trier. In: Campana, S., Forte, M. (eds.) Remote Sensing in Archaeology. From Space to Place, British Archaeological Reports Internat. Series 1568, pp. 395–400. Archaeopress, Oxford (2016)
28. Wefers, S., Karmacharya, A., Boochs, F.: Ontology-based knowledge representation for recommendation of optimal recording strategies – photogrammetry and laser scanning as examples. gis.Sci. 3, 105–113 (2017)
29. Decker, S.: Semantic web methods for knowledge management. Ph.D diss., Karlsruhe University, Diss. (2002)
30. Ricci, F., Rokach, L., Shapira, B.: Introduction to Recommender Systems Handbook. Springer, US (2011)
31. Middleton, Stuart E., Roure, D.D., Shadbolt, Nigel R.: Ontology-based recommender systems. In: Staab, S., Studer, R. (eds.) Handbook on Ontologies. IHIS, pp. 779–796. Springer, Heidelberg (2009). https://doi.org/10.1007/978-3-540-92673-3_35
32. Rodríguez-García, M.Á., Colombo-Mendoza, L.O., Valencia-García, R., Lopez-Lorca, Antonio A., Beydoun, G.: Ontology-based music recommender system. In: Omatu, S., Malluhi, Qutaibah M., Gonzalez, S.R., Bocewicz, G., Bucciarelli, E., Giulioni, G., Iqba, F. (eds.) Distributed Computing and Artificial Intelligence, 12th International Conference. AISC, vol. 373, pp. 39–46. Springer, Cham (2015). https://doi.org/10.1007/978-3-319-19638-1_5
33. Karmacharya, A., Wefers, S.: Ontology-based structuring of spectral and spatial recording strategies for cultural heritage assets. In: Bentkowska-Kafel, A., MacDonald, L. (eds.) Digital Techniques for Documenting and Preserving Cultural Heritage. Collection Devel-opment, Cultural Heritage and Digital Humanities series, pp. 157–172 (forthcoming)
34. Wefers, S., Karmacharya, A., Boochs, F., Pfarr-Harfst, M.: Digital 3D Reconstructed Models. Using Semantic Technologies for Recommendations in Visualisation Applications. In: Proceedings 21st Conference on Cultural Heritage and New Technologies, Vienna, 2016, Studies in Digital Heritage (forthcoming)

New Horizon of Digitization in Serbia Improvement of Digitization Through Cooperation with Leading World Institutions and the In-House Development of Digital Tools

Vasilije Milnovic[1]([✉]) and Aleksandar Jerkov[2]

[1] University Library Expert Associate in Scientific Center, Belgrade, Serbia
milnovic@unilib.rs
[2] University Library CEO, Belgrade, Serbia
jerkov@unilib.bg.ac.rs

Abstract. In 2016 the University Library "Svetozar Markovic" in cooperation with eight partner institutions started a project entitled "New Horizon of Digitization in Serbia", which was funded by the Ministry of Culture and Information of the Republic of Serbia. The aim of the project was to improve the main segments of digitization that were developed properly and to apply new digitization methods in as many institutions as possible in Serbia in a standardized way. The new digitization methods and approaches used in this project mostly come from the cooperation of the University Library "Svetozar Markovic" with leading world institutions or result from the in-house development of digital tools to improve segments of the digitization process. During 2016, the University Library "Svetozar Markovic" in cooperation with the British National Library carried out the project entitled "Safeguarding the fragile collection of the private archive of the Lazic family" within which it acquired rich experience in enhancing the digitization process. This paper presents several segments which show how the digitization process has been improved within the project. The paper also outlines the need for the full searchability of digital text in materials that are presented to patrons and that portray the University Library "Svetozar Markovic" experience through the example of a searchable collection of historical newspapers. Two methods for creating searchable texts are outlined: via the creation of METS-ALTO files in cooperation with the National Library of Luxembourg in the case of printed materials and via automatic recognition of the handwritten text in the Horizon 2020 READ project. Finally, the needs of patron groups in working with digital materials and possibilities for their display and promotion in the modern business environment of libraries are analyzed. This paper describes in detail the experience of using the promotional device Magic Box at the University Library "Svetozar Markovic" and outlines analysis and scenarios for its application in cultural institutions. This paper is an overview of the possibilities and first experiences of improving the digitization process which will mark the following development of the field in Serbia and the region.

Keywords: Digitization process · Digital tools
University library "svetozar markovic"

© Springer International Publishing AG, part of Springer Nature 2018
M. Ioannides et al. (Eds.): Digital Cultural Heritage 2017, LNCS 10754, pp. 78–88, 2018.
https://doi.org/10.1007/978-3-319-75789-6_6

1 Introduction

The University Library in Belgrade (ULB) as the central academic library in Serbia – which has gained invaluable experience in versatile EU funded digitization projects, the most notable being "Europeana Libraries" and "Europeana Newspapers" – coordinated the digitization project "Safeguarding the fragile collection of the private collection of the Lazić family" within the framework of the Endangered Archives Programme (EAP) of the British Library. With these endeavours, the ULB has positioned itself as the main innovative content provider for researchers in Serbia and one of the leading institutions in digitization.

It is anticipated that the information needs of researchers relating to their research will be met through the information available via digital technology. [7] So, the ability to access and use digital technologies is becoming a critical aspect of this contemporary science. Academic libraries are the places where researchers discover new information and where information literacy skills of researchers are being developed. [5] The role of such a library is to become an information hub where one can experiment with new technologies and where new concepts can be adopted. [4] This is especially important for humanities and social sciences researchers in Serbia who represent a deprived group that often struggles to acquire up-to-date information and knowledge.

The University Library "Svetozar Markovic" consolidated its digitization activities in the project entitled "New Horizons of Digitization in Serbia", carried out with eight partner institutions (National Library of Serbia, Military Archives, University Library Kragujevac, Biblical Institute of the Faculty of Orthodox Theology (University of Belgrade), City Library Novi Sad, Library "Milutin Bojic", Journalists' Association of Serbia and BITEF). This project was supported by the Ministry of Culture and Information of the Republic of Serbia. New digitization methods were applied in the project. New approaches to digitization were gradually adopted in the following ways: from the University Library "Svetozar Markovic" cooperation experience with the British National Library and the National Library of Luxembourg, as a result of the in-house development of the digital tools necessary for the application of certain improvements in the digitization process, and through the cooperation with partner institutions in the project and with other institutions in Serbia and the region.

As regards improvements of the digitization process, it should be noted that different segments of the process, from scanning to user interface, are enhanced in daily and project activities at the University Library. These segments are: implementation of colour and size references, user authentification of digital materials, full searchability of digital text via METS/ALTO files, docWorks, a system for storing digital copies and, therefore, a system for searching and displaying METS/ALTO files, as well as Magic Box, a new presentation device for digital materials. Additionally, the system is improved via participation in the HORIZON 2020 "READ" project.

2   Colour and Size References

So far in Serbia within the process of digitization, as a rule, international standards such as Technical Guidelines for Digitizing Cultural Heritage Materials[1] or standards recommended by UNESCO[2] have been consulted when drafting general recommendations until a wholesome national standard is tailored. In coordination with the British Library, the University Library "Svetozar Markovic" has adopted new digitization concepts which contain new standards.

The recommendations for creating digital copies of physical objects refer to the resolution, the minimum being 300 dpi (dots per inch), or to the format tiff (Tagged Image File Format). In addition to these widely known and broadly applied standards, by meeting the demands of the Endangered Archives Programme[3], we were introduced to the new practices and standards that helped us improve our own digitization guidelines. Above all, work on this project, has brought about two new dimensions: colour and length.

Just as a geographical map is closely determined by its dimensions and colour, a scan or a photograph (a picture of a digitized object) is more precisely determined with a ruler and a color calibration card. Thereby every scan or every photograph provides more precise data about the genuine physical characteristics of an object, by giving unquestionable information about its precise dimensions and colors. Simultaneously, the calibration card and colour scheme give a more precise insight into the colours of an object. This is especially prominent in old archival and physically damaged or endangered materials such as were digitized in the EAP project.

Different sources of light have different temperatures. Photographs which are taken under different conditions do not portray the precise colours of an object. To avoid this, we use White Balance, which is a source based correction. Colours corrected in such a way change balance between red, green and blue curves (RGB curves), but not their shape nor position. Therefore, what is changed in the photograph is the light, not the colour shades. Moreover, when photographs are taken with different devices, we do not get identical colours (Understanding color management, 2016). That is why colour management was developed to make such conversions more subtle and to improve the quality of the photograph.

One of the main colour management tools is a calibration card or a colour scheme. Adjusting colours on the photograph to portray the genuine colours of an object is a challenge in digital and analogue photography. A Swedish company from Gothenburg QP Cards AB developed a cost-effective and efficient solution which is based on an open correction software and calibration cards and which was used within the EAP project. There are several versions available.

---

[1] http://www.digitizationguidelines.gov/guidelines/FADGI_Still_Image_Tech_Guidelines_2016.pdf (accessed 27 Sept. 2017).

[2] http://www.unesco.org/new/fileadmin/MULTIMEDIA/HQ/CI/CI/pdf/mow/digitization_guidelines_for_web.pdf (accessed 27 Sept. 2017).

[3] Endangered Archives Programme. Guidelines for photographing and scanning archival material. Retrieved from http://eap.bl.uk/downloads/guidelines_copying.pdf, (accessed 01 Sept. 2017).

The QP Card is only one of the accepted models of calibration cards. These cards are industrially acquired, i.e. manufactured in factories, usually made of cardboard and cannot be printed through one's own efforts, especially if they should satisfy a particular standard. They usually contain a ruler and a colour scheme (Fig. 1).

Fig. 1. QP Card (Color figure Online)

Colour correction in pictures with a QP Card is done by the calibration software, QPcolorssoft 501, which can be downloaded from the manufacturer's website. This software and a QP Card set up in the scanning surface create a reference profile. They should be set up indirectly to the camera sensor, neither at an angle, nor in shade during the scanning. As the white balance is fixed and a suitable colour profile with given parameters created, a reference correction profile is created and all other pictures taken with the QP Card can be calibrated.

Calibration consists of the following steps: the QP Card is selected, it is adjusted to the colours of the card so that every colour takes the right place in the pattern, then a specific colour profile and a reference calibration profile are created. When the profile is created, all the pictures taken under the determined conditions and the same white balance can be corrected as a group.

If in addition to tiff, as a suitable format for pictures, 300 dpi resolution, as the basic minimum resolution, sufficient and necessary for OCR, completely covered surface of the scanned object, from edge to edge, a colour scheme with a ruler was included. A digital object created in such a way would represent an almost ideal picture of the physical object.

3 Quality Control of the Digitized Materials

Quality control and evaluation have to be carried out over the whole digitization process and the potential future standard. In the current project, the University Library followed the EAP guidelines and took the following measures:

- at the end of every workday it is necessary to carry out quality control of the scans;
- scans are copied to the external hard drive and stored at separate locations (back up);
- when the pictures are stored one needs to check if they are rotated properly so that the content can be read;
- prior to permanent storing of the material MD5 checksum is applied to detect errors.

The MD5 checksum for a file is a 128-bit value, something like a fingerprint of the file. There is a very small possibility of getting two identical checksums of two different files. This feature can be useful both for comparing the files and their integrity control.[4] To understand how this value works, one needs to imagine that there are two physically separated huge files for which it should be determined whether they are the same or different, but which cannot be joined or compared directly. With the MD5 checksum it is sufficient to calculate control sums for both files and then to compare them and determine whether the files are the same or different. One should note that the algorithm MD5 checksum, which was first used at the British Library and which is now a common practice there, was replaced with the algorithm SHA2, which is mostly used by institutions in America. The reason for this is security. Namely, the American algorithm is more secure and less prone to hacking.

4   METS/ALTO

Full searchability of digital texts is achieved via METS/ALTO files. An institution can adapt its digital objects, pictures, to searchable documents via these files. PDF documents offer very limited search possibilities by keywords. Important metadata such as title, subtitle, author or geometric lines of certain articles are not built into the PDF. [3] Searching a PDF results in a marked search term in the text, but not in the picture of the page, which makes locating the search term even harder. Therefore, the METS/ALTO standard was developed in newspaper and library communities. METS and ALTO standards were established for easier description of printed materials. The idea was to separate descriptive information from the content of materials in order to manipulate digital objects more easily because when all data are in an XML file (as with TEI – Text Encoding Initiative format), the XML file is huge. This standard has already proven its quality when it comes to preservation of digitized newspaper collections, and it is widely supported today. The University Library obtained the first such files via the Europeana Newspapers project. After further development of such files in cooperation with the National Library of Serbia, the University Library can produce boundless files.

METS (Metadata Encoding and Transmission Standard) is an XML-based open standard, established by the Library of Congress in Washington in 2001. It is used for storing permanent files that describe digital objects, printed media (books, newspapers, journals), audio and video material, etc. METS usually contains several types of metadata standards: descriptive, administrative, structural information, standards regarding physical and logical structure and links to other digital objects, pictures, audio-visual and textual files.

ALTO (Analyzed Layout and Text Object) is an XML-based open standard also established by the Library of Congress in Washington in 2001. It is used for digital description of the printed page layout so that the original page can be reconstructed. This file comprises the content of an individual page of a digital document and can contain tags with more data about the object. It describes styles, layout and the type of

---

[4] http://www.fastsum.com/support/md5-checksum-utility-faq/md5-checksum.php.

information blocks. All METS/ALTO are grouped in the system for browsing and displaying METS/ALTO files. The collection of these files is searchable and is displayed via open software. This was achieved in cooperation with the National Library of Luxembourg.

Digital objects structured in such a way will be much more operative and will provide a unique search – in the physical space, when it comes to new technologies such as Magic Box, and online, when it comes to a specialized digital repository – with results that will provide a detailed overview of collection contents to the user and a fast and easy search by keyword. In addition to the content of the digitized object, ready metadata and expert literature accompanying the theme of the object will be provided for users. Thereby, the book is not only digitized, but also datafied. Books become data sets, i.e. text corpora, and words become data points. Hence, machines become readers [6].

5   docWorks

The aforementioned transition of images into searchable documents is achieved via the docWorks application, which we implemented with the support of the Ministry of Culture and Information of the Republic of Serbia. The software docWorks, which is the main model of a programme for organizing contents in Magic Box, will be used for the preparation of that material (Fig. 2).

Fig. 2. docWorks

The preparation of material in docWorks[5] consists of the following steps:

- cropping page surfaces of some digital objects;

---

[5] http://content-conversion.com/#docworks-2.

- zoning objects by segmenting pages into blocks and columns with surfaces defined for OCR (Optical Character Recognition) and determining their type as regards the function in the object: titles, text, author, pictures, etc.;
- arranging the structure of the object (bullet, chapter, article) by connecting titles and contingent text;
- correcting text and metadata;
- creating ready objects in the form of METS/ALTO files suitable for display in Magic Box and the repository.
- All aforementioned steps imply an automatic analysis and then manual correction.

6 Therefore

During 2014, the University Library "Svetozar Markovic" carried out a project entitled "University Library "Svetozar Markovic" for the Network of Serbian Public Libraries: Knowledge, Content and Programme Delivery". Within that project, we developed a business solution for advancing library activity in the field of working with digital documents. The solution is based on the professional software platform Therefore and enables the functional connection of the scanning station, regardless of scanner type and software, with the system for the automation of library contents work (COBISS or BISIS), via repositories of digital objects with advanced functions. Therefore, the system was obtained in cooperation with the University Library Kragujevac and the City Library Novi Sad.

We developed the interface for automatic manipulation of metadata, both within the system where metadata for the automation of library contents are automatically paired with scanned objects and for connecting with entities outside this system via the OAI-PMH protocol. In addition, the system facilitates the management of business documentation and all other digital documents in the library. Within the system, one can create a timeline, map names and places which appear in metadata and create virtual exhibitions by linking objects, following certain criteria.

Within Therefore there are 7 applications:

Navigator: a client application which represents metadata basis and allows for their search;

Case viewer: an application which facilitates working with documents, creating templates, full text search, copying documents, etc.;

Viewer: serves for importing and editing metadata and also for downloading and overview of documents;

Capture Client: this application imports scanned material;

Solution: this application facilitates system administration and is located on the server, where the Library does not have access;

Console: administration of user accounts;

Loader: serves for creating scripts and importing scans and metadata into Therefore. This system is a part of a bigger picture and our idea to form a network of repositories that would introduce new library services such as, for instance, digital interlibrary loan.

7   Magic Box

The final phase of the digitization process is the presentation of digital documents. For this reason, the University Library acquired the very attractive cutting-edge technology called Magic Box. This device is the first in east Europe and our library is the third in the world to own it. It provides transparent browsing of digital material on a touch-screen while the physical object can be seen behind the screen (Fig. 3).

Fig. 3. Magic Box

Aware of the importance of the availability of information and open access, especially regarding cultural and scientific heritage, for establishing a knowledge society and the role of academic libraries in the dissemination of knowledge, the University Library will present digital collections to its patrons via these up-to-date technologies.

In its attempt to keep up with the new technological trends in librarianship, and bearing in mind the protection of rare books, the University Library bought Magic Box with the support of the Ministry of Culture and Information. This is a cabinet display which provides a virtual, yet a very real experience of leafing through the digitized and protected library collections.

This kind of technology has already become a pulsating window into the world of the interests of researchers and experts in the field of history, philology, sociology and also of the wider public, thereby encouraging their active participation. This smart device is suitable for the interactive display of materials that are too fragile to leaf through. In that way, permanently stored digital copies are less physically used, therefore less damaged, which ensures that they last longer. [1] Patrons can search through digital content in a completely transparent way, and in addition to digitized print media, Magic Box displays photo galleries, 3D objects and videos.

This means that all interested researchers will be able to search through invaluable archival and library collections in a sophisticated digital way as physical access to these materials is limited due to their fragility. For instance, one might consider certain materials within the EAP collection. A majority of them were published, but the largest part of the collection was published in small circulation, periodicals and calendars in particular. There were not as many readers at the time and many of these documents were destroyed after they were read. That is why they were printed on low quality paper prone to fraying. On the other hand, when it comes to Serbian war periodicals, they were also published in small circulation due to war and exile. For all these reasons, the majority of the digitized collections in the project, and many other from the rich University Library collection are labeled as rare and endangered and cannot be easily accessed. This display will provide a completely new and unique experience to all those interested in rare publications that have limited access because they were not produced for repeated use.

8   Horizon 2020

Participation in international projects is an invaluable experience. In that sense, we didn't have second thoughts about accepting participation in the HORIZON 2020 READ project[6], even though we have not received funding. The University Library acquired TRANSRIBUS within the project and developed methods and techniques for the automatic recognition of handwritten text.

This is especially beneficial to social sciences and humanities researchers who somehow always fall behind their colleagues in the natural and technical sciences due to lack of use of innovative technologies in their research, so they struggle to obtain up-to-date information.

The TRANSKRIBUS programme enables researchers to upload documents and pictures which are the subject of research and to manage them via this digital tool, to segment pictures and blocks of text that are the subject of research and to link text with appropriate pictures. Simultaneously, technically speaking, after retyping the first 20 pages of text, the algorithm recognizes the rest of the handwritten text.

This project will help our library to offer its patrons extremely useful work with valuable materials and yet to be able to control it. Our patrons will receive the opportunity to work with one of the most advanced transcription systems, which is very important. The created transcriptions of concrete handwritten documents (whose access is limited) will not be lost in the private computers of our patrons, but will enrich our digital collections with the possibility of integrating these transcriptions into the existing repositories in a standardized way. This is an ideal platform for crowd-sourcing projects, bearing in mind that within this project there is a crowd-sourcing interface which is easily managed.

---

[6] https://transkribus.eu/Transkribus/ (accessed 27 Sept. 2017).

9 Conclusion

Multilingual and multicultural Europe creates a challenge for those who provide users with easy and seamless browsing experiences when exploring digital collections. To meet this challenge is to translate digital collections into a live vivid experience in a transparent and objective way via new technologies. All the technologies described here were first implemented at the University Library. We plan to transfer these achievements and results to the academic institutions network and to all interested institutions in the public and private sector and among NGOs.

The importance of this undertaking is portrayed in the richer and more productive analysis of local historical and cultural events. By using the advantages of new technologies, the University Library aims to create innovative digital objects online and in physical space, which will attract patrons' attention and focus it toward high quality historical content. This content is connected with the need to establish wider and more defined scientific cooperation in the Balkans and in Europe which will be based on the global digitization process.

Our future goal and largest professional challenge will be connecting the displays of digital and physical objects and the patrons' experience in virtual and digital space.

New technologies should offer a significant breakthrough into various scientific disciplines via open access to cultural and scientific heritage. This is in accordance with the noticeable tendency to use e-infrastructure and innovative technologies as a clear indicator of progress in the field of cultural and national heritage, leading towards their full integration into the open science concept [2].

This should also contribute to the development of a highly qualified young workforce. Moreover, when it comes to the global presentation of library and archival material, such wider implications are of great importance.

References

1. De Stefano, P.: Selection for digital conversion. In: Kenney, A., Rieger, O. (eds.) Moving Theory into Practice: Digital Imaging for Libraries and Archives, pp. 11–23. Research Libraries Group, Mountain View (2000)
2. Fresa, A.: Digital cultural heritage roadmap for preservation. J. Humanit. Arts Comput. J. Digit. Humanit. 8, 107–123 (2014)
3. Geiger, B., Snyder, H., Zarndt, F.: Preserving and accessing born digital newspapers. In: Newspapers: Legal Deposit and Research in the Digital Era, pp. 31–36. De Gruyter Saur, Berlin (2011)
4. Jerkov, A., Sofronijevic, A., Stanisic, D.K.: Smart and sustainable library: information literacy hub of a New City. In: Kurbanoğlu, S., Boustany, J., Špiranec, S., Grassian, E., Mizrachi, D., Roy, L. (eds.) ECIL 2015. CCIS, vol. 552, pp. 22–30. Springer, Cham (2015). https://doi.org/10.1007/978-3-319-28197-1_3

5. Julien, H., Gross, M., Latham, D.: Survey of information literacy instructional practices in US academic libraries. Coll. Res. Libr. 17–1024 (2017)
6. Murrell, M.: The datafied book and the entanglements of digitization. Anthropol. Today **30** (5), 3–6 (2014)
7. Newtown, L.: Data-logging in practical science: research and reality. Int. J. Sci. Educ. **22**(12), 1247–1259 (2000)

An Application to Improve Smart Heritage City Experience

Adriana Mar$^{(\boxtimes)}$, Fernando Monteiro, Pedro Pereira, and João Martins

CTS – UNINOVA, Department of Electrical Engineering, Faculty of Science and
Technology, Universidade NOVA de Lisboa, 2829-516 Caparica, Portugal
am.jesus@campus.fct.unl.pt,
fernando.j.c.c.monteiro@gmail.com,
{pmrp,jf.martins}@fct.unl.pt

Abstract. Nowadays technologies relate to so many aspects in our daily life
that makes society eager for more and more ways of using it. To keep up with
this new technological world, all economic sectors, from industry to services,
are trying to adapt their products into this new reality. Presently, cultural heritage is already a field where the application of technology allows a static site to
be converted into an intelligent environment, with detailed information about a
specific monument or historical place, becoming more interesting, not only for
local habitants, but also for tourists. This paper describes an application that
allows tourists, managers and historical sites' habitants to experience a completely new way of discovering those places, offering a visit with detailed
real-time information taking into account their personal interests. Tourists will
have at their disposal a full set of optimized routes, combining their interests
with their visiting time.

Keywords: Smart city · Heritage · Monitoring · Tourists' application

1 Introduction

Naming a city "smart" has evolved in such a way meaning a city that has mitigated
problems generated by development, population growth and rapid urbanization. New
issues like scarcity of resources, air pollution, human health, inadequate, deterioration
and aging of infrastructures can be associated to several stakeholders, increasing the
social and political complexity of their interdependency. To ensure liveable conditions
within the context of such fast worldwide growth, a deep understanding of smart city
concept is required [1, 2]. Additionally, the rapid growth and development of new
technologies has led to a compulsive use, which can be advantageous for tourists,
during their time visiting a certain country/city, historical centres' managers or even to
the local commerce and infrastructures.

This work describes the merging of the smart city and heritage centres concepts.
This trend has been pushed up due to economic and ecological pression, and to the
existence of new technologies that gives tourists a new experience when visiting a city.

For tourists, the implementation of this concept can help them get around the city,
warn them if some monuments are overcrowded, if the waiting time is more than they

M. Ioannides et al. (Eds.): Digital Cultural Heritage 2017, LNCS 10754, pp. 89–103, 2018.
https://doi.org/10.1007/978-3-319-75789-6_7

are willing to spend, or simply let them know about new unusual paths that they would otherwise not know, and last but not least to promote local commerce. For managers, the decentralization of tourists over the entire heritage area will help them, decrease the stream of people at the same place, thus helping with preserving the monuments in structural terms. This work intends to potentiate an innovative way to manage historical centres, improving high quality tourism (taking into account the needs of visitors and monuments).

This article is organized in the following way: Sect. 2 introduces the smart city concept as well as relevant work that has been done over the heritage centres. In Sect. 3, the Smart Heritage City (SHCity) project, its main goals, problematics and system architecture definition, are presented. In Sect. 4, the highlight goes to the proposed Tourist Application, its structure and contents that users will have at their disposal. Section 5, introduces the main lines of the routing algorithm that will be used to create a circuit in accordance with tourist's requests. Finally, conclusions are offered in Sect. 6.

2   Concepts

This section introduces the meaning of Smart City (SC), describing its features and the main application domains. After defining the concept of SC, the merging between SC and Heritage is presented. Lastly, an analysis of technologies to create and/or optimize smart walking circuits through heritage cities, and get to know their history, is presented.

2.1   Smart City Concept and Its Application Domains

Although the smart city (SC) concept has grown in the last years, as a means to improve citizens' life quality, there is not yet a concrete definition of SC, being difficult to identify a common application.

Several definitions have been adopted for practical and academic usage by different authors. In [3, 4] the focus of a SC is pointed out on infrastructures, considering a smart city one that monitors and integrates conditions of all critical infrastructures such as roads, bridges, airports or subways, that can optimize the available resources, elaborate a preventive maintenance plan and monitor citizens' security. A smart city should interconnect physical, technological, social and economic infrastructures in an intelligent optimal way. On the other hand, [5] claims that the intelligent city vision involves the use of new technologies improving sustainability and habitability. Combining information and communication technologies (ICT) with other efforts to speed up processes and help find new and innovative solutions to city management.

In [6] it is alleged that SCs should optimize the use of tangible assets, such as transport or energy distribution infrastructure, and intangible ones, like human capital. This definition is mostly related with two aspects: one concerning the way cities adapt to do this optimization and another, and the most critical, connected with the intelligent usage of urban resources.

Energy grids and culture, are two key areas that can be identified and related with the presented work. In [7, 8] smart energy grids are the pillar of a smart city and the ones that use ICT to allow the exchange of information on consumption between users and suppliers, which will contribute to costs reduction and an improvement of energy systems clearness. This shows that the use of ICT brings, not only advantages from the point of view of a company (cost reduction and profits), but also social advantages such as costumers' awareness about their behaviour impact in their daily life. The culture area is another domain that can be taken into account and will be considered under the developed work presented in this chapter. Offering the user a system able to provide services according to their preferences, activities or needs when travelling, that's what is proposed in Piccialli's work [9]. The work presented by Piccialli offers a Context Evolution System that aims to help tourists during a visit through a museum. For that, a system was modulated with a group of features (sensors, knowledge, sources, monitoring, among others) in order to be able to observe the reality and create a dynamic cultural space.

2.2 Smart City and Cultural Heritage

Cultural Heritage represents an incalculable worldwide resource, attracting millions of visitors each year to monuments, museums, art exhibitions or cities. Indeed, in order to achieve a sustainable cultural space, it is necessary to create intelligent solutions for the interaction with visitors to enrich their visiting experience.

In one hand, there is the concern to provide the tourist with a better visit inside a monument or museum, helping him to understand why a particular object is in that specific location, how it interconnects with history, in what context was created or if it is the path for something more challenging. Taking that into account, some authors try to relate technologies and multimedia tools, such as tablets or smartphones and their applications, to improve tourist mobility and interest during a visit, providing relevant resources that can't be exposed but are essential for a better perception of monuments or artworks. The work presented in [10] is a good example, showing a system that turns cultural spaces, like museums or exhibitions, into an intelligent space. This system aims to give tourists a better understanding of what they are observing at monuments or museums.

On the other hand, helping tourists to select the most interesting places considering their personal interests, or when they have limited time to visit a certain place, is a current concern. Typically, tourists need to collect information from different sites such as websites, articles or guidebooks of different points of interest to plan their itinerary. In this planning they also consider different restrictions, some of them related with themselves other related with the sites to visit. This process may present some unexpected difficulties because certain information may be outdated or incorrect [11]. Thereby, one current trend involving decision makers and integrated network technology, offers to tourists a dynamic multimedia information that could help them with a more detailed visit. In [12] a hybrid multi-objective genetic algorithm was used on a mobile application to, smartly, generate feasible circuits for an orienteering problem, which plans circuits taking into account a predefined time window, i.e., opening hours of points of interest. For this propose, a group of locations and a start and end time are considered.

In [13, 14] the time dependence on tourism systems is considered, where time required to move from one location to another is considered in circuit planning. The system can generate, with a semantic matching technique, itineraries with dynamic updating considering the tourist visiting time.

The work presented in this paper goes a step forward on this concept, taking advantage of monuments' sensor data collection. Using data collected from cameras, placed on the monuments entry/exit, the described system uses real time information about the occupancy rate of each monument.

3 Smart Heritage City Project

With the ambition of integrating urban heritage centres with the smart city concept, an innovative challenge to create an open source tool was embraced within the Smart Heritage City project (SHCity), managing historical centres and helping responsible entities to take accurate decisions about their monuments management. The proposed solution aims to use data collected from a sensor network, which is inserted in urban areas, to control and have access to data related to buildings, its surrounding areas, which allows to prevent against existing risk factors. Based on a set of developed ICT tools and expert knowledge, in different areas of urban heritage management, the Smart City concept was extended to Smart Heritage City. Built on previous results coming from the SHBuildings project [15], the SHCity project scales it from a building level up to an urban area level.

SHCity is intended to contribute to the mitigation of failures detected on the SUDOE space (Portugal, Spain and France) related with i+d+I (investigation, development and innovation) and new ICT technologies, proposing a sustainable heritage management system, increasing job creation and improving citizens and visitors' life quality. The developed intelligent system is able to be deployed in any historical monument or city on the SUDOE space, improving technology transfer, promoting social innovation and public service applications as well as promoting the use of innovative technologies for a better environmental protection and more efficient usage of resources.

On the other hand, it is also intended to provide tourists with complete knowledge of the city, providing information related to unusual parts of the city that, although less touristic, are worth visiting.

3.1 Heritage Centres' Opportunities

Many historic urban centres, with great cultural and artistic values, are an element of identity and key factor of local economic development for the SUDOE space. Some of them own World Heritage status, while others are recognized by national or regional labels with the intention of aesthetical and functional preservation.

These historical centres have been losing inhabitants due to their characteristics, often inadequate to fulfil twenty-first century comfort standards, resulting in a degradation of both buildings and quality of life of those who live there. Thus, in order to change this paradigm and give a new life to the urban areas of cities, it is imperative to provide tools allowing a better management of historical centres as in the smart city paradigm.

For the SHCity project the integration of several heritage assets in the concept of smart city is its higher driven factor. For this propose, there is the need to equip buildings, and their surrounding areas, with useful technology in order to provide information that will facilitate their management, saving public resources and giving a more efficient return of investment. The project will deliver an economical enhancement, not only in the tourism industry but also on scientific and cultural developments, achieving innovation and economic creativity that will bring added value to social organizations and public in general.

The SHCity project SWOT analysis, where the main strengths and opportunities as well as weaknesses and threats are shown in Fig. 1.

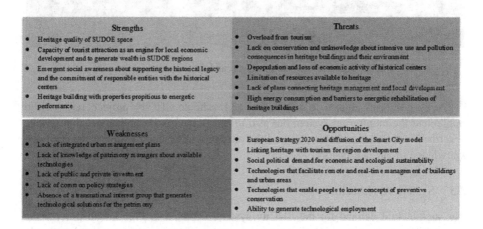

Fig. 1. SHCity SWOT analysis

3.2 Avila – Pilot City

Avila was declared a UNESCO World Heritage Site in 1985, which makes it one of the best places to implement an ICT tool for the management of historic sites. Avila is part of the Spanish Jewish Quarter Network since 2005, offering tourists several routes with great cultural heritage value, consequence of its history, architecture, inhabitants and landscapes.

This vast heritage of Avila requires a leisurely visit at different times of the day and, if possible, with the help of a good guide to understand an ancient, mediaeval and renaissance town with the subsequent recovery it suffered in the 19th century. As in other Spanish cities, Avila was the home of Jews, Muslims and Christians, which all left their mark and cultural legacy for the city.

Avila became a place of tradition, with many religious and traditional customs. Each quarter has its own festival, remembering past divisions when each of the groups who went to repopulate the town settled around a parish church, that attracts various tourists to participate not only in festivals but also to get to know the city. There has been made a considerable investment in heritage, as a tourist resource and development engine. Avila (Fig. 2) is part of the Spanish Network of Intelligent Cities and has several assets monitored, such as the wall or the cathedral, which facilitates the implementation of the SHCity project.

Fig. 2. Avila's view with the wall and the cathedral in the end

Avila has been chosen to implement and validate SHCity project, not only to implement the monitoring system but also to test the tourists' application, that will be described in the section below, around the city, providing them with a better visit and knowledge of Avila's history.

3.3 System Architecture

The architecture defined for the SHCity system, depicted in Fig. 3, will process the information of the city's 3D map and the data coming from the sensors' network, allowing to monitoring the different monuments. The data collected with these sensors (temperature, light, structural conditions, number of visitors) will be locally processed and stored into a cloud system, being available to be used in the heritage management system (managers app) as well in the tourist application (tourist app). The propose of the present work is to describe the structure and functionalities of the tourist application. The managers application will not be considered in this work.

With the purpose of creating a better and more complete heritage management system, but also to avoid damage inside heritage buildings, wired and wireless sensors are considered.

After being locally processed, the data will be stored and available at a cloud structure, providing access for the system's applications, as presented in Fig. 4. For each specific client/application, a communication system was developed based on standards, assuring entities and infrastructure integration. Java or C# are used to implement the infrastructure needed, as well as some communication modules and web services, that will be implemented in each entity to communicate with the cloud.

Finally, at the application layer two services are considered with different goals. The first one is dedicated to management, designed to help heritage managers on their daily and planning actions, using the information gathered from sensors. The second

Fig. 3. SHCity system definition

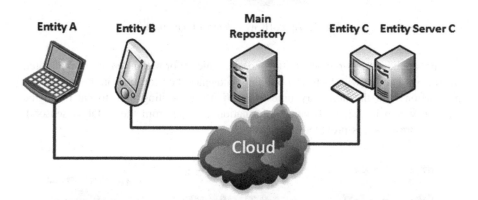

Fig. 4. Connection between cloud and clients/application

service is dedicated to the tourist application that aims to offer detailed information about monuments and/or suggestions regarding walking circuits, in order to promote a better city experience. In the next section, the tourist application will be described in detail.

4 Smart Heritage City Tourist Application

Being a tourist in an unacquainted city can be as challenging as difficult. Trying to diminish these difficulties, SHCity-Tourist application provides a set of information that allows tourist to better know not only famous monuments but also less mainstream points of interest. The information (whose front page is presented in Fig. 5) is provided in three categories, as listed below:

- List of monuments;
- Presentation of pre-established circuits;
- Walking circuit creation based on users provided data.

Fig. 5. App SHCity – Tourist home page

The application combines static and dynamic information on each monitored monument. The list with historical buildings indicates their location on the map (static information) and the necessary time to reach it, the waiting time to enter and the occupancy rate inside it (dynamic information coming from the installed sensors). Figure 6 presents this provided information:

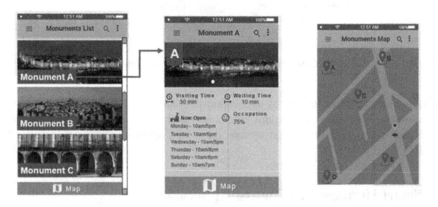

Fig. 6. Monument list and available information.

- Static information: location, visit hours and/or average visiting time;
- Dynamic information: occupancy rates, waiting time and/or time/distance to reach it.

Regarding the walking circuits, two options are available to the tourist: (i) pre-defined circuits of different duration and difficulty; (ii) the possibility of creating their own circuit. For the first option the tourist can find a list of predefined circuits with detailed information: walking time, number of considered monuments and difficulty level. Within each circuit, the user can access photos and videos or download the map with the location of the circuit's monuments, as presented in Fig. 7. Figure 7 also presents an example of a circuit to be made in two days, visiting eight monuments and with medium difficulty level. The circuits are classified accordingly to:

Fig. 7. Circuits list option with circuit characteristics.

- Difficulty level (easy, medium or hard);
- Duration (one or several days, plus night routes).

To establish their own circuit, tourists will have a menu at their disposal where they can insert the following information: total time of visit (1 h, 5 h, 1 day or more), the initial point and a priority list of monuments they are willing to see. The selected monuments will be shown on the map, as presented in Fig. 8. Considering real-time information, a dynamic circuit can be created through the use of evolutionary algorithms, aiming to optimize the circuit total time and maximizing the number of places to visit in accordance with tourist's requirements. The algorithm combines the distance and time between each one of the monuments (static information) with real-time information about occupancy rate, waiting time and average visiting time (dynamic information).

As an example, let us consider the following scenario, illustrated in Fig. 9:

- Starting location for the visit: point F;
- Available visiting time: 3 h;
- Mandatory visiting monuments: H and I;
- Average visit time of monument H: 70 min;
- Average visit time of monument I: 40 min;
- Entrance waiting time for monument I: 10 min (real time information at the moment the tourist asks the system to create its route);
- Entrance waiting time for monument H: 1 min (real time information at the moment the tourist asks the system to create its route).

Fig. 8. Circuit Creation

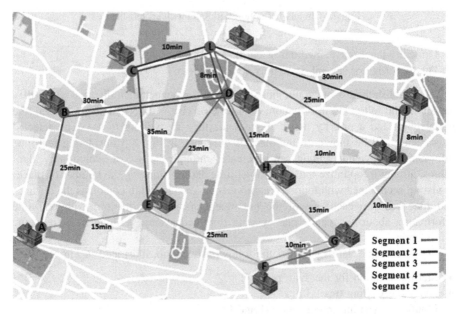

Fig. 9. Definition of different segments interconnecting city monuments

With this information, the best planned visit of the city will at point F then passing through point G in order to visit H and I. Considering the waiting time and time distance between monuments/places the tourist will have spent approximately 2 h 25 min. At this point, the artificial intelligence engine of the application suggests several options for the remaining time: the tourist can choose between monuments J or G, both with an average visit time of 20 min. Taking into account the information on occupancy rate, waiting time and distance, the application will suggest which would be the best choice to take. In case a tourist chooses a monument with a persistent huge waiting time it can be removed during the visit, and the application will re-route the circuit considering the remaining time and monuments already visited.

5 Routing Algorithm

Application Behaviour

The tourist application is based on an algorithm designed to create a circuit in accordance with user's requests (based on an Optimizing Personalized Touristic Itineraries [11]). As the main goal, such circuit will provide the largest number of places of interest to visit, during the available circuit time.

This is a real time and optimization problem with some requirements to take into account, such as user's inputs and real-time data acquisition. As illustrated in Fig. 10, the first step is to acquire information from the user side, namely:

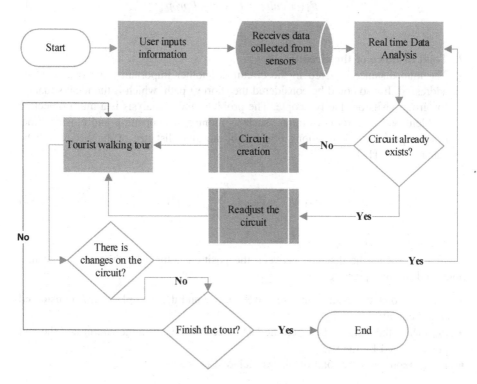

Fig. 10. Flowchart of the tourist application behaviour

- The available time for the circuit;
- The initial and final location;
- Priority places to visit (if any).

With this information and analysing the real-time data coming from the sensors, the algorithm will create the optimized circuit (minimizing the unused time and increasing the number of visited monuments). Being a real-time application, if a deviation to the initial plan occurs, the algorithm readjusts the circuit always taking into account the collected data and the places visited so far.

1. **Number of places required by the user and those proposed by the application:**
   The objective is to minimize the difference between the number of places to visit required by the user, inserted in the input requirements, denoted as P_{user}, and the number of places that effectively will be presented in the proposed circuit, denoted as P_{prop}. Taking into account other conditions, as the waiting time to entrance, the visiting time and the time from one point to another, the number of places to visit, P_{prop}, will be lower or equal to P_{user}, where the ideal circuit represents the one that includes all the places, making Eq. (1) equal to zero [11].

$$\Gamma_1(circuit) = Puser - Pprop \tag{1}$$

2. **Total distance of the circuit:**
   The total distance covered in the circuit is another important issue that must be addressed. It also could be considered the shortest path, which is the ideal situation for group visits or elderly people. The problem under analysis is a multi-objective problem with several constraints, such as monuments' opening and closing time, priority places to visit, among others. So, the total distance of the circuit will be calculated as [11]:

$$\Gamma_2(circuit) = d_{init} + \sum_{i=1}^{P_{circuit}} d_{i,i+1} + d_{fin} \tag{2}$$

Where:

d_{init} represents the distance between the position defined by the user as the first point and the first place to visit;

- $d_{i,i+1}$ denotes the distance between one place i and the next place, $i+1$, considered in the circuit;
- d_{fin} means the distance between the last place considered in the circuit and the end point defined by the user;
- $P_{circuit}$ represents the total of places included in the circuit.

3. **Total duration of the circuit:**

To analyse the total duration of the proposed circuit, will be take into account the following variables:

- $t_{i,j}$ indicating the necessary time to go from a place i to j, where j represents the successive place to i in the presented circuit;
- t_{wait_j} represents the waiting time to access the place j, bearing in mind real time information and data analysed from the database;
- t_{visit_j} denotes the visiting time of the place j;
- t_{end} means the time necessary to go from the last visited place to the ending point selected by the user;
- max_{time} represents the maximum time defined by the user to realize the circuit.

Considering these variables and knowing that the objective is maximize the duration of the circuit respecting the constraint $\Gamma_3(circuit) \leq max_{time}$, the total time is given by, [11]:

$$\Gamma_3(circuit) = \sum_{i=1}^{P_{circuit}} \left(\sum_{j=1}^{P_{circuit}} \left(t_{i,j} + t_{wait_j} + t_{visit_j} \right) \right) + t_{end} \qquad (3)$$

Optimization Methods

As mentioned above the problem under analysis infers multi-objectives for creating an optimal circuit that takes into account the user's requirements. Considering the optimization methods categorized in Fig. 11, it was possible to choose the most suitable method to be applied to this specific case study.

As shown, optimization methods can be linear or non-linear programming. As the name specifies, the linear programming is characterized by obtaining the best solution through the use of linear functions. Although, the non-linear programming regards to more complex problems that needs to be decomposed into multi-problems separately, where each problem can have different objective functions [16]. Due to the nature of the problem embraced in this work, a stochastic method was adopted, since it introduces randomness to the search process which means that there is no need of previous information concerning the problem being optimized. Moreover, this type of optimization methodology is also able to determine not only the best, but also some good solutions in accordance with user's inputs.

Between several stochastic methods, the evolutionary algorithms (EA) aims to find the best solution conceivable among the available possible solutions to a certain problem. The evolutionary search studies evolution of species and try to find the best among other possible solutions which can be suitable for computational and engineering problems that requires complex solutions with innumerable hypotheses [16].

Taking into account what was said about optimization methods and what is described in the literature, to the tourist application algorithm was considered the use of evolutionary algorithms, since this type of programming can search for the optimal solution of a problem with multi-objectives and presents more effective and quicker results than other methods that have a more exhaustive search methodology, i.e., the enumerative algorithms goes through every point of the search space and at each point

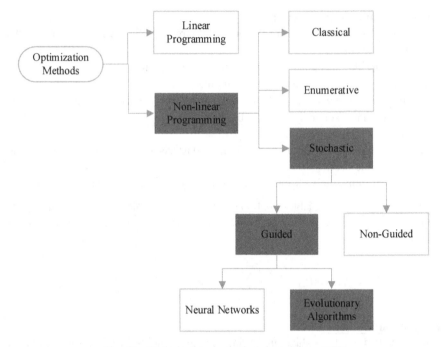

Fig. 11. Optimization methods (adapted from [17])

all solutions, which most of the times implies a prohibitive amount of time. This criterion is of major importance in real-time problems.

6 Conclusions

From the research conducted it was clear that a reasonable number of initiatives and studies, addressing new technological approaches on tourism, were already led in the research community. The literature review has allowed to identify opportunities concerning the smart city concept integrated in cultural heritage patrimony.

The work presented in this chapter aims to improve tourism from two distinct points of view, management and tourist side. Although the manager side was not approached in this work. In order to go a step forward in relation to the initiatives/projects that already exists, this work integrates intelligent sensors, which are placed in historical monuments, collecting data and make it available for both managers and tourists. From the tourist point of view, an application that aims to provide a new concept of travelling through the city learning about its monuments and history. Such application will offer real-time information about occupancy rates or waiting time entrance, as well as suggestions for walking circuits or giving tourists the opportunity of getting a personalized circuit in accordance with their preferences.

Acknowledgement. This work was supported by the INTERREG SUDOE Smart Heritage City SOE1/P1/E0332 project and the Portuguese National Funding through the FCT (Science and Technology Foundation) UID/EEA/00066/2013 project.

FCT Fundação para a Ciência e a Tecnologia

MINISTÉRIO DA EDUCAÇÃO E CIÊNCIA

References

1. Komninos, N.: Intelligent cities. Encycl. Digit. Gov. **5**, 1100–1104 (2007)
2. Chourabi, H., et al.: Understanding smart cities: an integrative framework. In: Proceedings of the Annual Hawaii International Conference on System Sciences, pp. 2289–2297 (2011)
3. Hall, R.E., Bowerman, B., Braverman, J., Taylor, J., Todosow, H.: The vision of a smart city. In: 2nd International Life Extension Technology Workshop, vol. 28, p. 7 (2000)
4. Harrison, C., et al.: Foundations for smarter cities. IBM J. Res. Dev. **54**(4), 1–16 (2010)
5. Toppeta, D.: How innovation and ICT the smart city vision: how innovation and ICT can build smart, liveable, sustainable cities. Think Rep. **5**, 1–9 (2010)
6. Neirotti, P., De Marco, A., Cagliano, A.C., Mangano, G., Scorrano, F.: Current trends in smart city initiatives: some stylised facts. Cities **38**, 25–36 (2014)
7. Correira, L.M., Wunstel, K.: Smart cities applications and requirements. City, 1–39 (2011)
8. Steria - Smart Cities will be enabled by Smart IT, pp. 1–12 (2011)
9. Chianese, A., Piccialli, F.: A smart system to manage the context evolution in the Cultural Heritage domain. Comput. Electr. Eng., 1–12 (2015)
10. Chianese, A., Piccialli, F., Valente, I.: Smart environments and Cultural Heritage: a novel approach to create *intelligent* cultural spaces. J. Locat. Based Serv. **9**(3), 209–234 (2015)
11. De Falco, I., Scafuri, U., Tarantino, E.: Optimizing personalized touristic itineraries by a multiobjective evolutionary algorithm. Int. J. Inf. Technol. Decis. Mak. **15**, 1–44 (2016)
12. Diosteanu, A., Coftas, L., Smeureanu, A., Dumitrescu, S.: Natural language processing applied in itinerary recommender systems. In: The 10th WSEAS International Conference on Applied Computer and Applied Computational Science (ACACOS 2011), pp. 260–265 (2011)
13. Cotfas, L.A.: Collaborative itinerary recommender systems. Econ. Inform. J. **11**(1), 191–200 (2011)
14. Cotfas, L.A., Diosteanu, A., Dumitrescu, S.D., Smeureanu, A.: Semantic search itinerary recommender system. Int. J. Comput. **5**(3), 370–377 (2011)
15. SHbuildings. http://www.shbuildings.es/. Accessed 17 Oct 2017
16. Luenberger, D., Ye, Y.: Linear and non-linear Programming, Third. vol. 4 (1992)
17. Pereira, P., Fino, M.H.: Optimization Based Design of LC Voltage Controlled Oscillators (2013)

Interactive Gallery: Enhance Social Interaction for Elders by Story Sharing

Cun Li$^{(\boxtimes)}$, Xu Lin, Kai Kang, Jun Hu, Bart Hengeveld,
Caroline Hummels, and Matthias Rauterberg

Eindhoven University of Technology, Eindhoven, Netherlands
Cun.li@tue.nl

Abstract. At present, the most effective way to deal with the demographic shift of elders is encouraging them to live in nursing homes for more effective health care. However, such move dramatically increases their risk of social isolation. A contextual inquiry in a local nursing home revealed that most elderly people have few connections with the outside environment because of their decreased mobility and have difficulty establishing relationships with fellow residents. In addition, they show great interests in sharing stories. Based on the above findings, we present Interactive Gallery, a system consisting of a cluster of specially designed camera kits and a gallery-like interactive installation utilized with the metaphor of gallery and postcards. This system aims to make the elders feel more connected to the outside environment, stimulate them to reminisce, and further facilitate their sharing of stories with fellow residents and citizens from local communities.

Keywords: Elderly · Story · Social interaction · Interactive installation
Tangible interface

1 Introduction

An increasing number of older people spend their lives in nursing institutions. While living in a nursing home benefits the elderly, it has disadvantages as well. On one hand, a nursing home is a relatively enclosed environment that elderly people cannot leave without supervision. On the other hand, elderly people are disconnected from the mainstream social circles due to the lack of technology and devices that resonate with them [1]. This disconnection is because mainstream user interactions are not based on existing mental models of technology that the elderly already understand [2], which intensifies the possibility of the elderly living in nursing homes to suffer from social isolation.

According to previous studies, people lacking social contacts are more susceptible to diseases, infarction, stroke, and the onset of Alzheimer's disease [3, 4]. Loneliness and social isolation among elderly people are of significant concern.

Recently, more researchers have explored how social technologies can be used to alleviate the elderly's experience of loneliness and social interaction, especially with the development and popularization of the Internet of Things (IoT). The idea that the convergence of the IoT and the social network world is possible, or even advisable, is gaining momentum [5].

© Springer International Publishing AG, part of Springer Nature 2018
M. Ioannides et al. (Eds.): Digital Cultural Heritage 2017, LNCS 10754, pp. 104–116, 2018.
https://doi.org/10.1007/978-3-319-75789-6_8

In the current paper, we introduce an interactive gallery consisting of a group of specially designed camera kits and a gallery-like interactive installation combined with IOT technologies to facilitate the story-sharing of elderly people in nursing homes with fellow residents and citizens from local communities. We first discuss related theories and representative relevant cases. In the contextual inquiry section, interviews with the caregivers and elderly are conducted. Then, the design requirements are specified, followed by the details of project design and implementation. Conclusions, limitations, and recommendations for future work are found in the final part of this paper. The research methodology includes contextual inquiry, scenario creation, and prototyping.

2   Related Work

The study project links the following areas of research: social interaction of the elderly, life-story, reminiscing, and storytelling. The range of studies within these areas is extensive. In this section, we first discuss related theories, such as memory cues of reminiscence and place attachment theory and then briefly discuss some representative related cases.

2.1   Memory Cues of Reminiscence

Psychologist Webster defined "reminiscence" as: the process of recalling memories from our personal past that is an activity engaged in by adults of all ages at different points throughout their lives [6]. Humans have memory triggers that set off very strong recollections of past experiences. Memory cues are significant aspects of reminiscence and a broad range of external memory cues could be employed as triggers to evoke memory and experiences.

According to S. Tejaswi Peesapati's research, common memory cues are classified as: things, places, people and experiences, as shown in Table 1 [7].

Table 1. Memory cues by category.

Things	Places	People	Experiences
Entertainment: *Music, Books, Games*	Homes	Family: *Parents, Siblings, Pets*	Medical
Technology	Outdoors	Loved ones	School
Appearance	School/Work	Friends	Work
Food			Travel
Events: *Sports, Parties*			

Interactive devices can support reminiscing using captured images and other data as memory cues, provided design efforts are based on a solid understanding of what makes people remember their past [8].

2.2   Place Attachment Theory

Before elderly people moved into nursing homes, they live in the city for many years and are familiar with the city, lots of places in the city keeps memories and stories of them. Their lives and personal memories are punctuated by meaningful interactions with places. However, when the elderly move into nursing institution, they couldn't leave easily for the lack of mobility.

According to the place attachment theory, a place is not simply a bounded geographical area, it is a space which is imbued with meaning or resonance to an individual or a collective [9]. Place contains a wealth of different experiences and stories especially for the elderly. A place is vibrant and ever transforming and can take differing forms to every individual or collective who experiences it [10].

2.3   The Elderly and Social Technology

Much research has been carried out in theory and practice on how to increase the social connections for the elderly by lowering the threshold of the elderly getting access to social technology. Related research in this area can be summarized into 3 aspects: (1) Increase the elderly's social connections with intergenerational family members: Audio-Enhanced Paper Photos is a hybrid paper-digital approach to sharing photos that is a tool for intergenerational communication, reminiscence, and social engagement [11]. (2) Facilitate social interaction between fellow residents in nursing home: "Bring Dichein" is a local, service-oriented collaborative consumption platform called with the purpose of facilitating social interaction across generations as well as the trade of peer-to-peer services [12]. (3) Meet the needs of keeping up with far-away relatives and friends: "insight" invites elderlies to interact with their loved ones in a playful, intuitive, and non–intrusive manner, all achieved through the utilization of a simple interface metaphor [13].

2.4   Reminiscence of the Elderly

Most of current related research consider reminiscence as a way of therapy for people with AD and other forms of dementia because reminiscence therapy is a proven method of stimulating long-term memory to evoke communication.

Many interactive systems provide digital memory cues to evoke the user to recall memories: Picgo is a game-based reminiscence service that enables elders to capture memories, annotate photos, and iteratively reinforce the annotation of photos in a storytelling process. Which is able to provide meaningful reminiscent materials to caregivers and occupational therapists in reminiscence therapy [14]. Vardit Sarne-Fleischmann introduces a personalized reminiscence program, which was developed specifically for use by patients and their caregivers in the treatment of mild to moderate Alzheimer's disease [15].

2.5 Storytelling of the Elderly

Based on the facts that the elderly have abundant life memories and experiences, they prefer to express themselves in terms of their life achievements and life stories, they love to tell and share their own stories. Some studies try to aid the elderly to tell stories either by interactive installation: Storycubes is a system that helps residents of independent living communities make connections through sharing stories, and express their identity in terms of their unique background, interests, and values [16]. Some others are by the means of tangible interfaces: TopoTiles [10] employs Tangible User Interfaces, which is designed to aid storytelling, reminiscence and community building in care homes. Aiming to use tangible interfaces to aid storytelling and further encourage inclusivity in group sharing situations in an indirect or peripheral manner.

3 Contextual Inquiry

To understand the patterns of socialization of elderly people, interviews were individually conducted with the caregivers and elders in a local nursing home in a contextual inquiry phase. Caregivers have the most contact with the elderly and could provide us information from a relatively objective perspective, whereas the elderly in nursing homes serves as the target group that could provide firsthand feelings and experiences of their social lives.

3.1 Interview with the Caregivers

Four semi-structured interviews were conducted with caregivers in a local nursing home, and each interview was audio-recorded. The main goal in this phase of interview is to obtain information on the following aspects: major roles and responsibilities of the caregivers, collective activities in the nursing home, abilities of reading and writing of the elders, daily routines of the elders, and their connections with their fellow residents and the outside environment.

Table 2. Daily routine of a typical resident under care service.

8:00	Wake up and take a shower
8:30	Cook breakfast by themselves
10:00	If they stay in their apartment, they usually have nothing to do
12:00	Some have lunch in the canteen, and others need a caregiver to deliver the food to them
13:00	After eating, most return to their apartments, while some stay in the canteen
17:00	Dinner
22:00	Bed time

Information gathered from the caregivers are summarized as follows:

(1) The daily routines of elderly people remain the same. They move from sleeping area to eating area, as shown in Table 2.

(2) Most of the elderly prefer to do nothing in their own rooms rather than attend collective activities.
(3) Elderly people encounter difficulty in connecting with their fellow residents.
(4) Elderly people would like to share their lives and stories with the caregivers, though in most cases the stories are the same.

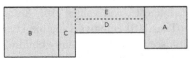

A:library B:canteen C:meeting room D:corridor E:resting area

Fig. 1. Layout of the ground floor in the nursing home.

Fig. 2. Canteen and meeting room in the nursing home.

(5) Elderly people often feel depressed because they could not do some things they could before (Figs. 1 and 2).

3.2 Interview with the Elderly

A total of 11 semi-structured interviews were conducted with older adults (65 years or older) in the local nursing home, and each interview was audio-recorded. Our main objective for this phase is to obtain information from the following aspects: their familiarization with technology, their way of obtaining information, and their connections with fellow residents and the outside environment.

The interviews indicate that although every elderly person knows their fellow residents, the relationships between them are not profound and there are no close bonds. For instance, when talking about whether they had someone to talk with in the nursing home, one interviewee said:

It's always "Good morning," "Good afternoon," "Did you have a nice meal?", or something like that. But real talking? No. They are all very friendly and do it very well, but a real friend? No.

One of the reasons for such disconnection is that they do not understand each other's backgrounds and hobbies, and therefore have no mutual topic to start a conversation. For example, when asked why he/she did not talk too much, one interviewee said: *Well, they're all strangers. There are a couple of people who play cards on the table and we meet very often. But I don't like playing cards.*

Another interviewee said:

Usually it's like "how are you" and so forth. I don't know their hobbies; if you know something about them you might be able to talk about that, but I don't know any of that. I quickly get emotional as well. Then you have no idea how to get through it.

Lack of mobility caused by physical decline also leads elderly people to stay in their own rooms. For instance, one interviewee said:

Every day I hear the same nonsense. As I am also not that mobile anymore, I'd rather stay in my own room. It's always the same topic and so boring.

Information gathered from the elderly are summarized as follows:

Elderly people in the nursing home have alienated relationships with their fellow residents.

Although most of the elderly people's family members visit them at least once a week, the residents feel lonely again when family members leave.

In the nursing home, the only chance for interaction for the elderly people is the time for collective activities. They are connected because they play together; however, there is no significant interaction between them and the activities do not match their interests. Thus, collective activities could not be a medium to establish social connections.

Most elderly people suffer from decreased mobility, which prevents them from leaving the nursing home without the company of caregivers or family members. The nearest supermarket is the maximum distance to reach independently for most elderly people. In short, the nursing home is a relatively closed living environment.

Moreover, most elderly people are greatly interested in sharing stories with others to express their rich life memories and experiences.

3.3   Summary of Contextual Inquiry

Major findings in the above contextual inquiry could be summarized as follows: (1) nursing home internal social interactions comprise the relationships between residents, and (2) nursing home external social connections comprise the social connections between nursing home and outside environment.

In terms of nursing home internal communication, most residents have difficulty establishing meaningful relationships with fellow residents.

With respect to the connection with the outside environment, most elderly people are rarely connected with the outside environment because of their decreased mobility.

Furthermore, the strong desire of the elderly to share their stories could be the breakthrough subject of our design concept.

4   Design of Interactive Gallery

We could construct a design concept based on the findings acquired from the above interviews:

(1) We could enhance the elderly people's connections with the outside environment by transmitting real-time scenery photos to the nursing home.

(2) Based on the findings that elderly people enjoy telling and sharing their own stories, we could enhance their understanding of one another by story sharing and further build and improve their social interactions with fellow residents.

(3) Citizens from local communities could also be involved as volunteers sharing sceneries with elderly people as well as receivers of stories told by the elderly.

(4) Scenery photos attached with locations could motivate elderly people to reminisce.

4.1 Design Requirements of Interactive Gallery

Elderly people are a special group that lacks experience in using digital devices and suffer from age-related physical decline. Additional design requirements must be considered.

(1) Tangible interface: physicality
The first concern in designing for the elderly is accessibility and usability, as most interviewees do not use computers or smartphones. Elderly people still rely on paper and prefer physical interaction and operation. Therefore, a tangible interface could be employed to overcome the challenges of traditional screen-based interfaces and lower the threshold of manipulating an interactive installation.
(2) Metaphor: familiarity and simplicity
Elderly people are greatly interested in traditional physical objects such as handicrafts and radios. They also prefer simple interaction channels like letters and handwritings. Interaction should be based on existing interaction styles that elderly people could rely on to help them manipulate the devices easily [2]. A metaphor could be employed in the design to enhance familiarity and simplicity.
(3) Share: collaboration and delivery
On one hand, story sharing is a rewarding and engaging process, and it makes sense only when the stories are being listened to. On the other hand, one elderly person telling a story could also cause others to recall their memories. The process is not solitary but collaborative. Thus, the design must provide a way to deliver and share the stories effectively.

4.2 Usage Scenario

As illustrated in the previous section, photos facilitate communication and support reminiscence, while locations contain different experiences and stories. They are both effective methods to trigger our memory and experience of the past. In the concept of Interactive Gallery, scenery photos attached with locations shared from local citizens spark reminiscence for elderly people.

Interactive Gallery is a system consisting of a cluster of specially designed camera kits and a gallery-like interactive installation employed with the metaphor of gallery and postcards. The system aims to make the elderly feel more connected to the outside environment, stimulate them to reminiscence, and further facilitate their sharing of stories with fellow residents and citizens from local communities.

Interactive Gallery consists of two parts: the scenery-collectors and an interactive gallery. The former is distributed to the citizens to share outside sceneries, while the latter is placed in the nursing home and used by the elderly people. The design concept and usage scenario of Interactive Gallery are illustrated in the following storyboard (Fig. 3).

(1) Scenery-collectors are distributed to the citizens from local communities.
(2) Citizens could put the scenery-collectors wherever they want to share sceneries with the elderly people in nursing homes. Scenery-collectors automatically take pictures of outside views at certain intervals and transmit these to the interactive gallery in the nursing home.
(3) The interactive gallery displays the scenery photos attached with locations transferred from scenery-collectors. The elderly could print photos in the form of postcards by pressing the installation button. If the scenery photo reminds elderly people of memories and experiences related to the photos, the elderly could write them down on the back of the postcards.

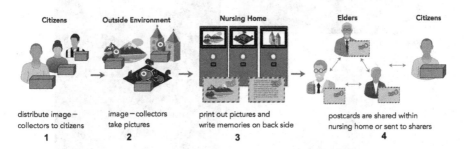

Fig. 3. Storyboard of interactive gallery system.

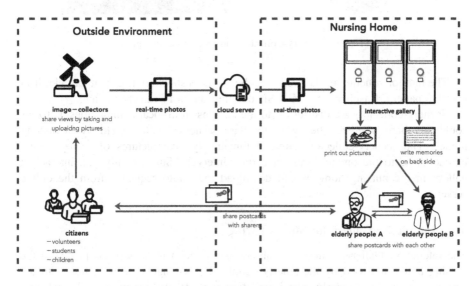

Fig. 4. System architecture of interactive gallery.

(4) Then, the postcards could be either exchanged with the elderly people in the nursing home or sent to the citizens who share the view (Fig. 4).

4.3 Scenery-Collectors for View Sharing

Scenery-collector is a group of specially designed camera kits. The appearance of the scenery-collector is a brick-like cuboid, which is portable and easy to carry. The shell is made of transparent acrylic covered with cement which is waterproof and unobtrusive in an outdoor environment.

Fig. 5. Scenery-Collector and its interior structure

The interior structure of the scenery-collector is as shown in Fig. 5; it has a built-in portable battery, Raspberry Pi, 3G USB dongles, and a Pi camera module.

Scenery-collectors are distributed to the citizens from local communities. Citizens could put them wherever they want to share sceneries with the elderly in nursing homes. The scenery-collectors could automatically take pictures of sceneries and upload these to the online server at certain intervals. Subsequently, the interactive gallery in the nursing home would download the photo sequence from the online server.

4.4 Interactive Gallery for Story Sharing

The Interactive Gallery, which is a cabinet-like wooden installation, is placed in the nursing home and used by the elderly people. The vintage style is in line with the aesthetic view of the elderly. The installation consists of three units, with each unit equipped with one high-definition monitor decorated with a frame and a large button. A simple interaction channel and the metaphor of gallery and postcards are the two features of the Interactive Gallery, which is easily accessible and easy to use for elderly people.

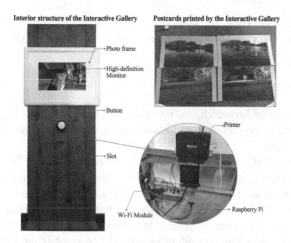

Fig. 6. Interactive gallery and its interior structure

The interior structure of the Interactive Gallery is as shown in Fig. 6; it has a built-in Raspberry Pi, Wi-Fi module, printer, and button.

The interactive gallery displays the scenery photos attached with locations transferred from scenery-collectors. Elderly people could print photos in the form of postcards just by pressing the button on the gallery. If the scenery photo reminds the elderly of past memories and experiences, the elderly could write these down on the

Fig. 7. Implementation of the interactive galley.

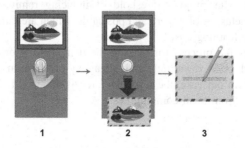

Fig. 8. Interaction process of printing postcards by the interactive gallery.

back of the postcards. Then, the postcards can be either exchanged with the elderly people in nursing home or sent to the citizens who share the view (Fig. 8).

5　Conclusions

Through a user-centered research, we find two prominent problems of elderly people living in a nursing home and attempt to alleviate the problems by design, resulting in the Interactive Gallery.

The Interactive Gallery has two corresponding core functions: (1) Scenery photos attached with locations, which generates reminiscence; (2) and Interactive gallery and post cards, which act as the medium to facilitate the sharing process.

This installation system explores the contents created by elderly people to build and enhance the social interaction of their fellow residents and the citizens from local communities. Two significant considerations should be emphasized during the entire process: triggers and share.

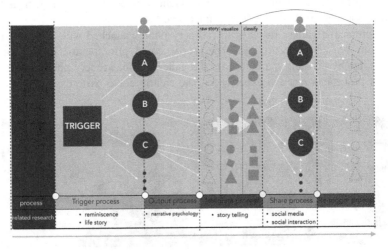

Fig. 9. Five steps for triggering and sharing stories.

Triggers lower the technology threshold of inducing reminiscence for elderly people. We use the metaphor of gallery and postcards, which are familiar to the elderly people, to reduce the learning cost.

Sharing facilitates the process for making the delivery of stories more effective. Story-sharing should be a rewarding and engaging process, in which responsive receivers are needed. In our case, the responsive receivers are elderly people's fellow residents and citizens from local communities.

Figure 7 shows that the process could be further abstracted as a model that involves the following steps:

(1) Trigger process: The process of selecting appropriate memory cues as triggers to evoke reminiscence.
(2) Output process: The various forms (e.g., text, audio, drawing) of the story-creation process.
(3) Integration process: The process of classifying and visualizing the raw stories.
(4) Share process: The process in which the created stories are delivered to the audience.
(5) Re-trigger process: The process in which the stories created by someone could be a new trigger to others (Fig. 9).

6 Limitations and Future Work

Despite the considerable enthusiasm of the elderly people in using the installation, the attraction of the interactive gallery gradually declines. In addition, how to encourage volunteers to share sceneries with the elderly people and sustain the entire process in a long-term and containable way must be considered.

Usability and user experience of the installation must be improved in future iterations. For the current version, although the installation is simple enough, not all the elderly people feel comfortable understanding and using it.

In addition to employing photos and locations as memory triggers, this work will continue exploring the interactive gallery in a variety of triggers in subsequent studies. The first step is using photos of different subjects to explore the most effective trigger for the elderly, and the next is using other types of triggers such as physical objects and music.

References

1. Waycott, J. et al.: Older adults as digital content producers. In: Proceedings of the SIGCHI Conference on Human Factors in Computing Systems, pp. 39–48 (2013)
2. Van De Watering, M.: The impact of computer technology on the elderly, vol. 29, no. 2008, p. 12, June 2005
3. Sorkin, D., Rook, K.S., Lu, J.L.: Loneliness, lack of emotional support, lack of companionship, and the likelihood of having a heart condition in an elderly sample. Ann. Behav. Med. 24(4), 290–298 (2002)
4. Tomaka, J.: The relation of social isolation, loneliness, and social support to disease outcomes among the elderly. J. Aging Health 18(3), 359–384 (2006)
5. Atzori, L., Iera, A., Morabito, G., Nitti, M.: The Social Internet of Things (SIoT) – when social networks meet the internet of things: concept, architecture and network characterization. Comput. Netw. 56(16), 3594–3608 (2012)
6. Webster, J.D.: Construction and validation of the reminiscence functions scale. J. Gerontol. 48(5), P256–P262 (1993)

7. Peesapati, S.T., Schwanda, V., Schultz, J., Lepage, M., Jeong, S., Cosley, D.: Pensieve: supporting everyday reminiscence. In: Proceedings of the SIGCHI Conference on Human Factors in Computing Systems, pp. 2027–2036 (2010)
8. van Gennip, D., van den Hoven, E., Markopoulos, P.: Things that make us reminisce: everyday memory cues as opportunities for interaction design, pp. 3443–3452 (2015)
9. Tuan, Y.: Topophilia: A Study of Environmental Perception, Attitudes, and Values. Prentice-Hall, Englewood Cliffs (1974)
10. Bennett, P. et al.: TopoTiles: storytelling in care homes with topographic tangibles, pp. 911–916 (2015)
11. Piper, A.M., Weibel, N., Hollan, J.: Audio-enhanced paper photos: encouraging social interaction at age 105. In: Proceedings of the 2013 Conference on Computer Supported Cooperative Work, pp. 215–224 (2013)
12. Koene, P., Köbler, F., Esch, S., Leimeister, J.M., Krcmar, H.: Design and evaluation of a service-oriented collaborative consumption platform for the elderly. In: CHI 2012 Extended Abstracts on Human Factors in Computing Systems, pp. 2537–2542 (2012)
13. Loh, Z., Zhang, E., Lim, Z.Y.: InSight: Kick-Starting Communications for Elderlies Ageing in Place, pp. 25–30 (2015)
14. Lee, H.-C., Cheng, Y.F., Cho, S.Y., Tang, H.-H., Hsu, J., Chen, C.-H.: Picgo: designing reminiscence and storytelling for the elderly with photo annotation, pp. 9–12 (2014)
15. Sarne-Fleischmann, V., Tractinsky, N., Dwolatzky, T., Rief, I.: Personalized reminiscence therapy for patients with Alzheimer's disease using a computerized system. In: Proceedings of the 4th International Conference on Pervasive Technologies Related to Assistive Environments, New York, NY, USA, pp. 48:1–48:4 (2011)
16. Linnemeier, M., Lin, Y.-Y., Laput, G., Vijjapurapu, R.: StoryCubes: connecting elders in independent living through storytelling. In: CHI 2012 Extended Abstracts on Human Factors in Computing Systems, pp. 1321–1326 (2012)

PLUGGY: A Pluggable Social Platform
for Cultural Heritage Awareness
and Participation

Veranika Lim[1(✉)], Nikos Frangakis[2], Luis Molina Tanco[3],
and Lorenzo Picinali[1]

[1] Imperial College London, London, UK
{v.lim,l.picinali}@imperial.ac.uk
[2] Institute of Computer and Communication Systems, Zografou, Greece
nikos.frangakis@iccs.gr
[3] University of Malaga, Malaga, Spain
imtanco@uma.es

Abstract. One of the preconditions for genuine sustainability is a heritage that is present anywhere and anytime in everyday life. We present PLUGGY, a Pluggable Social Platform for Heritage Awareness and Participation. PLUGGY will address the need of society to be actively involved in cultural heritage activities, not only as an observer but also as a creator and a major influencing factor. With PLUGGY, we aim to bridge this gap by providing the tools needed to allow users to share their local knowledge and everyday experience with others, together with the contribution of cultural institutions. Users will be able to build extensive networks around a common area of interest, connecting the past, the present and the future. It will be powered by its users and puts people's values, aspirations and needs first. Users of PLUGGY will be the providers of information about cultural heritage in the everyday and ordinary, real life. Through its social platform and by using its innovative curation tools, designed to solely focus on a niche area in social media, citizens will be able to act as skilled storytellers by creating fascinating personalised stories and share them through social networking with friends, associates and professionals. In this paper, we describe a structured formative and summative evaluative approach of PLUGGY's core concepts, which results will be used to inform and improve its design.

Keywords: Distributed curation · Social media · Cultural heritage
Mobile applications · 3D audio · Virtual and augmented reality
Collaborative games · Geolocation

1 Introduction

1.1 A New Paradigm in Cultural Heritage

The Faro Convention argues that a heritage that is everywhere, and relevant to everyday life, is likely to be one of the preconditions for genuine sustainability. This is certainly the case at the social and cultural levels, but also at the economic and environmental ones [9]. The convention itself stresses the importance of heritage communities, deemed

© Springer International Publishing AG, part of Springer Nature 2018
M. Ioannides et al. (Eds.): Digital Cultural Heritage 2017, LNCS 10754, pp. 117–129, 2018.
https://doi.org/10.1007/978-3-319-75789-6_9

as social groups who value specific aspects of cultural heritage which they wish to sustain and transmit to future generations within the framework of public action [7]. The Faro Convention outlines a framework for considering the role of citizens in the definition, decision-making and management processes related to the cultural environment in which communities operate and evolve. Citizen participation has become an ethical obligation and a political necessity. It revitalises society, strengthens democracy and creates governance that can renew the conditions for living together, encouraging wellbeing and a better quality of life. Thus, a new heritage paradigm is becoming visible. In the traditional view, material things were privileged, and values were based on supposedly intrinsic properties or represented a national history. This was a paradigm that encouraged the reduction of heritage to tourism and consumption. In contrast, the emerging new paradigm puts the production of heritage in the foreground, and aims to encompass greater democratic participative action, with greater concern for the local and the everyday. It uses the concept of landscape that is promoted by the European Landscape Convention (which is increasingly popular in academia and policy) as a global frame for heritage, recognising that heritage assets and objects offer fundamental social and economic values and benefits far beyond those traditionally recognised [9].

1.2   Enablers of the Paradigm Shift

Policy. The role of culture as a component of sustainable development is being increasingly discussed in policy debates. UNESCO emphasised the importance of culture during the Decade of Culture and Development (1988 - 1998) and through its Conventions (e.g., on the Protection and Promotion of the Diversity of Cultural Expressions in 2005; for the Safeguarding of the Intangible Cultural Heritage in 2003; and concerning the Protection of the World Cultural and Natural Heritage in 1972). It is currently working towards the objective of including culture in the UN Post 2015 Millennium Development Goals (UNESCO Hangzhou Declaration in May 2013). In Europe, both the Council of Europe's Landscape Convention and its Faro Convention imply more culturally-sensitive approaches [9].

Inclusivity. One key approach to cultural heritage is inclusivity. Heritage is most often represented by the best buildings and monuments. Rarely are these located where most people live, *'here'*. Too often they are — it seems almost by definition — somewhere else, *'there'*. People might visit them on holiday, but this type of heritage is not part of the everyday landscape of their normal lives. If heritage is thus defined as *elsewhere*, there is a risk that it will unintentionally become an instrument of exclusion. It can, however, become an instrument of inclusion and commonality if, following Faro, it is defined contextually as local, lived-in, ordinary, if it is seen as a legacy from our predecessors rather than more narrowly from ancestors, and if it is recognised as an element of both shared identity and differentiation [15]. Furthermore, the modern accepted concept of heritage is much more extensive, including tangible, natural and intangible heritage. In 2003, following a strong debate [2], the General Conference of the Unesco established the foundations for the safeguarding of the intangible cultural heritage. As a result, Unesco extended the previously accepted definition of cultural heritage, restricted to monuments, buildings and sites and included oral traditions and expressions including language, performing arts, social practices, rituals and festive events, knowledge and practices and traditional craftsmanship. Thence, heritage is not just anywhere since it involves communities playing a central role in safeguarding activities of intangible cultural heritage. States were asked to ensure the widest possible involvement of communities and individuals in the creation, transmission and even management of such heritage. After the Faro Convention, the paradigm shift moved beyond considering inclusivity at the heart of current heritage policies. Inclusivity is now the goal, and participatory creation, transmission and management of cultural heritage are the means to that goal.

Technology. Because of careful planning of mobile technology manufacturers and operators [8], we have reached an *always-connected* society. The combination of almost ubiquitous access to multimedia content and information with the consolidation of crowdsourcing, creates great opportunities to develop technological tools to further enable this paradigm shift in cultural heritage, such as PLUGGY. Crowdsourcing is a phenomenon by which citizen communities have accepted to freely provide this content and information [13].

2 PLUGGY

Currently, limited ICT tools exist to provide better support to citizens in their everyday activities in shaping cultural heritage and being shaped by it. There are important initiatives to build applications and repositories for heritage dissemination which compile collections from museums, libraries and other institutions through virtualization (e.g., Europeana, Google Cultural Institute). However, these have been top-down driven by institutions and have so far not succeeded at involving citizens in the creation of heritage communities around them. In contrast, current social platforms have demonstrated their potential to build networks through the individual and distributed contributions of users. However, their possibilities have not been fully exploited with regards to cultural heritage promotion and integration in people's everyday life. PLUGGY aims to bridge this gap by providing the necessary tools to allow users to share their local knowledge and everyday experience with others together with the contribution of cultural institutions such as museums. This joint effort builds extensive networks around a common interest in connecting the past, the present and the future. This is in accordance to Flinn [10], who emphasized the importance of diversity within our national histories and archives, and that we all, professional and non-professionals, need to find a way of ensuring that community histories and archives are preserved.

The objectives in this project are to: (1) design, develop and implement a heritage centric social platform; (2) design an architecture of the social platform to allow the easy integration of applications; the scalability of the platform and the support of specialized devices (e.g., AR/VR/trackers etc.); (3) design, develop and implement the integration of the PLUGGY Social Platform with online digital collections and other social media; (4) design, develop and implement the curatorial tool for creating stories with meaningful narratives resulting to Virtual Exhibitions around specific topics;

(5) design, develop and implement 4 different applications, utilizing the social platform and the curatorial tool, in order to showcase the potential of the platform and to be used to kick start applications for the after project life of the platform; and finally (6) evaluate the impact of PLUGGY and the pluggable applications in a variety of case studies.

3 Background

3.1 The Role of Communities

According to Giaccardi et al. [11], contemporary heritage studies teach us that values are not attached to just artefacts, buildings or sites. Nor are they frozen in time. Instead, they are the results of ongoing interactions in the lived world of ordinary people. Giaccardi et al. emphasizes that heritage is something we socially construct in the context of our own lives as a way of meaningfully interacting with our past and shaping our vision of the future. Fortunately, digital and social technologies are facilitating distributed forms of curatorial practice, which can be harnessed to democratize history [16]. Although, we still need to understand better whether and how ubiquitous and communication technologies like social media shape and sustain a shared sense of identity and belonging for current and future generations [11], there are examples of previous work in cultural heritage where social media plays a central role, e.g. in distributed curation and personalization (further discussed below).

3.2 Distributed Curation

Liu [16] describes distributed curation as a socio-technical practice involving people, cultural artefacts, and information and communication technology. It's a collaborative and distributed practice, creating shared ownership over the stewardship of the living heritage through transparency, which further allows other parties to partake in the curatorial process. One well-known social media channel, generally accepted and used by communities, is Instagram. Instagram allows creative practices from non-elite social contexts and communication that relies on everyday competencies rather than a formal artistic education (Burgess, 2006 as described in [19]). In making selections as to what to display and which narrative to tell, Instagrammers somehow act as virtual curators (Hogan, 2010 as described in [19]), extending the reach of the museum beyond its walls [19]. In supporting rural community heritage, the CURIOS project [18] explored how digital archives for rural community heritage groups can be made more sustainable so that volunteer members can maintain a lasting digital presence. It was developing software tools to help remote rural communities to collaboratively maintain and present information about their cultural heritage using open linked data. This approach is attuned to the specificity of a local heritage but can also take advantage of already collected materials from elsewhere. Yelmi et al. [20] evaluated soundscapes as an intangible cultural heritage element and introduced the Soundsslike Project; a crowd-sourced online sound archive which invites people to record symbolic urban sounds and upload them to the online sound archive. This online platform was built and displayed in an exhibition by means of an interactive table top interface to learn more from users and contributors, and to enrich the archive content by raising public awareness of urban sounds.

3.3 Personalization in Cultural Encounters

Social media can also play a role in the personalization of information technologies. People are often overloaded with an increasing amount and variety of cultural items making it difficult to identify what is interesting. Therefore, there is a need to personalize visits to cultural objects, to visitors' knowledge and connections, to ensure interactions are effective. For example, ArtLinks was developed to provide a guidance system based on a public display in museum exhibits that allowed visitors to create and use tags to help guide other visitors [5]. ArtLinks aimed at encouraging social interactions and enhancing experiences by supporting visualization of people, words and their connections related to an exhibition. Similarly, MobiTag [6] is an electronic guide that supports semantic, social, and spatial navigation in museums by allowing visitors to create and vote for tags. Furthermore, Han et al. [12] developed a mobile application called Lost State College (LSC) and showed that users utilized social features as a way of learning local history and interacting with others, co-creating digital traces and rich layers of local history information. Users shared information using social features, which allowed different types of connection to the local history.

Personalization, derived through interactions between visitors of cultural environments, has also been supported using data from popular available social media sources such as Twitter, Instagram, Wikipedia and Flickr. For example, McGookin and Brewster designed PULSE [14] to allow users to gain a vibe (i.e., an intrinsic understanding of the people, places and activities around their current location) using Twitter data. As users moved, PULSE downloaded public messages (tweets) generated by any user in the current location. Then, PULSE would select the closest tweet and insert it in a virtual 3D auditory environment: users heard tweets as whispered conversations. Bellens et al. [1] explored how social media data can be employed to study tourism on European Cultural Routes and showed its potential for investigating a complex touristic object such as a cultural route. They combined text related to photos on Instagram with Wikipedia for geographical places. This allowed them to identify the most popular stops and localities related to the cultural route. Bujari et al. [4] proposed PhotoTrip, an interactive tool able to autonomously recommend cultural heritage locations along travel itineraries even if those locations were not mainstream. PhotoTrip identified points of interest by gathering pictures and related information from Flickr and Wikipedia and then providing the user with suggestions and recommendations.

Related work has demonstrated how digital cultural heritage transforms the way of experiencing or learning community heritage through social media. The community are being more and more involved through distributed curation, i.e., where technologies mediates and allows them to contribute to our histories, and personalization, i.e., where communities' online activities are used to aid in decision-making. Current social platforms have demonstrated their potential to build networks through the individual and distributed contributions of users. To our knowledge, however, their possibilities have not been fully exploited with regards to cultural heritage promotion and integration in people's everyday life.

4   Methodology

4.1   PLUGGY Technologies

The Social Platform. PLUGGY will be built around a heritage-centric social platform ensuring that citizens are at the heart of PLUGGY. The social platform will be the place where citizens, heritage communities and professionals are able to share their curated Virtual Exhibitions, visit Virtual Museums and browse the Digital Collections created by others. Users of the social platform will upload, tag, categorize and describe assets in the form of high quality images and videos, text, 3D models and 3D audio that will be experienced through the pluggable applications. The platform will interface with Europeana, the British Museum's Collection OnLine and other existing online Digital Collections to allow citizens to experience and relate tangible, intangible and natural heritage collections through PLUGGYs browsing functionalities. The social platform will deploy artificial intelligence methods for the semantic tagging of its content and the Virtual Exhibitions, facilitating also an automated way of creating Virtual Museums by grouping Virtual Exhibitions. See Fig. 1.

The Curatorial Tool. The Curatorial Tool will allow users to create Virtual Exhibitions hosted on the social platform. The Curatorial Tool allows the curation of stories, which link the digital collections uploaded within the social platform and those available through the interfaces to the Digital Collections. Users of PLUGGY curate content that can be accessed using novel interfaces (Augmented Reality, Geolocation), and thus experience stories in new engaging ways. The Curatorial Tool has an open architecture that allows for development of future applications with interfaces which have not yet been developed.

Pluggable Applications. Through the Pluggable Applications, the users experience the stories created and hosted on PLUGGY's social platform. Applications have two sides to them: on the one hand, they allow users to experience the content of the Virtual Museums in novel and engaging ways. On the other, they extend the Curation Tool through their curation application interfaces. The Pluggable Applications can be combined for a rich multi-sensory experience. A total of 4 applications showcase the potential of PLUGGY's content.

Augmented Reality Application. This application allows stories to be experienced through virtual models and overlaid information, on live video streams. The application authoring interface extends the Curation Tool to allow association of assets and behaviours to markers for augmenting real exhibitions and other experiences with virtual content.

3D Audio Application. The 3D Audio application allows for the creation and interactive playback of 3D sonic narratives and, more generally, the creation of 3D audio content within PLUGGY. In addition to a 3D sound spatialization tool (both for loudspeakers and headphone playback), the application will integrate functions/modules for selecting, editing and mixing audio from existing sources (e.g., import audio-les), and for applying sound effects (e.g., reverberators, spatial spread algorithms, etc.).

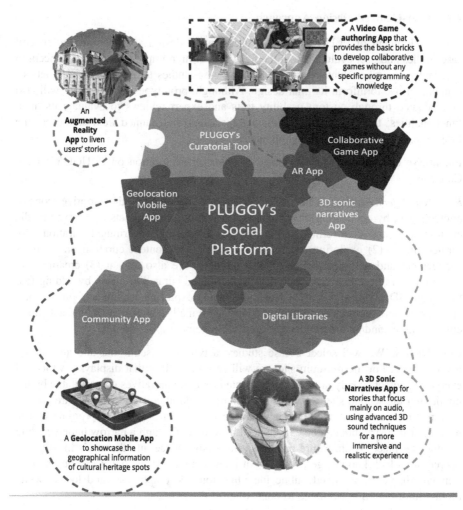

Fig. 1. PLUGGY's concept structure of the social platform, curatorial tool and pluggable applications.

Collaborative Game Application. The Collaborative Game application allows for video game authoring by providing the basic bricks (i.e., rules, routes) to develop collaborative games. This application does not require programming knowledge and enables participants to engage in asset and story discovering through challenges and other gamification-based engagement techniques.

Geolocation Application. The Mobile Geolocation application targets outdoor activities. With this application, geo-located stories are made available to users when they are physically near the coordinates of assets where they are virtually situated. The application extends the Curation Tool by allowing curators to situate virtual content geographically on a map at specific coordinates.

4.2   User-Centred Design Approach

The development of PLUGGY takes a user-centred design approach around several case studies and user evaluations in the field. It is of high importance for the concept to be adapted to and evaluated through different case studies to account for a variety of contexts of use to inform its final design. Although, prototypes of PLUGGY will also be evaluated through custom usability tests and expert reviews to evaluate its main functionalities, this concept paper mainly discusses the planned field studies in the formative and summative evaluation stages.

Formative evaluation. The first stage contains an exploration on PLUGGY's Core Concepts.

Research Objectives. In this first stage, we aim at (1) broadening the narrative scope of artefacts, i.e., by connecting physical artefacts with digital artefacts in a mixed media environment, and connecting people and stories through distributed curation. We further aim at (2) exploring the impact of distributed content curation on people's engagement and participation in cultural heritage. We also aim at (3) creating and promoting a more immersive approach to distributed curated artefacts by adding features e.g., 3D audio and Virtual Reality, and (4) exploring its impacts on visitor's engagement and participation in cultural heritage. Finally, we aim at (5) understanding commonalities and/or differences between socio-demographic groups.

Case Studies. We will select 2 case studies: a typical museum site and an outdoor historical site. For the museum site, we will select a gallery that displays a variety of everyday artefacts. Daily artefacts are expected to invite narratives contributable by the public. For the second site, we will select an architectural collection, which are usually very popular tourist attractions. They can be used as an artefact to promote ethics, history, or industry, but can be experienced by visitors through a narrow understanding of time and place. Architecture can be an immersive space into the city's history, but people often lack knowledge about it. An interesting aspect is that it can be an environment shared by a mixed public including tourists, employees, and locals, while limited information is available to contextualize the artefacts.

Study Design. For each site, 3 to 4 artefacts will be selected for the study. The artefacts will be exhibited in different display design conditions, e.g., each display design is presented for a week:
Condition 1: the artefacts are presented with the current curator's information only. This forms the baseline from which evaluations will be made.
Condition 2: the artefacts are presented with the current curator's information as well as visitor's curated content using Instagram or Medium centralized into a website. Visitors will be triggered with open questions such as: *"What does this artefact/building remind you of?", "What influences do you see?", and "Can you identify any specific artistic/architectural features?".*

- Curating stories: Visitors will be asked to use Instagram or Medium for sharing their answers or stories. They will be asked to use one specific hashtags (for Instagram) and tags (for Medium), for the study project and artefact. Stories shared on Medium will be accessible through a custom WordPress website (one per case study). Each website will contain a link to each artefact and each artefact page will have a list of links to shared stories in Medium on the specific artefact). Participants' own devices can be used to curate information.

- Accessing stories: Answers and stories shared using Instagram, will be accessible by using the specific hashtag with the Instagram application. Answers and stories shared in Medium will be accessible through the custom WordPress website using a QR code or a link. Participants' own devices can be used to access information.

Condition 3a and b: each artefact page will contain 3D audio narratives of selected 'quotes' from the different stories and/or 3D soundscapes. Audio narratives and soundscapes are accessible on visitors own devices as well as on a tablet publicly available.

Condition 4: each artefact contains a 3D virtual image accessible on visitors own devices as well as on the tablet publicly available.

Technological equipment. To conduct the study, the following equipment will be used: (1) laminated information labels with the questions, hashtags and tags, a QR code and a link to the project website. A video camera will be used to record interactions. 3 tablets will be made available for those who do not wish to use their own devices. These tablets will have Wi-Fi access and will be secured on a standalone tablet stand near each artefact. Each tablet will include acoustic speakers and custom earplugs for 3D augmented audio. One tablet will be used for post questionnaires.

Procedures. For each condition described above, visitors will be shadowed and observed during their interactions with the artefacts and available digital information. A map of the test site will be used to annotate navigation, touch points, and note behavioural insights. In a post-test measurement, upon exiting the site, visitors will be invited to participate in an online questionnaire and sign informed consents. Visitors will also be asked general information such as their demographics, where they came from, what brought them to the site, where they are going, what they know about the site, what they would like to know about the site, about their everyday technology use, and their social media use. They will be given an information sheet for a debriefing on the objectives of the study.

Study outcome measures. The study will provide insights on the narrative scope of artefacts and will underline to what extent distributed content curation have an impact on visitor engagement. Engagement is measured using the standardized MEC spatial presence questionnaire [17], through structured observations, and online activities. The study will also provide insights into the additional impact of 3D audio and virtual reality on visitor engagement and participation in cultural heritage. Findings from this stage will be used to inform the initial design of PLUGGY which will undergo a summative evaluation.

Participants entry. Visitors will be triggered with a link to the displays, which they can voluntarily use. Upon exiting the site, visitors will be approached to fill out the questionnaires and informed consent form. A random and opportunity sampling technique will be applied. Visitors will not be obliged to participate and can opt out of participating in the study at any time. For the video-recorded observations, all individuals will be anonymized by blurring facial images.

Data analysis. Collected data will be compared between the display conditions. A thematic analysis will be performed on the stories and pictures posted in Instagram and Medium. A quantitative analysis will be performed on the observed behaviours around the artefacts. Data from questionnaires will be analysed quantitatively and thematically.

Summative Evaluation. The second stage contains an exploration on the user experience around PLUGGY's final technologies.

Research Objectives. In this stage, we aim at (1) exploring the use, usability, and impact of PLUGGY's social platform, curatorial tool and mobile applications on people's engagement and participation in cultural heritage. We also aim at (2) understanding commonalities and/or differences between socio-demographic groups.

Case Studies. We will select a number of case studies, including typical museum sites, outdoor historical sites, and individuals with tangible and intangible collections not necessarily related to specific sites. In addition to the selected case studies in the formative evaluation, we will involve the museums as part of the project, which are the Open-Air Water Power Museum in Greece, the Environment Museum in Greece, the Museum of Silversmithing in Greece, and the East Slovakian Museum in Slovakia. These case studies will be run for a period of at least 6 months.

Study Design. For each site, 3 to 4 artefacts will be selected for the study. The artefacts will be displayed in different display design conditions:
Condition 1: the artefacts are presented as is with the curator's information only. This will form the baseline against which comparisons can be made.
Condition 2: the artefacts are presented as is with the curator's information, as well as visitor's curated content when using PLUGGY's Social Platform. The public will be able to curate stories using the Curatorial Tool. For each artefact, the suite of mobile applications can be used for 3D audio narratives and soundscapes, 3D augmented reality, geolocation (only for outdoor test sites), and collaborative games. Visitors in both museum and historical sites and individuals with tangible and intangible collections not necessarily related to specific sites will be asked to use PLUGGY's technology in any way they wish.

Technological equipment. To conduct the study in the selected museums and historical sites, the following equipment will be used: (1) laminated information labels with hashtags and tags, and a QR code linking to the study project's website. A video camera will be used to record interactions. Optionally, 3 tablets will be made available for those who do not wish to use their own devices. These tablets will have Wi-Fi access and will be secured on a standalone tablet stand near each artefact. Each tablet will include acoustic speakers and custom earplugs for 3D audio. One tablet will be used for post questionnaires. Individuals with tangible and intangible collections not necessarily related to specific sites will be using PLUGGY's technologies on their own devices.

Procedures. The same procedures as in the formative evaluation will be applied for the selected test sites. The following procedures apply to individuals with tangible and intangible collections not necessarily related to specific sites. First, the participant will be given an information sheet on the objectives and procedures of the study and an informed consent form. They will be asked to use the PLUGGY in any way they wish. Intermittently and in a post-test measurement, individuals will be invited to participate in online questionnaires.

Study outcome measures. The study will provide insights in the narrative scope of artefacts and to what extend PLUGGY's technologies have impact on visitor's engagement and participation in cultural heritage. Engagement and participation is measured using the standardized MEC spatial presence questionnaire (relevant only for the test sites) [17], experience narratives, through structured observations (relevant only for the test sites), and online activities. Other questionnaires aim at collecting users' positive and negative experiences of specific functionalities and at exploring perceived usability of the technologies using the System Usability Scale (SUS) [3]).

Participants entry. Museum and historical site visitors will be asked to voluntarily participate upon entering and exiting the site. A random and opportunity sampling technique will be applied. Visitors will not be obliged to participate. They can refuse participation or withdraw anytime without repercussions. Individuals will be recruited on site, and through professional and social networks.

Data analysis. PLUGGY's usage will be analysed through descriptives. A quantitative and qualitative analysis will be performed on the online and offline (i.e., observations relevant only for the test sites) interactions between users of PLUGGY. A quantitative analysis will be performed on the data from the questionnaires. Thematic analysis will be performed on the experience narratives.

5 Conclusion, Challenges and Impacts

With PLUGGY, we aim to transfer the responsibility towards cultural heritage from the exclusive domain of experts to individuals and heritage communities, giving them the opportunity to expose and transmit their values to anyone sharing their interests, visions and concerns. With PLUGGY's social platform, Curatorial Tool and pluggable applications, any sensitized individual will be able to enrich the cultural heritage of their focal point by uploading materials (i.e. audio, video, images, text, 3D models) and use these in combination with what is already available in the platform to create a more personalized, interactive, and to-the-point story which can then be shared online. PLUGGY, however, will face several challenges. For example, is there room for yet another social platform? And what is the value of having a centralized social platform specifically for cultural heritage over the potential of the various social media services already in use? Moreover, it might be argued that PLUGGY also faces the challenges inherent to the paradigm shift in cultural heritage [2]; institutions and professionals trained to safeguard traditional cultural heritage may have difficulties in applying their skills to safeguard intangible heritage (or any other type of heritage) due to differences in perceptions or truths held in society. On the other hand, it will allow for a diversity of ways to look at history. This will further extend to the issue of trust. What mechanisms should be implemented to gain trust in content and content creators for an effective use of a platform like PLUGGY? Nevertheless, we expect PLUGGY to have significant impacts socially, economically and ecologically. First, it can promote wider understanding of heritage. Second, it can improve innovation capacity and integration of new knowledge as it will mobilize the economic sectors, i.e., tourism and the creative industries, indirectly promoting local development and entrepreneurship. Finally, it is expected to promote cultural diversity.

Acknowledgement. This work is a part of the PLUGGY project. PLUGGY has received funding from the European Union's Horizon 2020 Research & Innovation Programme under grant agreement no 726765. Content reflects only the author's view and European Commission is not responsible for any use that may be made of the information it contains.

References

1. Bellens, A., Grabar, N., Valmond Le Banc, N., Kergosien, E., Eloire, F., Severo, M.: Social media and European cultural routes: Instagram networks on the Via Francigena. In: The International Conference on Management of Computational and Collective Intelligence in Digital EcoSystems, pp. 122–128. ACM, New York (2016)
2. Bortolotto, C.: Le Trouble Du Patrimoine Culturel Immatériel, Terrain (2011)
3. Brooke, J.: SUS: a quick and dirty usability scale. In: Jordan, P.W., Thomas, B., Weerdmeester, B.A., McClelland, I.L. (eds.) Usability evaluation in industry, pp. 189–194. Taylor & Francis, London (1996)
4. Bujari, A., Ciman, M., Gaggi, O., Palazzi, C.E.: Using gamification to discover cultural heritage locations from geo-tagged photos. Pers. Ubiquitous Comput. **21**, 23–252 (2017)
5. Cosley, D., Lewenstein, J., Herman, A., Holloway, J., Baxter, J., Nomua, S., Boehner, K., Gay, G.: ArtLinks: fostering social awareness and reflection in museums. In: Proceedings of the SIGCHI Conference on Human Factors in Computing Systems, pp. 403–412. ACM, New York (2008)
6. Cosley, D., Baxter, J., Lee, S., Alson, B., Nomura, S., Adams, P., Sarabu, C., Gay, G.: A tag in the hand: supporting semantic, social, and spatial navigation in museums. In: Proceedings of the SIGCHI Conference on Human Factors in Computing Systems, pp. 1953–1962. ACM, New York (2009)
7. Council of Europe Treaty Series - No. 199 (2005). https://rm.coe.int/1680083746. Accessed 01 June 2017
8. Cushing, B.: Always connected. beyond broadband - what comes next? In: Broadband Services, Applications, and Networks: Enabling Technologies and Business Models, pp. 15–23. Professional Education International Inc., Chicago (2011)
9. Fairclough, G., et al.: The faro convention, a new paradigm for socially - and culturally - sustainable heritage action? In: Културa/Culture, pp. 9–19 (2014)
10. Flinn, A.: Community histories, community archives: some opportunities and challenges. J. Soc. Archivists **20**(2), 151–176 (2007)
11. Giaccardi, E., Churchill, E., Liu, S.: Heritage matters: designing for current and future values through digital and social technologies. In: Extended Abstracts on Human Factors in Computing Systems, pp. 2783–2786. ACM, New York (2012)

12. Han, H., Shih, P.C., Rosson, M.B., Carroll, J.M.: Enhancing community awareness of and participation in local heritage with a mobile application. In: Proceedings of the 17th ACM Conference on Computer Supported Cooperative Work & Social Computing, pp. 1144–1155. ACM, New York (2014)

13. Howe, J.: The rise of crowdsourcing. In: Wired Magazine (2006)

14. Mcgookin, D., Brewster, S.: PULSE: an auditory display provide a social vibe. In: Proceedings of Interacting with Sound Workshop: Exploring Context-Aware, Local and Social Audio Applications, pp. 12–15. ACM, New York (2012)

15. Wolferstan, S., Fairclough, G.: Common European heritage: reinventing identity through landscape and heritage? In: Callebaut, D., Mařík, J., Maříková-Kubková, J. (eds.) Heritage Reinvents Europe, EAC Occasional Papers, pp. 43–54. European Archaeological Council/ Archaeolingua, Budapest, Hungary (2013)

16. Liu, S.L.: Grassroot Heritage: A multi-method Investigation of how Social Media Sustain the Living Heritage of Historic Crises. Ph.D thesis (2011)

17. Vorderer, P., Wirth, W., Gouveia, F.R., Biocca, F., Saari, T., Jäncke, F., Böcking, S., Schramm, H., Gysbers, A., Hartmann, T., Klimmt, C., Laarni, J., Ravaja, N., Sacau, A., Baumgartner, T., Jäncke, P.: MEC Spatial Presence Questionnaire (MECSPQ): Short Documentation and Instructions for Application. Report to the European Community, Project Presence: MEC (IST-2001-37661) (2004). http://www.ijk.hmt-hannover.de/presence

18. Webster, G., Nguyen, H.H., Beel, D.E., Mellish, C., Wallace, C.D., Pan, P.: CURIOS: connecting community heritage through linked data. In: Proceedings of the 17th ACM Conference on Computer Supported Cooperative Work & Social Computing, pp. 639–648. ACM, New York (2015)

19. Weilenmann, A., Hillman, T., Jungselius, B.: Instagram at the museum: communicating the museum experience through social photo sharing. In: Proceedings of the SIGCHI Conference on Human Factors in Computing Systems, pp. 1843–1852. ACM, New York (2013)

20. Yelmi, P., Kuscu, H., Yantac, A.E.: Towards a sustainable crowdsourced sound heritage archive by public participation: the soundsslike project. In: Proceedings of the 9th Nordic Conference on Human-Computer Interaction, vol. 71. ACM, New York (2016)

Interactive Lapidarium – Opportunities for Research and Training

Valeria Fol, Oleg Konstantinov$^{(\boxtimes)}$ ⓘ, and Kalin Stoev

University of Library Studies and Information Technologies, 119 Tzarigradsko shousse Blvd, 1784 Sofia, Bulgaria
{v.fol, o.konstantinov, k.stoev}@unibit.bg

Abstract. The presentation of cultural heritage is a difficult, comprehensive and constantly updated topic. Researchers often focus more on the different techniques to digitize artifacts of cultural heritage. This work focuses on the overall shape and structure of a multimedia application, called "Interactive Lapidarium", whose specificity is determined by the topic – the ancient inscriptions. Below is presented the structure and content-based information available for specific ancient inscriptions in the lands of modern Bulgaria. The main concept of the multimedia application is to be used in teaching programs related to cultural heritage and history of antiquity in universities. The aim of designers is that it can be modified easy for use in museums also. The Interactive Lapidarium application is in the process of being developed. At this point, several objects have been added just to illustrate the full functionality that future users will have.

Keywords: Ancient inscriptions · Multimedia content
Multimedia application · Interactive map · E-learning · Cultural heritage

1 Introduction

The ancient inscriptions are probably the most important source for everyday life, administration, society and religion of the ancient societies. Especially valuable are the epigraphic monuments of the European "classical" and postclassical past, i.e. the history of the Roman Empire and its provinces. The multicultural Roman society stretched from what is now Portugal to the banks of Euphrates has left more than 300 000 inscriptions [1] that cover multitude of aspects of its life – from the minutiae of everyday life to the laws and records of the Emperors themselves. This epigraphic evidence is exploited mainly by the scholars and meanwhile developed itself into a separate discourse within the broader scholarly field of Roman history and archaeology.

Sadly however, the ancient inscriptions belong to the most underestimated artifacts of the cultural heritage. In this respect, they can look back to a long history of damaging and plundering beginning from the Late Antiquity or early mediaeval times, when they were often replaced from their original sites and were reused as a building material for later constructions, thus losing part of their scientific and cultural significance. Nowadays only a relative smaller number of the epigraphic monuments from the Antiquity could be found by excavations in their original archaeological context.

M. Ioannides et al. (Eds.): Digital Cultural Heritage 2017, LNCS 10754, pp. 130–140, 2018.
https://doi.org/10.1007/978-3-319-75789-6_10

In present days, the inscriptions were given a central position in the museums or special attention by the teaching only in exceptional cases. The main reasons for this seem to be two: in the first place, the lack of knowledge of ancient languages by most of the receptors of the cultural product is a considerable obstacle for the popularization of monuments of this kind. Secondly, the ancient Greek and Roman inscriptions are great in numbers in the lands of modern Bulgaria and thus and their multitude and variety makes any classification approach, not to mention the way in which they should be preserved and exposed in the museums, a hard task.

Consequently, the inscriptions not only lack the attractiveness of some other archaeological artifacts, but they are hard to manage with respect to teaching, but also in matters of organizing and preserving cultural heritage. These circumstances determine the need for a vivid, content-based information of the inscriptions, who will achieve the removal of the barriers between the common user or student and the epigraphic material. The main goal of the project is to achieve a transmission of sufficient information about a variety of inscription types, their context and historical and archaeological background, while at the same time it manages to keep a complex historical and archaeological information understandable enough for a broader audience by providing pictures, comments and translations of the inscriptions and including.

The main method that was used by the classical science of 19 and 20th century for encompassing epigraphic information was the publishing of *corpora*, which followed the pattern of the famous *Corpus inscriptionum latinarum*, first published in Berlin in 1862. The following 17 volumes of this collection, compiled according to the geographical distribution, include the known Latin inscriptions from the times of the Roman Empire. In the beginning of this endeavour, correspondents from different countries informed the editorial board about the newly found inscriptions. This approach is also used by the most famous bulletin for epigraphy – *Annee epigraphique*. Soon, the different states that share territories of the former Roman Empire began to publish *corpora* for their own epigraphical material. In Bulgaria this task was carried out by the distinguished scholars Georgi Mihailov (for the Greek inscriptions, 1956–1995) and Boris Gerov (for the Latin ones), who, unfortunately could only publish the latin monuments between the Rivers Oescus and Iatrus (1989) in Northern Bulgaria.

Such collections, although still of high scientific value, are often inaccessible for the common scholar and sometimes have some inaccuracies in the readings. In lot of cases the photos are not good enough and hamper the correct juxtaposition with the published text of the inscription. Since the epigraphic corpora concentrate on the inscribed text, the archaeological context is sometimes neglected, or just briefly mentioned. Considerable weakness of this approach is the steadily growing number of newly found and unpublished inscriptions the paper body could not catch on.

Thus, the digitalization, the quick access to the collected epigraphic information about the ancient society is a goal that has been pursued by other European countries and research centres. Today there is a variety of online resources that offer search possibilities in terms of geographical distribution or with key words from the inscription content (EpiDoc content). Such an example is http://www.manfredclauss. de/. Many of these offer possibilities for tracing the geographical distribution of the monuments according to their grouping in a certain region.

Our project offers a similar decision by the main focus being on the artifacts in the museums. Although the material in the now existing databases is encompassing also some monuments that are being preserved in the museums, there is no attempt for digitalization and categorization of the content of specific museums – this will contribute not only to the introduction of the inscriptions to the broader scientific audience, but also to the socialization of the cultural-historical heritage in terms of visualization of hardly accessible (and hence available only to fewer people) monuments, which is the main concept of the project.

In broader terms, the resources that now exist are offering mostly an access to the material that will eventually serve the scientist in their scholarly attempts. In this project the digitalized inscriptions will be accompanied by a scientific commentary (analysis), which aims at a contribution to several problems from the field of ancient roman provincial history and archaeology. A very specific and complicated aspect of the modern epigraphic discourse – and probably the most important – is the understanding of the still unsolved puzzle of ethnical and migrational patterns in the provinces of the Roman Empire, including the processes of assimilation and Romanization.

The epigraphic monuments are a material of high value for the investigation of a large spectrum of problems in connection with the population, demography, ethnical and social identities in the Roman Empire. As long as the most epigraphic databases are integrating inscriptions from the whole Empire, their criteria hardly match to the specifics of every single province. This make the need for specific database, which concentrates on the multicultural society of Moesia and Thracia especially visible, for the population of this provinces consists of Romans and Romanised peregrines, Thracians, Greeks, who are often mutually connected through social relations or marriages.

The approaches that we propose place the research endeavour of the project in the vanguard of the ancient and Roman provincial studies, where the topics as the social networking in the Roman and Late Roman world broadens gradually. In more specific terms, the attempted categorization of inscriptions will be used for evaluation of the so called "epigraphic habit" – a definition that is since long created to point at the social manifestation of Roman or pre-Roman identities and developed itself into starting point for most of the epigraphic researches that concentrate on the patterns of veneration through inscriptions.

Thus, using the modern scientific approach, the project will create a database that could be used for easy access to the abundant epigraphic material that encompasses the various social layers and ethnic groups represented by the "epigraphic habit", and could offer possibilities for summarizing it. Further, this collection will enable conclusions about the density of the Romanized population represented on the inscriptions and about its grouping and networking in social entities and influential groups, both in provincial and imperial context.

The project is a considerable attempt for a new approach to the presentation and research of a specific type of monuments, integral and important part of the historical heritage, which haven't received until now the deserved attention as cultural and historical artefacts. It will bring the research in the field of ancient society and culture on a new level. The Project will be a contribution to the growth of the interest in these monuments and their enhanced scientific research and exposure in the museums. The results will reach a maximal number of scientists, students and lovers of the antiquities due to the fact that the database will be bilingual – in Bulgarian and English languages.

2   Cultural Heritage Education – The Role of ICT

Cultural heritage education in most European countries was based for a long time on traditional teaching methods such as face-to-face classroom lessons using mainly printed materials (texts and images), and very seldom watching videos [2]. Strangely enough, such innovativeness has not yet reflected openness to the introduction of ICT (Information and Communication Technology) in teaching and learning methods, which has, on the contrary, characterized other disciplines in the last few years. As a matter of fact, no specific reference was directly made in the recommendation, as far as the use of ICT to support and enhance Cultural Heritage Education [3]. Consequently, nowadays ICT, while being increasingly employed in the field of cultural heritage to produce large archives of materials [4], to support scientific research and to foster the maintenance/preservation of cultural heritage artifacts [5], has not yet affected the approaches to teaching and learning in cultural heritage education enough.

Immersive technologies such as virtual environments and augmented reality have a clear potential to support the experiencing of cultural heritage by the large public, complementing the current tools and practices based on tangible goods such as museums, exhibitions, books and visual content. Serious games – videogames designed for educational objectives – and multimedia applications appear as a new tools to learn cultural content in an engaging way [6].

3   Examples

The further lines intend to demonstrate the values of the *interactive lapidarium* for the research and visualizing of specific topics from the history, culture and religion of the ancient Thracian and Roman society in the lands of present-day Bulgaria. We have chosen four texts that exemplify the role of the inscriptions as testimonies of the multi-national society, which emerged after the Roman conquest of these lands. For a common feature in these testimonies we have chosen the name *Pyr(u)merulas* that belonged to a native Thracian deity, which was venerated also under the Roman rule – both by Thracian soldiers that had been romanized in the Roman army and Roman officials.

The first inscription (Fig. 1) is engraved on vessels from a treasure that consists of a cylindrical vessel and five dippers with a total weight of 1.650 kg; chemical analyses show that it was made of the highest grade silver [7]. It was found in a place named Zhidovets, located on the southern slope of a ridge to the north of the Golyama Brestnitsa village, which had been populated already in the pre-Roman period and in all probability it flourished during the first three centuries of the first millennium, which is also suggested by the coin hoards found in the region [8]. The treasure was found accidentally during trenching of a vineyard (1958), hence the archaeological context is unclear, with the exception of the fact that the five dippers had been placed inside the bowl and they were buried in the ground in that way [7, 9].

Fig. 1. Inscription engraved on vessel from a treasure found in a place named Zhidovets, located on the southern slope of a ridge to the north of the Golyama Brestnitsa village. Photo: Nikolai Genov

The making of the vessels is dated to the end of the 1st or the beginning of the 2nd century, and its burying is associated with the barbarian incursions and more specifically with the late 3rd century. This dating is also corroborated by the written form of the *nomen gentile* of the dedicator – *Flavius*, perceived more as a *praenomen* and a sign for military rank or affiliation and thus mostly abbreviated as *Fl.* in the inscriptions at the close of the 3rd century AD and later.

The inscription has been commented many times. The prevalent opinion on the meaning of the epithet *Pyrumerulas* is "big/brilliant fire" [9–12], and the name of the beneficiary *Flavius Mestrianos* – as Latinised Thracian name [13, 14]. A votive tablet of the Thracian Hero with the same epithet as the one in the inscriptions on the bowl and on the handle of one of the dippers originates from the same region where the treasure was found [13].

The treasure was found accidentally during trenching of a vineyard (1958), hence the archaeological context is unclear, with the exception of the fact that the five dippers had been placed inside the bowl and they were buried in the ground in that way [7]. There is evidence of such arranging of vessels also from the people who had found the Panagyurishte gold treasure, who reported that the rhytons and the amphora had been placed in the phiale [11]. It is not possible for the descriptions to have been influenced by one another and this suggests seeking symbolism in the arranging of the vessels, all the more that the treasures comply with the theme of the ritual deposition of valuable objects, which has been repeatedly discussed in the specialised literature. The act of burying treasures in the ground is interpreted as a gift to the Great Goddess-Mother in connection with inauguration or with the aim of acquiring or confirming autochthonous status as marking of territories and as an act of symbolic hierogamous relation with the Goddess-Earth [9, 11]. However, the set from Golyama Brestnitsa is a gift for the ruler-hero *Purumerulas* – most probably an equine deity with a fiery-solar nature (i.e., connected with light) and the arranging of the vessels before they were buried tends to suggest a ritual act recreating a hierogamous relation between the fiery equine deity and the Great Goddess-Earth. From the time of the first publication of the set it was assumed to have been used for drinking wine during some rite. Sets made of precious metals and bronze are generally associated in specialised literature with drinking wine or libations with it, ignoring the other ritual liquids: water, milk, honey and blood. However, the set found near the Golyama Brestnitsa village suggests another hypothesis as well, because it was found near a spring the water from which flows into the Panega River (on the sanctuary near Glava Zlatna Panega see [15]). There is a very high probability that the spring was worshipped as sacred in the search for the water–fire opposition (on account of the fiery nature of the worshipped deity). Purifying rites were mandatory, especially those involving washing with and drinking of the sacred liquid prior to entering the sacred space and performing sacred acts.

Bearing in mind that inscriptions with epithet *Pyrmerulas, Pyrmerylas, Pirmerulas, Pyrymerylas* and *Purumerulas* occurred to the south of the Balkan Range [16] and along the Struma River, it may be assumed that the donor of the treasure with dedication to the horseman-deity (and hunter) with fiery-solar characteristics originated from there, and that the epithet was transferred to the north by Thracians who settled in the region after their military service (see also [9]). Most probably Mestrianos was a son from a typical soldier's family of Romanized Thracians (see below).

We have the rare chance to find the name of the supposed father of *Flavius Mestrianos* on an inscription of completely different kind. It is found in the very same place, called "Zhidovec" by the village of Malka Brestnica (now Brestnica), Lovech Province, Northern Bulgaria, in other words in the very same region as the treasure. Most probably the votive plate was once dedicated in a sanctuary of the Heros. The monument is partially preserved: a lower part of a marble anaglyptic image of the Thracian Rider. The inscription on it reveals the name *Flavius Mestrius Iustus*. *Flavius Mestrianos* (see above) obviously received his father's *nomen* (the latinized Thracian Name *Mestrius*) transformed by the suffix – *ianus* to a derivative *cognomen* (*Mestrianus*) in order to underline his descent from a father's kin (more on this naming in [17]).

Both pieces of evidence reveal a military family of Thracians that had kept the religion of their ancestors. The father *Flavius Mestrius* was probably recruited for *cohors II Lucensium* from the lands where its camp *Germania* (now Sapareva banja) was situated at the first decades of 3rd century. As a son of a soldier, Mestrianos was recruited for more prestigious military unit – one of the Moesian legions (most probably *legio I Italica*), where he eventually reached the high-rank of a *beneficiarius*.

Apart from the lands of the province Lower Moesia (now North Bulgaria), we posses other testimonies for the cult of *Purmerulas*: one of them [18] is particularly interesting. It is found in the church of the village Kovacevo, Sandanski region, SW Bulgaria. The dedicator, or an ancestor of him, is mentioned in an inscription from

Rome [19]. *Cestius* was most probably a Roman official, with still unknown function in the Thracian "fasti". Nevertheless, he pays homage to the local Deity of *Pyrmerulas*, which is mentioned not as a Heros or Master (see above), but as a Great God. According to the inscription, the Roman official *L. Cestius* was inspired – by a vision or a by a dream - by *Pyrmerulas* to made a dedication to him, which shows that the deity was without doubt very popular among the local Thracian population and *Cestius* felt obliged to show his religious piety by dedicating an altar to him.

4   Possibilities

As it was shown, the interactive database provides possibility to trace the geographical distribution of monuments that inform about a specific problem of the past and about a specific type of cultural relict. The interactive map creates possibilities for tracking (through hyperlinks) the inscriptions with a similar content and leads the user through different archaeological and cultural context of the inscriptions.

In the interactive application, the approach is based on geo-positioning the ancient inscriptions. The main menu is in the form of a map and each location is a button (hyperlink), leading to an internal page dedicated to proper inscription (Fig. 2). Within the home page, links will also include information for authors, a common bibliography, and a search engine.

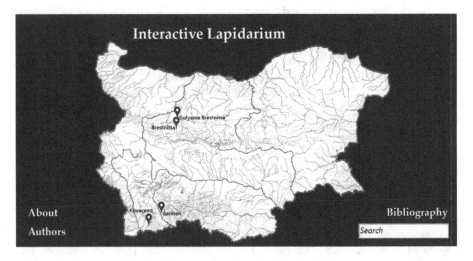

Fig. 2. Home screen of multimedia application

At an inner level the interface includes description of the object, context, bibliography, text of inscription, translation, date, commentary, hyperlink to the site of the institution where the artefact is stored, 3D model of object and pictures (Fig. 3). To develop the product are used programming languages ActionScript and Lua. The product will be distributed among the students through the learning management

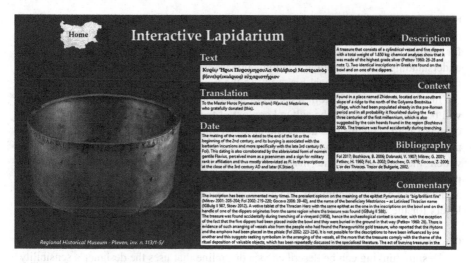

Fig. 3. Inner level screen of multimedia application

systems (e.g. Moodle, ILIAS etc.) as a separate exe-file for download (now the application is only available for PC users).

5   Research Methodology and Techniques

The interdisciplinary approach of the project determines the use of various research techniques. The main scientific method of the study of the epigraphic material is the text analysis of the monuments and the comparative epigraphic analysis of their contents. It takes place in several stages. The first one aims at familiarising with the actual preserved text of the monument, eventually correcting previous erroneous readings or omissions. Text content acquires a broader historical context by comparison with other inscriptions that mention similar names, divinities, and other realia. After the end of this stage - clarification of its written and correct normalization, a digital version with a photo of the monument and normalized text would be included in the database. If the region's inscriptions described by earlier researchers are now lost, instead of a photo a drawing or schematic presentation of the inscription text will be applied. Normalization serves to convert the raw epigraphic text often found on the stone in abbreviations in the Latin monuments (sigla), sometimes in Greek as well as without other necessary clarifications, punctuation marks in the ancient text. For Latin monuments, the Leidner Klammersystem conventions system will be used that is common in epigraphic publications, and which during the normalization phase correctly translates the characteristics of the original text.

In the next step, a content-based text analysis of the monuments is used, which analyzes the historical context and significance of the monuments. The methods of prosopography and historical anthroponomy apply to the personal names and composition of the population known owing to the monuments: grouping the population by monuments according to different criteria and examining the relative influence they have in society and on the historical process through the dissemination data of the names and families in the various areas of the Empire. This methodology is classical for studies on the provincial history of the Roman Empire and contributes to the understanding of demographic relations, processes of Romanisation and acculturation, migration, and socio-political hierarchy in the regions the monuments originate from.

In addition, methods from the field of archaeology, cultural studies, and art studies will be used to determine the cultural context of the finds, exploration of monuments as objects of art, conclusions about the spiritual life and the culture of the mentioned population. Their use is particularly important in defining the different workshops in which the inscriptions are made. This would allow to determine the economic parameters of the spread of the epigraphic habit. For the definition of the atelier, as well as the dating of the monuments, the palaeographic method, which uses the shape of the letters for the dating of the monuments, is of particular importance.

The development of the interactive application will follow the method of design thinking with its six-step process.

Design thinking can be described as a discipline that uses the designer's sensibility and methods to match people's needs with what is technologically feasible and what a viable business strategy can convert into customer value and market opportunity. (Tim Brown, CEO of IDEO, HBR, 2009).

The design thinking process consists of the following several stages: Empathize, Define, Ideate, Prototype and Test. Within these steps, problems can be framed, the right questions can be asked, more ideas can be created, and the best answers can be chosen. The steps aren't linear; they can occur simultaneously and can be repeated.

On the other hand, the interactive application is an instrument to respond to particular human and research needs. Its functionalities in response to these needs should be very well defined and planned, prototypes should be created at fast-paced iterations in order to test every step and functionality until a fully functional final product is created within the limited time-frame of the respective Working Package. Added value to the design thinking process is the multidisciplinarity of the scientific team, as this would allow to analyse the application's functionalities and content from all necessary points of view – both scientific, IT, as well as with regard to the needs of the direct and indirect target groups.

6   Conclusions

The project has the ambition to encompass the inscriptions from the times of the Roman rule in modern day Bulgaria. The next stages of the work could incorporate also evidence from broader regions of the South-Eastern Europe, e.g. the region of Ancient Thrace, which is now divided between Bulgaria, Greece and Turkey, thus showing the multicultural past of the region in the ancient times. The idea will result in a *full-scale interactive map*, which should be usable not only by scholars and students, but also by the institutions responsible for the cultural heritage, tourists and everyone that needs quick and easy virtual access for scientific or learning purposes, or for the goals of the management of the cultural heritage.

References

1. Keppie, L.: Understanding Roman Inscriptions, Baltimore, p. 9 (1991)
2. Konstantinov, O., Kovatcheva, E., Fol, V., Nikolov, R.: Discover the thracians – an approach for use of 2D and 3D technologies for digitization of cultural heritage in the field of e-learning. In: Pavlov, R., Stanchev, P. (eds.) Proceedings of The International Conference on Digital Presentation and Preservation of Cultural and Scientific Heritage – DiPP2012, pp. 167–171, Institute of Mathematics and Informatics – BAS, Sofia (2012)
3. Ott, M., Pozzi, F.: Towards a new era for cultural heritage education: discussing the role of ICT. Comput. Hum. Behav. **27**, 1365–1371 (2011)
4. Meyer, É., Grussenmeyer, P., Perrin, J.P., Durand, A., Drap, P.A.: Web information system for the management and the dissemination of cultural heritage data. J. Cult. Heritage **8**(4), 396–411 (2007)
5. Lytras, M.D., Ordóñez de Pablos, P.: Social web evolution. Integrating semantic applications and web 2.0 technologies. IGI-Global (2009)
6. Mortara, M., Catalano, C.E., Bellotti, F., Fiucci, G., Houry-Panchetti, M., Petridis, P.: Learning cultural heritage by serious games. J. Cult. Heritage **15**(3), 318–325 (2014)
7. Petkov, H.: The newly discovered treasure from the village of Golyama Brestnitsa, Pleven. Archeology 1, 26–28 (1960). (Петков, Хр.: Новооткритото съкровище от с. Голяма Брестница, Плевенско. – Археология 1, 26–28)
8. Bozhkova, B.: Coin treasure (II-III c.) from the village of Golyama Brestnitsa. Numismatics, clusters and epigraphy 3, part 1, 121–130 (2006). (Божкова, Б.: Монетно съкровище (II-III в.) от с. Голяма Брестница. Нумизматика, сфрагистика и епиграфика 3, част 1, 121–130)
9. Fol, V.: The Treasure from the Golyama Brestnitsa Village and the Relation: Sacred Object – Rite – Faith. Orphaeus 22 (in print) (2017)
10. Mitrev, G.: The names in the Medina Struma valley and religion as a factor for the formation of the name system in the I – III c. Seminarium Thracicum 5. Second Academic Readings in Memory of Academician Gavril Katsarov, pp. 199–210, Sofia (2001). (Митрев, Г.: Имената в долината на Средна Струма и религията като фактор за формирането на именната система през I – III в. – Seminarium Thracicum 5. Втори академични четения в памет на академик Гаврил Кацаров. София, 199–210)
11. Fol, A.: Thracian Dionysus. Book Three. Naming and Faith, pp. 208–224, Sofia (2002). (Фол, Ал.: Тракийският Дионис. Книга трета. Назоваване и вяра. София)
12. Gočeva, Z.: Die örtlichen funktionalen Epitheta des Thrakischen Reiters. Orpheus. J. Indo-Eur. Thracian Stud. **16**, 33–41 (2006)
13. Mihailov, G.: Inscriptiones Graecae in Bulgaria repertae.Vol. II. Academia Litterarum Bulgarica. Serdicae, pp. 587–588 (1958)
14. Stoev, K.: Being a Roman in Moesia. Anthroponymy and Prosopography of the Romanized Population in Upper and Lower Moesia, Sofia (2017). (Стоев, К.: Да бъдеш римлянин в Мизия. Антропонимия и просопография на романизираното население в Горна и Долна Мизия. София)
15. Dobruski, V.: Thracian sanctuary of Asclepius next to Glava Panega village. Archaeological Announcements of the National Museum in Sofia, 1, 3–86 (1907). (Добруски, В.: Тракийско светилище на Асклепий до Глава Панега – Археологически известия на Народния музей в София,1, 3–86)
16. Detschew, D.: Die Thrakischen Sprachreste. Verlag der Österreichischen Akademie der Wissenschaften, Wien (1976)

17. Stoev, K.: The hereditary nomenclature and its value as a source for the study of identities. In: Gavrielatos, A. (ed.), Self-presentation and Identity in the Roman World, pp. 162–210. Cambridge Scholars Publishing (2017)
18. Mihailov, G.: Inscriptiones Graecae in Bulgaria repertae, vol. IV. Academia Litterarum Bulgarica. Serdicae, p. 2304 (1966)
19. L'Epigraphic Database Roma (EDR030416). https://goo.gl/KYNre9. Accessed 25 May 2017

Ontologizing the Heritage Building Domain

Andrej Tibaut[1]([ ])(iD), Branko Kaučič[2](iD), Daniela Dvornik Perhavec[1](iD),
Piero Tiano[3](iD), and João Martins[4](iD)

[1] Faculty of Civil Engineering, Transportation Engineering and Architecture,
University of Maribor, Maribor, Slovenia
andrej.tibaut@um.si
[2] Initut, Institute of Information Technology Ltd., Maribor, Slovenia
[3] National Research Council, Institute for the Conservation
and Valorization of Cultural Heritage, Florence, Italy
[4] Electrical Engineering Department, Faculty of Sciences and Technology,
Universidade Nova de Lisboa, Lisbon, Portugal

Abstract. New challenges for cultural heritage have arisen from the expansion of digitalization, the broader range of available applications, and the increase in individuals and organizations interested in obtaining and sharing heritage knowledge. Supporting digital knowledge sharing relating to cultural heritage entails the challenges of structuring and transforming of data to information, information to knowledge and knowledge to application, etc. Digital cultural heritage processes must be knowledge-based and interoperable. Knowledge-based approaches using the concepts of linked data and ontologies are recognized as a basis for efficient solutions.

The paper investigates the development of ontology for the domain of heritage buildings as part of the wider domain of cultural heritage. A two-iterations-based process is presented.

Keywords: Heritage buildings · Ontologies · Ontologization · AECO

1 Introduction

Knowledge exists in many forms, but three general categories are recognised: tacit, implicit and explicit [40]. Also, different and overlapping knowledge relating to similar or related matters exists, for example, knowledge about buildings, about building structures, or building materials. Occasionally, facts and databases containing facts are considered as knowledge to some extent. The same knowledge can also be structured differently. Therefore, the process of the conceptualization and structuring of information is extremely important for the transformation of information to knowledge, which can then support the resolution of problems. This paper researches the process of ontologization for the domain of heritage buildings (HB), considering different methodologies and different input knowledge. The goal of the process is to provide an interoperable knowledge model (ontology) for HB.

© Springer International Publishing AG, part of Springer Nature 2018
M. Ioannides et al. (Eds.): Digital Cultural Heritage 2017, LNCS 10754, pp. 141–161, 2018.
https://doi.org/10.1007/978-3-319-75789-6_11

The process of data transformation from the physical to digital world is an ongoing digitalization process where databases and, recently, also knowledge bases are created. Both are collections of digital artefacts gathered and transformed from real world physical facts with some level of digitalization, which varies in scope, structure and accessibility. The process is best compared with the cognition process of humans, where individuals systematically learn new facts, relate them to other facts, memorize them and apply them in different daily situations. Information becomes new knowledge when it is applied. Most new knowledge is created during interaction and exchange between information holders (individuals, organizations, software etc.). If the new knowledge is properly managed, then it can also improve future processes.

There is always a dilemma as to whether or not to start the process for a new domain knowledge model as we have decided to do for the HB domain. These questions are very similar for any community or research group that aims to undertake this development. To fully address the dilemma, one should learn from similar projects (e.g. [CIDOC CRM or ISO 21127:2014]) in order to answer questions about the goals and results of the conceptualization process, the technical use of the knowledge model, etc.

Additionally, documentation as an HB process is specific and has changed enormously in terms of amount, details, organization, supporting tools, services, etc. Still, the huge amount and variety of the existing HB documentation and gaps due to missing or lost documentation calls for a holistic knowledge-based approach in treating HB documentation and its content. In the paper relevant research and professional sources have been selected, studied, and their results (documentation, taxonomies, ontologies) reused and upgraded. All this significantly influences the period in which knowledge-based solutions contribute to the development of the Semantic Web for more interoperable and interconnected IT solutions. The amount of "unknown" and "not understood" is decreasing, while on the other hand humans appreciate knowing that one's knowledge can be linked to the knowledge utilized by digital systems. This leads to the realization of the Data-Information-Knowledge-Wisdom concept (DIKW) [27].

Characteristics of knowledge engineering for the HB domain are:

- Understanding of the general benefits of ontology creation (ontologization), which include [5,6] clarifying the structure of knowledge and enabling knowledge sharing. Ontology also supports better integration between technical and organizational aspects and addresses the dichotomy between tacit and explicit knowledge.
- Human understanding extended to digital understanding of common concepts (i.e. temporal activities for HBs: construction, modification, conservation, preservation, reconstruction, refitting, rehabilitation, replacement, restoration, reuse, transformation, valorisation are related to the existing concept of "part addition" and "part removal" (from CIDOC CRM)).
- Transformation of unpredictable HB events (restoration sites etc.) into predictable solutions.

- Evolution of old information assets into new knowledge assets means the massive ontologization [36] of historical data, which will eventually lead to an explosive growth of distributed but digitally linked knowledge sources such as museums, archives and sites.
- Practically, HB stakeholders will still enjoy the comfort of "accessing the database", but technically, the knowledge based approach is more than just data crunching, therefore the knowledge bases for the 21st century will be used [17].
- The knowledge modelling horizon problem explains that for the HB domain one should not model the whole world, but rather just the parts which are relevant to the sub-domain tasks [29].

The goal of this paper is to research the ontologization process for the new open Heritage Building ontology, which will provide consolidated core knowledge about HBs domain and will utilize all the potentials of ontology engineering (classes, object properties, data properties, rules) while reusing existing ontologies.

1.1   Motivation

In the last decade, digitalization has undoubtedly been the most important transformation in many areas. In addition, it is also an important goal on the European Commission's digital agenda and generally recognized as a key element in market competitiveness. Nowadays, almost all stakeholders have access to digital technologies, information services are already well populated, access and usage of knowledge from digitized information is quick and effective, information and related knowledge constructs can be effectively recognized, revised, analyzed, used and improved in vast areas of interest.

The digitalization of the Architecture, Engineering, Construction and Operation (AECO) domain also includes the domain of HB, ranging from world, national, regional or local heritage importance. Problematic issues with historical buildings such as houses, bridges, industrial buildings, etc. are: (a) documentation for HB is dispersed because their parts are archived by numerous public and private owners, (b) lack of digitized documentation about HB, (c) incomplete documentation causes undesirable data gaps, which also result in incomplete interpretations of HB. All these issues have a negative effect on research in this domain, especially on the digitalization of HB.

To understand the need and rationale behind the digitalization of the HB domain, one has to understand the theory of information and its pyramid of knowledge [1], Fig. 1. The pyramid is an important conceptualization, which teaches us that data chunks can be transformed into meaningful information and further into knowledge assets. A revised pyramid of knowledge [27] extends the original with the explanation of the influence of Big Data on data-information-knowledge. The process of making sense and making meaning from Big Data increases the number of information artefacts, which in turn increase the number of knowledge artefacts, etc. The new pyramid of knowledge emphasizes the

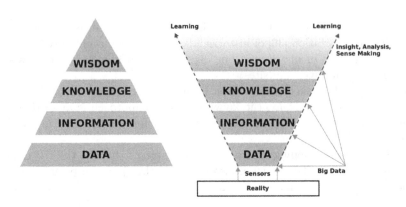

Fig. 1. The pyramid of knowledge

importance of knowledge technologies also for the HB domain. Therefore, in this paper, we use knowledge engineering technologies for HBs to diminish the negative effect of the aforementioned problematic issues.

1.2 Ontologization

Information embedded in the documentation poses a challenge for information extraction and the construction of an appropriate ontology. Several researchers have presented cases of constructing ontologies from different sources of information for different topics, and a few researchers have proposed methodologies for developing ontologies for different domains [44]. In general, there is a need to identify key elements, important and related information and, consequently, the relevant knowledge structures of concepts and relations among them. At the same time, there is also a need to identify which information represents perturbation or noise and accordingly include or filter it out from the knowledge model. This is generally referred to as the ontologization process [36], or, as defined by the dictionary, "to ontologize" means "to convert into ontological entities or express ontologically". Similarly, Zouaq refers to ontologization as "the ability to build a bridge between the natural language level and the abstract/conceptual level" [45].

The most commonly mentioned methodologies for building ontologies are Uschold's and Grunninger's Skeletal methodology, Grunninger & Fox's TOVE methodology, METHONTOLOGY [18], Noy & McGuinness's Seven-Step method, and a 5-step recipe by Gavrilova et al. [44,45].

The results of the ontologization processes are ontologies, structured sets of terms and concepts presenting the meaning of information domains, formed as a hierarchy of concept descriptions related by subsumption relationships with added axioms in the more complicated ones [39].

As an explicit specification of conceptualization, the term ontology was first defined by Gruber in 1993 [23]; several other definitions emerged later (see [39] for a selection of them). The formalization of knowledge in ontologies is based on five components: classes (or concepts), relations (or properties) between classes, relations for data assignment, functions and instances (or individuals). Typically, ontologies are (re)used for: merging between two or more ontologies, creating a unique ontology by ontology integration, mapping between ontologies, alignment/matching between ontologies, and handling changes in ontology versioning [39].

Skeletal methodology defines four main phases: (1) identifying a purpose and scope; (2) building the ontology: ontology capture, ontology coding, integrating existing ontologies; (3) evaluation (verification and validation); and (4) documentation. TOVE methodology consists of six phases: (1) identification of motivating scenario(s) for understanding the need and use of ontology; (2) preparation of set of questions (called informal competency questions) for evaluation of ontological commitments that have been made; (3) specification of the terminology of the ontology by using first-order logic (first the relevant objects are identified, then attributes of these objects are defined and relations among the objects are defined); (4) definition of formal set of competency questions; (5) definition of axioms necessary and sufficient enough to express the competency questions and their solutions; (6) definition of completeness theorems that define the conditions under which the solutions to the questions are complete. METHONTOLOGY resists on three flows: management phase, development phase and maintain phase all in 6 steps: (1) specifying the purpose of the ontology, the level of formality and the scope of the ontology; (2) collecting all the knowledge; (3) conceptualization phase, first building a glossary of terms with all possibly useful knowledge for the treated domain, grouping these terms according to concepts and verbs and gathering them in tables, formulas and rules; (4) checking if there are any existing ontologies that can and should be used; (5) implementation phase producing ontology defined in a formal language that can be evaluated according to selected references; (6) documentation of the ontology developed so far. Seven-Step method is oriented towards application of the Protégé tool [34] and consists of seven steps: (1) determination of the domain and scope of the ontology; (2) reuse of possible existing ontologies; (3) enumeration of important terms in the ontology; (4) definition of the classes and the class hierarchy; (5) definition of the properties of classes called slots; (6) definition of the facets of the slots; (7) creation of instances. Lastly, a 5-step recipe proposal: (1) development of glossary; (2) laddering; (3) disintegration; (4) categorization; (5) refinement. For more details, the reader is referred to [44].

1.3   Contribution

Contributions of the paper are (a) besides [25] and [24] this is more general and extensive ontologization research for HBs, (b) demonstrates the application of the first four steps of the METHONTOLOGY approach: (1) specifying the purpose of the ontology, (2) extracting and collecting knowledge, (3) conceptualization phase (glossary of terms), (4) check for existing ontologies, (c) research and analysis of core elementary ontologies that can be reused for a new ontology for HB, and (d) very early draft of HB ontology.

2   Sources of Knowledge About Heritage Buildings

All of the elements mentioned in the motivation section of this paper have led us to the development of a knowledge-based system (KBS) for HBs based on ontology integrated into an efficient IT tool. The ontology used will be prepared by an "HB data capturing" process (Fig. 2, presenting the information sources and actors in the ontologization process).

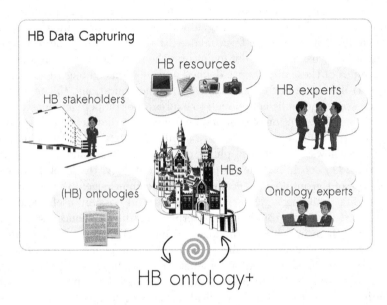

Fig. 2. HB data capture (revised image from [42])

Ontologization, and therefore also HB data capturing, is a continuing repetitive process, where each repetition can be seen as an iteration and can produce a new version of the ontology. The main objective is to produce an ontology, i.e. a final ontology for that iteration which best represents HBs and HB related processes and activities.

The main objects of interest are HBs. They are considered as a source of knowledge to some extent and a valuable source of possible new information that can be structured into knowledge. Typically, some work has already been carried out on HBs and some documentation perhaps already exists, while new needs for new knowledge may arise at any moment. As indicated before in the paper, there is a vast variety of resources in different forms, formats, ownership/possession, accessibility and quantities, and also at various levels of digitalization and aggregation (e.g. paper documents, voice recordings, video materials, images, database records, etc. forming data collections). It is usually prepared and/or used by various HB experts (e.g. from fields of reconstruction, renovation, conservations, bio-deterioration, etc.) and stakeholders. In general, stakeholders have some influence or relation toward the HB and vice-versa (individuals, groups and organizations, e.g. owners of HBs or lands, private funders, finance institutions, legislation institutions, data providers, HB service providers, and other various HB related stakeholders).

Several researchers, organizations and projects have produced ontologies or preliminary steps toward ontologies (e.g. data collections [16], metadata description of collections, taxonomies [32]). It is believed that each ontology presents a valuable view on the related knowledge domain and not all the work needs to be done from scratch when producing a final ontology. Therefore, ontology experts usually search for related ontologies and consider their contribution to the final result. Some ontologies can be directly connected to HB, some can be indirectly (e.g. ontology about building materials, which is useful for all types of buildings and therefore also HBs), and some serve as supporting core ontologies in the representation of core elements (e.g. time, location, person, etc.). In addition, some ontologies are appropriate entirely, some partially, some need some changes or improvements, and some are inappropriate. All considered ontologies contribute to the *final* ontology.

When a version of the *final* ontology is produced in current process iteration, that ontology is usually revised by HB experts and interested stakeholders. Based on the review feedback, a new iteration of the process might begin. For example, experts may identify missing chunks of information, which results in activities through which some HB related service provider will provide that information (e.g. by analyzing HB and preparing documentation). This results in the consideration and integration of new information and knowledge resulting in the new final ontology. The same issue of starting a new process iteration is also used when new requests or demands about some HB process or activity are identified. In order to produce the best possible ontologies with the minimal number of iterations, a set of methodologies (mentioned in Sect. 1.2) has been proposed.

Continuously improving the ontology according to new tacit and explicit knowledge corresponds to the well-known knowledge spiral [31]. At the end of each iteration, the best ontology is produced (and then used in the corresponding KBS). Regardless of the number of iterations, the problem of horizon is an integral part of this process. With each iteration, experts include new or transform existing knowledge, most likely expanding the horizon of knowledge, leading ultimately to new horizons.

2.1 Documentation

Our research included HB documentation specific for one country, Slovenia, which was obtained from regional archives, the building cadastre, digital HB repositories, and one real HB project.

Building Cadastre. In the Republic of Slovenia, over 1.1 million buildings and over 1.7 million parts of buildings from over 1.2 million owners are registered in the building cadastre. Databases on existing buildings are developed and maintained by The Surveying and Mapping Authority of the Republic of Slovenia [43] through the free access application e-Surveying Data [13]. Although some information in the building cadastre is generalized, it serves as valuable information for identifying the properties of classes and knowledge modelling (e.g. identification, owner, administrator if owned by the state, position and form, area (ground floor area, usable ground floor area, area for different purposes), actual use, apartment number or number of commercial space, link to land cadaster, link to real estate register, link to land registry, etc.).

Legislation and Rules. The obligatory rules for construction were issued in the Austro-Hungarian Empire. Before that, the basic principles of construction were collected and given to the Emperor as guidelines for maintenance.

In Slovenia buildings were built by various nations: the Romans, Turks, Habsburgs, Kingdom of Serbs, Croats, Slovenians, Yugoslavia (FLRJ, SFRJ) and, finally, the Republic of Slovenia as an EU member. Slovenia had no specific regulations for the construction domain until 1783 when the process of centralization in construction began. Centralization included residential buildings, public buildings, schools, roads, bridges, walls, hydroelectric power plants, ports and sacred objects. The methods and form of construction for single family-houses were described in the so-called Imperial Decrees. In 1786 the "Normalpläne" directive, a standard for the preparation of construction plans, including designs for particular types of objects, was issued. The first handbook (guide), a collection of all the regulations for building construction, titled "Der praktische Baubeamte", was published in Vienna in 1800 by Matthew Fortunat Koller. The handbook also included prices and labour costs. In 1807, the eminent road designer Jozef Maria Schemerl published several guides for the construction of roads and engineering structures. The first special regulations for the construction and reconstruction of new buildings, which was applied in all Styrian territories (except in Graz) was adopted in 1857 [3]. In 1905 the construction rules for industrial buildings were added [8]. Certain construction rules had already been summarized in a range of fire orders focusing on fire-resistant construction. In 1782 a Styrian fire order was issued and in 1822 a fire order for the capital city of Graz (capital city at that time) followed. A construction order for the territory of Styria remained in force after the end of the First World War and was confirmed with its publication in the Official Journal of the Kingdom of Serbs in 1920. It remained unchanged until 1931 when the Construction Act was accepted [9]. In 1933 general instructions for the production of implementation regulations of control plan and construction regulations were issued [21].

Structural rules in legislation and other related documents are a valuable asset in the conceptualization of buildings from specific time periods. For example, buildings, according to the 1857 Building Order for the Territory of Styria, were limited by the following rule "Masonry bricks bound by mortar must be

290 mm length, 140 mm width and 65 mm high" or "the thickness of load bearing wall in higher floor with span length <6,3 m must be 45 cm".

Archives. Archives are established memory institutions and retain extremely valuable sources of information, such as large amounts of original material (mostly written and visual) in historical order, such as administrational records, important letters, photographic collections, etc. [10]. Some of them are public, while others are private. In Slovenia cultural heritage archives are maintained in one national, three historical, three regional, and four diocesan institutions, with various aspects of informations related to HBs.

For the research considered in this paper, the most important source for construction history after 1850 was the Regional Archives Maribor established in 1933 (under a different name at that time).

2.2   Reference Ontologies and Other Sources

Ontology reuse is an important concept in ontology engineering (i.e. Semantic Web). It can be defined as the process in which already existing (core ontological) knowledge is employed as input to creation of new ontologies. The purpose of inclusion of core ontologies into a target domain ontology is to remove duplicated components (concepts, properties) in the domain ontology and replace them with references to existing concepts from external core ontologies.

Since ontology modelling is an iterative process the reuse of core ontologies is an important ontology revision step.

Core Ontologies for Reuse. The reuse of well-thought-out concepts follows the rule for "not reinventing the wheel", which means not duplicating basic concepts that have already been defined by well-known international communities and organisations. The grassroots concepts are recommended best practice because they are the result of a long standardization process and therefore ensure long term usability, growth and maintenance and are unlikely to change meaning over time. In our research they are considered core concept dependencies on which HB ontology stands.

Core ontologies from the following initiatives were researched:

- Dublin Core Metadata Initiative [11] for metadata terms inside ontology,
- FOAF Vocabulary Specification [20] for use of concepts (foaf:Agent, foaf: familyName, foaf:givenName, foaf:name etc.) for linking people (owners, architects) to HB information,
- OWL-Time Ontology in OWL by The World Wide Web Consortium (W3C) [48] for use of temporal concepts (time:TemporalEntity, time:Instant, time: Interval etc.) for describing the temporal properties of resources in the HB world,
- ISA Programme Location Core Vocabulary by W3C [46] for use of concepts (locn:Address, locn:Geometry etc.) for describing any place in terms of its name, address or geometry in relation to HB, and

– ISA Programme Person Core Vocabulary by W3C [47] for use of concepts like person:Person to define minimum set of classes and properties for describing a natural person for all individuals related to HB.

CIDOC CRM - ISO 21127. The CIDOC Conceptual Reference Model (CRM) is currently the furthest developed ontology for the integration of cultural heritage information [10] and is intended to promote a shared understanding of cultural heritage information by providing a common and extensible semantic framework to which any cultural heritage information can be mapped [7]. It is intended to be a common language for domain experts and implementers to formulate requirements for information systems and to serve as a guide for conceptual modelling good practice. As such, it provides definitions and a formal structure for describing the implicit and explicit concepts and relationships used in cultural heritage documentation. In this way, it can provide the "semantic glue" needed to mediate between different sources of cultural heritage information, published by museums, libraries and archives. It was developed by an interdisciplinary teams of experts, from fields such as computer science, archaeology, museum documentation, history of arts, natural history, library science, physics and philosophy, under the aegis of the International Committee for Documentation (CIDOC) of the International Council of Museums (ICOM). The CIDOC Documentation Standards Working Group and CIDOC CRM SIG, which are working groups of CIDOC, have been in operation for over 10 years. Until 1994 the product of these activities was the CIDOC Relational Data Model. Later they decided to engage in an object-oriented approach in order to benefit from its expressive power and extensibility for dealing with the necessary diversity and complexity of data structures in the domain, the result of which was the first edition of the CIDOC CRM in 1999. The continuation of this process took place under the aegis of the International Standard Organisation (ISO) and since 9/12/2006 CIDOC CRM it has been known as the official standard ISO 21127:2006.

Concerning the process of ontologization, the team of experts applied strict principles to admit only concepts that serve the functionality of global information integration, and other, more philosophical restrictions about the kind of discourse to be supported [10]. The application of these principles was successful in two ways. On the one hand, the model became extremely compact without compromising adequacy, and on the other, the more schemata were analyzed, the fewer changes were required in the resulting model.

The present version, CIDOC CRM 6.2, announced in May 2015, contains 85 classes and 275 object properties and 12 data properties [7], incorporating the semantics of an extensive set of different schemata.

AECO Ontology. The AECO ontology has been in development since 2009 at University of Maribor (FGPA) as a knowledge model for every construction project, which generally involves Architecture, Engineering, Construction and Operation. It was meant to facilitate organization and understanding of large volumes of information contained in construction works projects [41]. Latest version of the ontology (namespace http://www.fgpa.um.si/ontologies/aeco#) contains 194 concepts, 44 object properties and 5 data properties (Fig. 3).

Input for the ontology is mainly As-Built documentation from different AECO projects obtained from consultants and main contractors based on which the ontologization was done. A distinguishing value of the ontology is that it maintains links to the buildingSMART concepts as contained in the buildingS-MART Data Dictionary [4].

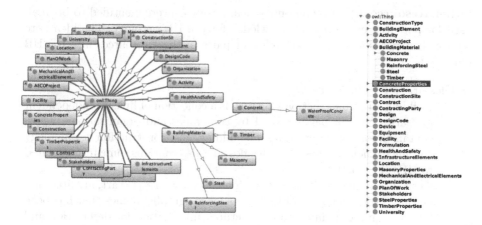

Fig. 3. AECO ontology (Protégé visualization)

The AECO ontology represented a reference for the HB ontology since its concepts cover the AECO domain which overlaps with HB domain.

2.3 Domain Ontology for Construction Knowledge

The ontology categorizes construction knowledge across three main dimensions: concept, modality, and context. Concept encompasses five key terms: entity (further subdivided into generic and secondary), environmental element, abstract concept, attribute, and system (combinations of the previous four types) [15].

Cultural Heritage Ontology for Cantabria. The project Cantabria's Cultural Heritage Ontology (CCHO) was initiative for the construction of an ontology for cultural heritage of specific region, Cantabria in Spain [25], that is based on CIDOC CRM, Dublin Core etc. Ontology was populated with knowledge from information sources with different formats (standardized and some proprietary formats) such as Encoded Archival Description files, Encoded Archival Guide files, Machine Readable Cataloging (MARC) 21 records, Dublin Core records, official webpages of Cantabria government, Excel sheets and relational databases.

Yorùbá Cultural Heritage Ontology. The ontology formally documents the African Yorùbá heritage knowledge obtained from embedded knowledge in the museums and monuments of Yorùbá antiquities and their narratives. The aim of the ontology was to design and implement an ontology representing knowledge embedded in Yorùbá Cultural Heritage (YCH) as a digital (documentation) resource. A combination of observation, consultation, documented materials and prototyping was used for the knowledge elicitation from domain experts [24]. The ontology contains 237 concepts, 9 properties and 900 individuals.

Other Resources. Other non-ontological resources were identified to be analysed for potential extraction of knowledge for the HB ontology. The idea is to analyse if it possible to integrate relevant parts of these resources into the HB ontology:

- Glossaries, Terminologies:
  - Building and Construction Glossary is a collection of links to independent glossaries on web pages hosted by companies and organizations, which contain informal descriptions of building and construction terminology specific to their business [2]. The glossary also contains some terms related to HBs (i.e. castle).
  - Getty Vocabularies [22] is a collection of vocabularies for art, architecture, cultural object names and thesaurus for geographic names that has been long recognized as important structured information for description and indexing of cultural materials [28].
  - FISH Vocabularies [19] by Forum on Information Standards in Heritage (FISH) represents a collection of thesauruses for archaeological objects, archaeological sciences, building materials, components and structural elements of buildings or monuments, archaeological events, remains of monuments, types of crimes and incidents against heritage assets, etc.
- Taxonomies, Classification systems:
  - ISO 12006-2:2015 (Building construction – Organization of information about construction works – Part 2: Framework for classification) defines a framework for the development of built environment classification systems. It identifies a set of recommended classification table titles for a range of information object classes according to particular views, e.g. by form or function, supported by definitions. It shows how the object classes classified in each table are related, as a series of systems and sub-systems, e.g. in a building information model. It does not provide a complete operational classification system, nor does it provide the content of the tables, though it does give examples. It is intended for use by organizations which develop and publish such classification systems and tables, which may vary in detail to suit local needs.
  - WAND Building and Construction Management Taxonomy [49] has 3,402 terms and over 700 synonyms of concepts, equipment, processes, and types of documents for any building and construction project. It suggests to tag

and organize project documents. It is linked to the WAND Product and Service Taxonomy (materials, equipment, and supplies) [50].

- Data, Conceptual Schemas:
  - EN ISO 12006-3:2016 (Building construction - Organization of information about construction works - Part 3: Framework for object-oriented information (ISO 12006-3:2007)) specifies a language-independent information model which can be used for the development of dictionaries used to store or provide information about construction works. It enables classification systems, information models, object models and process models to be referenced from within a common framework. Applications of this standard are buildingSMART Data Dictionary, LeXiCon (Netherlands) and BARBi (Norway).
  - EU-CHIC project developed a documentation proposal for historic buildings called Building Identity Card [33], which suggests a database schema with following 8 entities: names and references, location, functional type, dating, construction, current physical condition, protection/legal status and major risks.
- Data collections (catalogues) of HBs, databases:
  - Europeana.eu - EU digital platform for cultural heritage [16].
  - Eheritage.si - digital content of Slovenian cultural heritage [12].
  - SIRAnet - search engine of six Slovene regional archives [37].
  - SIstory - access to historical content relevant to study of Slovenian history by Research Infrastructure of Slovenian Historiography [38].
- Information models:
  - EN ISO 16739:2016 (Industry Foundation Classes (IFC) version 4) for data sharing in the construction and facility management industries (ISO 16739:2013 [26]) specifies a conceptual data schema and an exchange file format for Building Information Model (BIM).
  - Heritage Building Information Model (HBIM) is getting popularity but it is nothing more than BIM.

3   Ontologization Approach for Heritage Buildings

The iterative and incremental development (spiral) refines ontology through each iteration around the spiral. During the first iteration initial set of documentation about HB was studied and then initial ontology was created from the two already existing ontologies. In the second iteration, initial knowledge from the group of domain experts was collected and analysed for additional missing concepts and potential addition to the HB ontology. Both iterations are described in the next sections.

3.1   First Iteration

According to the statistical data (Republic of Slovenia, Ministry of Infrastructure and Spatial Planning, The Surveying and Mapping Authority of the Republic of Slovenia), Maribor has 4508 buildings which were built before 1918, but not all projects can be found in the archive. In the first phase we focused on domestic houses with a basement, ground floor and first floor, constructed between 1857–1931. We studied the legislation and acts from Archives of the Republic of Slovenia, legislation documents of Directorate of Cultural Heritage at Ministry of Culture of Republic of Slovenia, some books and research studies in libraries and museums, some documentation at Inspectorate for Culture, documentation of some proprietary reconstruction and conservation projects, and hundreds of images in archives. Special focus was given to floor plans and related data (permits, owners, architects, investors, researchers, etc.). More than 50 old projects in the Regional Archives Maribor were considered. The projects were categorised according to the number of floors. Examples of such design plans are shown in Fig. 4.

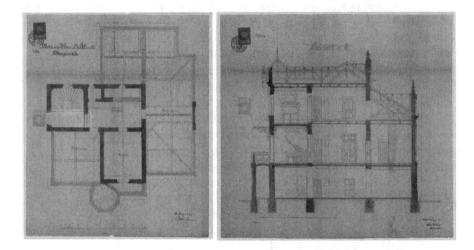

Fig. 4. Examples of design plans from Regional Archives in Maribor

For the ontologization process considered in this paper, 20 projects and their design plans were selected for further identification of location, ownership, number of floors, different building's basic structural elements such as main load bearing walls, its thickness and characteristics of building material. Few experts for archiving, reconstruction and conservation were contacted for additional informations.

From all gathered information, the ontology was prepared. The Protégé software tool [34] was used for the development of two connected ontologies in Resource Description Framework (RDF) format, namely material ontology and HB ontology.

The HB ontology was populated with knowledge about 12 actual building projects and referenced the material ontology (Fig. 5). From these building projects, the Baroness' House reconstruction project [30] was used for the observation of the legislative influence on construction. Figure 6 shows the concepts and the diagram for the HB ontology.

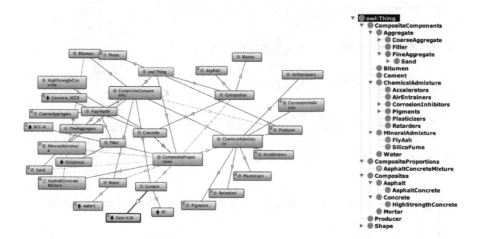

Fig. 5. First iteration HB ontology: the material ontology (Protégé visualization)

The HB ontology reused the Location [46], OWL-Time [48] and Person [47] ontologies through the import mechanism, i.e. the concepts of the three ontologies are loaded from their URLs and eventually their concepts populated the target HB ontology.

The Location ontology contains only three concepts (locn:Location, locn:Address and locn:Geometry) and all of them can be reused by HB ontology. Practically, each HB is mapped to its locn:Location with the object property locn:location, to its geographical position locn:Geometry with the object property locn:geometry. Generally, each HB also has some kind of address representation locn:Address, which can be represented with different spatial concepts like country, region, municipality, address area, post code, street name and address number. Another, more informal address representation is to write the complete address as a string, with or without formatting, and in this case the data property locn:fullAddress can be used.

The OWL-Time ontology contains temporal concepts, which are important for the HB ontology, because HB related activities (i.e. management, conservation, restoration etc.) are temporal activities. Preventive conservation, for example, starts at some point in time and is completed after some duration. Therefore, the HB ontology reuses the concept time:Interval, which is temporal concept with an extent or duration. The duration is constrained with two object properties, time:hasBeginning for start and time:hasEnd for the end of activity. The two object properties map time:Interval (domain) to time:Instant (range). The time:Instant defines point in time (interval with zero length). The concept

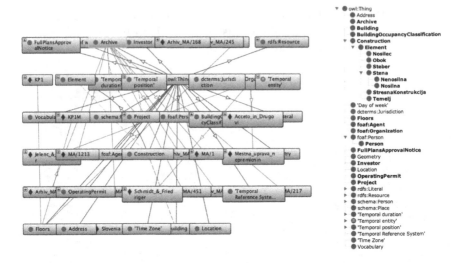

Fig. 6. First iteration HB ontology: the HB ontology (Protégé visualization)

is useful if the date of the change of ownership of a HB must be traced. We can express this with time:Instant.

From the Person ontology, the HB ontology reuses important concepts and properties for describing identity of a real person (individual) person:Person (i.e. Otto von Habsburg) related to a HB, which may be dead or alive, but not imaginary. Imaginary characters (i.e. Count Dracula) can be expressed with foaf:Person, which covers imaginary and real people. If owner of the HB is not a person but an organization (i.e. Catholic Church) or group (i.e. HB Friends) this can be modelled with foaf:Organization and foaf:Group respectively.

The efficiency of ontology and readiness for use by experts was tested by several SPARQL queries.

3.2   Second Iteration

In the second iteration of the ontologization a questionnaire was prepared for selected group of HB experts to obtain functional requirements for the ontology. Experts were asked to report on common issues (problems) related to their own HB use cases. The questionnaire contained the following set of questions:

- name of the HB issue (i.e. physical compatibility of materials), where experts were asked to select the issue according to the given list of categories (i.e. First expertise analysis, Preventive Conservation, Economic exploitation, Promotion, Social impact etc.),
- to what specific type of HB is the issue related (i.e. churches from 16th century in Mediterranean region),
- description of the issue where experts were expected to use their expert language and therefore they were given a glossary of terms,

– description of inputs (resources) for managing and resolving the issue related to the HB use case (i.e. causes, circumstances, temporal, environmental, etc.),
– specific actions (actors, equipment, etc.) needed to be taken to manage and resolve the issue, and
– results (outputs; documents etc.) of the actions taken.

Experts were given an initial list of representative well known HBs discussed among expert community. The goal was to achieve exact match between an expert and the representative HB to which also other expert activities can be related. The interdisciplinary expert team involved individuals with knowledge from the following HB important domains: owners and managers, historical and restoration value, social sciences, natural sciences, risk analysis, and economic issues. For development of the next iterative version of the HB ontology the following sub-topics as described by domain experts were identified:

– identification of suitable restoration techniques and materials to control and remediate deterioration processes and decay phenomena, lichenology and biodeterioration, evaluation of stone weathering and durability, recognition of the biodiversity on HB or in heritage sites as an additional cultural value,
– HB management (e.g. reconstruction of roof),
– social assessment of HBs and their surroundings,
– structural analysis, visual analysis (damage classification and state of usability), documentary analysis, in-situ tests, expected hazard and risk analysis, records about restoration, archiva documentation, historical analysis, photographic records, monitoring of conservation parameters, analysis of external issues, etc., and
– economic aspects of a HB.

Figure 7 shows the additional Activity concepts added to the HB ontology derived from the questionnaires results.

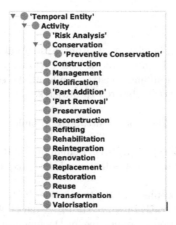

Fig. 7. Second iteration HB ontology: added Activity concepts

4   Conclusions

The ontologization research for HB domain as a subdomain of cultural heritage was the focus of the paper. The HB subdomain can inherit conceptualization from the cultural heritage domain. The research adopted the METHONTOL-OGY as the most appropriate methodology for development of the HB ontology. In the research we implemented four of the six development steps: (a) specification of the purpose and scope of the ontology, (b) collection of available knowledge for the domain including domain experts, (c) conceptualization phase that resulted in initial set of concepts and properties, and (d) reuse of existing ontologies. The steps (b) and (c) iterated two times. In the first iteration documentation from local regional archive in Maribor, Slovenia was collected and analysed, and in the second iteration, initial knowledge from the group of domain experts was collected and analysed for additional missing concepts and potential addition to the HB ontology. The resulting initial HB ontology is the first draft that reuses the CIDOC-CRM (Conceptual Reference Model), Location Ontology, OWL-Time and Person Ontology.

Research results have proved the initial research design and confirmed past ontology research experiences that ontology development is an ongoing spiral and iterative, but unavoidably, back-and-forth process, which must allow enough time for participation of different views. Therefore, our future work will include further development iterations that will include active involvement of domain experts that participated in the questionnaire, decision about further (deeper) specialization of the ontology, reuse of new core ontologies to minimize number of core concepts in the HB ontology, implementation of ontology in a knowledge based system, users' evaluation and validation in real projects.

Acknowledgement. The research was motivated by the project COST TD1406 - Innovation in Intelligent Management of Heritage Buildings, Work Group 2 - Interoperability for Heritage Building's Sustainability.

References

1. Ackoff, R.L.: From data to wisdom. J. Appl. Syst. Anal. **16**, 3–9 (1989)
2. Building Construction Terms, Lexicon and Dictionary. https://www.ats-group.net/glossaries/glossary-building-construction.html. Accessed 30 Sept 2017
3. Building order for Styria/Stavbni red za Štajersko. Deželno vladni list (1857). (in Slovene)
4. buildingSMART Data Dictionary. http://bsdd.buildingsmart.org. Accessed 30 Sept 2017
5. Chandrasekaran, B., Josephson, J.R., Benjamins, V.R.: Ontology of tasks and methods. In: Proceedings of Banff Knowledge Acquisition Workshop, Banff, Canada (1998)
6. Chandrasekaran, B., Josephson, J.R., Benjamins, V.R.: What are ontologies, and why do we need them? IEEE Intell. Syst. **14**, 20–26 (1999)
7. CIDOC CRM - International Committee for Documentation Conceptual Reference Model. http://www.cidoc-crm.org. Accessed 30 Sept 2017

8. Cizelj-Zajc, I.: Construction order for Styria/Gradbeni red za Štajersko. Glasilo Arhivskega društva in arhivov Slovenij, pp. 55–57 (1991). (in Slovene)
9. Construction law/Gradbeni zakon. Službeni list Kraljevine banske uprave Dravske banovine (1931). (in Slovene)
10. Doerr, M.: Ontologies for cultural heritage. In: Staab, S., Studer, R. (eds.) Handbook on Ontologies, pp. 463–486. Springer, Heidelberg (2009). https://doi.org/10. 1007/978-3-540-92673-3_21
11. Dublin Core Metadata Initiative. http://dublincore.org/specifications. Accessed 30 Sept 2017
12. Eheritage.si - digital content of Slovenia cultural heritage. http://www.eheritage. si/apl. Accessed 30 Sept 2017
13. E-Surveying Data Slovenia. http://egp.gu.gov.si/egp/?lang=en. Accessed 30 Sept 2017
14. El-Diraby, T.A., Lima, C., Feis, B.: Domain taxonomy for construction concepts: toward a formal ontology for construction knowledge. J. Comput. Civil Eng. 19, 394–406 (2005). https://doi.org/10.1061/(ASCE)0887-3801(2005)19:4(394)
15. El-Diraby, T.A.: Domain ontology for construction knowledge. J. Constr. Eng. Manage. 139(7), 768–784 (2013). https://doi.org/10.1061/(ASCE)CO.1943-7862. 0000646
16. Europeana.eu - EU digital platform for cultural heritage. https://www.europeana. eu/portal/en. Accessed 30 Sept 2017
17. Fensel, D.: Ontologies: A Silver Bullet for Knowledge Management and Electronic Commerce. Springer, Heidelberg (2004). https://doi.org/10.1007/978-3-662-09083-1. ISBN 3540003029
18. Fernández-López, M., Gómez-Pérez, A., Juristo, N.: METHONTOLOGY: from ontological art towards ontological engineering. In: AAAI 1997 Spring Symposium Series, SS-97-06, pp. 33–40 (1997). https://doi.org/10.1109/AXMEDIS.2007.19
19. FISH Vocabularies. http://heritage-standards.org.uk/fish-vocabularies. Accessed 30 Sept 2017
20. FOAF Vocabulary Specification. http://xmlns.com/foaf/spec. Accessed 30 Sept 2017
21. General instructions for the preparation of a regulation on the implementation of the regulation plan and building regulations/Splošna navodila za izdelavo uredbe o izvajanju regulacijskega načrta in gradbenega pravilnika. Službeni list Kraljevine banske uprave Dravske banovine (1933). (in Slovene)
22. Getty Vocabularies. http://www.getty.edu/research/tools/vocabularies. Accessed 30 Sept 2017
23. Gruber, T.: A translation approach to portable ontology specifications. ACM Knowl. Acquis. 5(2), 199–220 (1993). Special issue: Current issues in knowledge modeling
24. Hassan, J.A., Odéjóbí, O.A., Ògúnfolákàn, B.A., Adéjùwón, A.: Ontology engineering in Yorùbá cultural heritage domain. Afr. J. Comput. ICT 6(5), 181–198 (2013)
25. Hernández, F., Rodrigo, L., Contreras, J., Carbone, F.: Building a cultural heritage ontology for Cantabria. In: Proceedings of 2008 Annual Conference of CIDOC, Athens, 15–18 September 2008
26. ISO 16739:2013 Industry Foundation Classes (IFC) for data sharing in the construction and facility management industries. https://www.iso.org/standard/ 51622.html. Accessed 30 Sept 2017
27. Jennex, M.E., Bartczak, S.E.: A revised knowledge pyramid. Int. J. Knowl. Manag. 9, 19–30 (2013). https://doi.org/10.4018/ijkm.2013070102

28. Lanzi, E.: Introduction to Vocabularies: Enhancing Access to Cultural Heritage Information. Getty Information Institute, Los Angeles (1999). ISBN 0-89236-544-7

29. Lytras, M., Sicilia, M.-A., Davies, J., Kashyap, V.: Digital libraries in the knowledge era: Knowledge management and Semantic Web technologies. Libr. Manage. **26**(4/5), 170–175 (2005). https://doi.org/10.1108/01435120510596026

30. Mišič, D., Nahtigal, N., Kocutar, S., Mulec, M., Mlakar, D., Dugonik, B., Hojnik, D.: Baroničina hiša = Baroness' house: 1902–2015. Faculty of Electrical Engineering and Computer Science, University of Maribor, Maribor (2015)

31. Nonaka, I., Takeuchi, H.: The Knowledge Creating Company: How Japanese Companies Create the Dynamics of Innovation. Oxford University Press, New York (1995). ISBN 978-0-19-509269-1

32. Project Cultural Heritage Identity Card (EU-CHIC). http://www.eu-chic.eu. Accessed 30 Sept 2017

33. Rajčić, V., Vodopivec, B., Žarnić, R., Kippes, W.: EU-CHIC: European cultural heritage identity card - towards an integrative approach to documenting cultural heritage. In: Proceedings of the European Workshop on Cultural Heritage Preservation, EWCHP 2011, Berlin, Germany, 14–21 September 2011 (2011)

34. Protégé - ontology editor and framework for building intelligent systems. https://protege.stanford.edu. Accessed 30 Sept 2017

35. RDF 1.1 Turtle. https://www.w3.org/TR/turtle. Accessed 30 Sept 2017

36. Saab, D.J., Riss, U.V.: Information as ontologization. J. Am. Soc. Inf. Sci. Technol. **62**(11), 2236–2246 (2011). https://doi.org/10.1002/asi.21615

37. SIRAnet - Slovene regional archives search engine. http://www.siranet.si. Accessed 30 Sept 2017

38. SIstory - historical content of Slovenian history. http://www.sistory.si. Accessed 30 Sept 2017

39. Slimani, T.: A study investigating typical concepts and guidelines for ontology building. J. Emerg. Trends Comput. Inf. Sci. **5**(12), 886–893 (2014)

40. Smith, M.K.: Michael Polanyi and tacit knowledge. The Encyclopedia of Informal Education (2003). http://infed.org/mobi/michael-polanyi-and-tacit-knowledge. Accessed 30 Sept 2017

41. Tibaut, A., Jakoša, D.: Development of knowledge model for construction projects. In: Uden, L., Heričko, M., Ting, I.-H. (eds.) KMO 2015. LNBIP, vol. 224, pp. 248–259. Springer, Cham (2015). https://doi.org/10.1007/978-3-319-21009-4_19

42. Tibaut, A., Kaučič, B., Dvornik Perhavec, D.: Ontology-based data collection for heritage buildings. In: Lecture Notes - ITN-DCH Digital Heritage 2017 Conference, Olimje, Slovenia (2017, to be published)

43. The surveying and mapping authority of the Republic of Slovenia. http://www.gu.gov.si/en. Accessed 30 Sept 2017

44. Yun, H., Xu, J., Xiong, J., Wei, M.: A knowledge engineering approach to develop domain ontology, Chap. 4. In: Kumar, V., Lin, F. (eds.) System and Technology Advancement in Distance Learning. Information Science Reference, Hershey (2013)

45. Zouaq, A., Gašević, D., Hatala M.: Ontologizing concept maps using graph theory. In: Proceedings of SAC 2011, TaiChung, Taiwan, March 2011 (2011)

46. W3C ISA Programme Location Core Vocabulary. https://www.w3.org/ns/locn. Accessed 30 Sept 2017

47. W3C ISA Programme Person Core Vocabulary. https://www.w3.org/ns/person. Accessed 30 Sept 2017

48. W3C Time Ontology. https://www.w3.org/TR/owl-time. Accessed 30 Sept 2017

49. WAND Building and Construction Management Taxonomy. http://www.wandinc.com/wand-building-and-construction-management-taxonomy.aspx. Accessed 30 Sept 2017
50. WAND Product and Service Taxonomy. http://www.wandinc.com/wand-product-and-service-taxonomy.aspx. Accessed 30 Sept 2017

Designing Postdigital Curators: Establishing an Interdisciplinary Games and Mixed Reality Cultural Heritage Network

Lissa Holloway-Attaway[1] and Rebecca Rouse[2(✉)]

[1] University of Skövde, Box 408, 54128 Skövde, Sweden
`lissa.holloway-attaway@his.se`
[2] Rensselaer Polytechnic Institute, 110 8th Street, Troy, NY 12180, USA
`rouser@rpi.edu`

Abstract. As digital technologies have become more integrated in museum and cultural heritage contexts over the past decade, digital museums enter a new phase of coming into their own. This opens up opportunities for the incorporation of cutting-edge multiplayer gaming technologies and immersive mixed reality (MR) systems. To support nuanced and original engagement with the newly pervasive nature of the digital in museums, an interdisciplinary group of international researchers, designers, and museum professionals have established a new network: the Designing Digital Heritage Network (DDHN). The network operates to support research, design production, interdisciplinary collaboration, and the development of innovative new pedagogies and programs to 'design' the postdigital curators of the future. This paper outlines the mission and vision of the DDHN, and suggests initial directions for future research in the postdigital heritage field focused on interdisciplinary, performative, and game design approaches to production and exhibition.

Keywords: Games · Cultural heritage · Performative · Postdigital museum
Curator

1 Introduction

As digital technologies have become more integrated (and expected) in museum and cultural heritage contexts over the past decade, a critical mass of scholarship on the digital museum has developed. Museum Studies scholar Ross Parry's landmark history of computing in museums [1] can be seen as a major starting point for scholarship in the field. Ten years on from this seminal publication, a wealth of literature has centered around topics including networking, participation/interactivity, the role of authenticity in the digital museum, education and evaluation [2–4]. As digital museums enter a new phase of coming into their own, opportunities have opened for the integration of cutting-edge multiplayer gaming technologies and immersive mixed reality (MR) systems. This new phase has been described by Parry as *postdigital* – meaning the integration of digital technology has become so pervasive throughout the museum or heritage institution, that using the phrase 'digital museum' has become almost as redundant as the phrase 'paper museum' [5]. Parry's concept of the digital in

© Springer International Publishing AG, part of Springer Nature 2018
M. Ioannides et al. (Eds.): Digital Cultural Heritage 2017, LNCS 10754, pp. 162–173, 2018.
https://doi.org/10.1007/978-3-319-75789-6_12

contemporary museums as fully normative is based on his extensive research with multiple national museums in the UK. This postdigital viewpoint is presented as freeing us from the rhetoric of the new or the revolutionary, which allows us space and critical distance to bring our focus away from the technology or object, and back to the body and experience of the visitor. This opportunity could allow for new approaches in curation design and pedagogy, with possibilities for democratization of the politics of display in unique ways.

Games, Mixed Reality technologies (MR), and Critical Design approaches have particular advantages to offer the cultural heritage and museum context. Like museums, games have long been established as participatory, performative, storytelling spaces with potential for great cultural and social impact [6–8]. Several studies have sought at points to summarize the state of the use of digital gaming technologies in the heritage and museum fields. Anderson et al. [9] provided a technologically focused review of hardware, software, and graphics pipeline techniques in use across museums, heritage sites, and the commercial games sector creating entertainment applications inspired by historical content. Reflective of the time period in which this study was produced the authors provide a fascinating snapshot of the 2009-era, which could be seen as on the brink of the post-digital environment described by Parry above. There is a heavy focus in the Anderson study on massive multiplayer online game spaces and open sandbox worlds, such as SecondLife, as well as perhaps less relevant emphasis on commercial 'historical' games, all of which are war games. A more recent state-of-the field study from Mortara et al. [10] surveys a wide sample of contemporary serious games for cultural heritage, examining 51 projects in total. Beyond the valuable contribution of cataloguing so many contemporary works, this study also suggests the beginning of a taxonomy for understanding the aims of games for heritage across the following three broad categories of (1) cultural awareness, (2) historical reconstruction, and (3) heritage awareness. In addition, Mortara et al. call for the much-needed development of graduate programs focused in this area, a topic of urgency that will be discussed below with respect to current projects underway via the Designing Digital Heritage Network.

In addition to approaches from game design and game technologies, MR provides a uniquely layered approach for creating synergies and juxtapositions across physical and digital artifacts and spaces, encouraging polysemic experiences that can support curators' and historians' desires to tell ever more complex and connected stories for museum and heritage site visitors, even involving visitors' own voices in new ways. In combination, game design approaches and MR technologies, within the museum context, help re-center historical experience on the visitor's body, voice, and agency, shifting emphasis away from the object. This re-centering of design focus on the user's embodied experience with MR has been discussed across a variety of heritage, museum, entertainment, and participatory design examples in Rouse et al. [11].

Focusing museum and heritage site experience design on the body of the visitor can enable the creation of performative, liminal experiences that actively transform space into place, and provide deep kinesthetic meaning-making outcomes. Examples of this are discussed by Vosinakis et al. [12], Barba et al. [13] and Rouse [14]. A deep connection with site is often of core importance for exhibit design at cultural heritage locations. A major task of exhibit design and curation at these sites is to transform visitors' experience of space (as abstract; impersonal) into one of place, (imbued with value; personal), as discussed by Tuan [15, p. 6]. Tuan develops these concepts in ways directly relevant to museum design - space is understood as volume one moves through, whereas place-making necessitates a pause. The pause is also necessary for critical distance to develop, and for learning to occur. This re-centering on the body of the visitor in immersive space brings a new relevance to traditional architectural and museum design scholarship on the movement of the visitor through space, and the perceptual field or 'isovist' enacted by the visitor [16–18]. Further, the re-centering of the museum experience on the visitor's body also allows for connection with another set of influential scholarship on the digital and embodied experience, strongly influenced by affective and phenomenological approaches, currently underexplored in museum and heritage studies (Kozel, Grusin, Hansen) [19–21].

Finally, a post-colonial or critical approach in the design of games and MR experiences is a burgeoning subfield relevant to heritage work, found across scholars in Design Research (Bardzell and Bardzell) [22], Human-Computer Interaction (Irani et al.) [23], and Media Studies [24] (Engberg). The Bardzells' work is of particular note for the careful unpacking of the concept of criticality in design as ranging across a spectrum from work that is simply new or boundary pushing, to work that results from a critical theory approach, to work stemming from artistic critique. Irani et al. make the point that to design from a postcolonial perspective methods must shift from the traditional user profiling, ideation, and iteration to a new process centered on engagement, articulation and translation. Engberg goes even further to describe a design process centered on the concept of care, as in taking care not to re-inscribe violence and erasures previously done to colonized subjects, and instead seeking to both acknowledge and to some extent even heal these imperialist wounds.

Reflecting on the postdigital state of museums and heritage sites, and the panoply of technologies and techniques available to designers, it becomes clear that simply presenting a didactic display of historical facts is not enough to create a meaningful connection for many visitors to a heritage site. Unlike a museum, certain sites such as battlefields and burial grounds may be particularly opaque to the visitor. A performative intervention is needed to transform the space into a place with lasting resonance. Strategies, methods, and techniques from such interventions can also enliven design within the museum gallery space. Game design techniques, MR technologies, and critically infused approaches are now helping to make this a reality at heritage sites and museums across the world, and likewise advanced degree programs are being developed to 'design' the postdigital curators of tomorrow.

2   Postdigital Museums and Interdisciplinary Networks for Design

Given this postdigital potential for a uniquely robust approach to design and implementation in museum contexts, creating sustainable contexts to facilitate such interdisciplinary interventions is key. In other words, beyond shifts in design and curatorial acts within the museum itself, advancements must also be centered on educational and research initiatives to generate these complex, new museum experiences. We clearly, then, support Parry's central claim that digital technologies have become *normative* in museums and that currently we find ourselves in the age of the *postdigital*. Here "critical scrutiny" is key and necessary to mark this advanced state of change [5, p. 24]. For Parry this is an opportune, yet delicate juncture that requires a radical deepening of our understanding of the museums' relationship to digital tools:

> Postdigitality in the museum necessitates a rethinking of upon what museological and digital heritage research is predicated and on how its inquiry progresses. Plainly put, we have a space now (a duty even) to reframe our intellectual inquiry of digital in the museum to accommodate the postdigital condition. [5, p. 36]

Moving beyond the accepted fact that digital tools have been adopted and ubiquitously assimilated in museums and heritage sites, we must now focus on the contextualized practices in which these technologies will inevitably engage designers and users. Curation and exhibition design must be carefully crafted to support the experiences of users as they performatively engage postdigital museum sites. Nuanced forms of interdisciplinary research are needed to address these complex sites of exchange and development, where the mere presence of technology is not seen as revolutionary, but rather it is "naturalized, ambient and augmented" [5, p. 37]. At this level, it is even more critical to understand the ways in which communication and storytelling happen in deeply integrated and embedded user/technology relationships. Here, there is a "new contract between the connected institution and the connected viewer" where digital media is "familiar and expected," comprising a blended relationship, or "an embodied augmentation of one with the other" [5, p. 37], and it is also here where we focus our interest.

To this end, we propose that contemporary research in the fields of game design and mixed reality offers a foundation for thinking about these blended relationships within cultural heritage exhibitions and experiences, in the spirit of the postdigital museum that Parry proposes. We find three fundamental (and intersecting) areas critical for the future advancement of digital heritage projects:

1. Pedagogy
2. Research in Practice
3. Scholarship

To further development across these intersecting fields, in 2014 the Designing Digital Heritage Network (DDHN) was established at the University of Skövde in Skövde, Sweden. The network was founded by Associate Professor Lissa Holloway-Attaway and Lecturer Lupita Maria Guadalupe Alvarez Diaz, with funding provided by The Swedish Higher Education Authority ("Universitetskanslersämbetet" or "UKÄ").

Organized initially around two international seminars (in 2014 and 2015) exploring the connections between games, MR technologies and cultural heritage, the DDHN has continued to develop in more concrete and sustainable initiatives to support the three aims of the network's mission. Following Parry's call to adapt critical inquiry to the current postdigital condition, we chose to not showcase existing tools or exhibitions, but rather to examine the core challenges for the field as it advances. Thus, the 2014–2015 seminars served to provide a first-stage critical platform for postdigital conditions by developing a strategic international cross-section of cultural heritage and museum specialists, curators, exhibition designers, technology application designers, digital media and game design researchers, and others in related culture media industries. Importantly network collaborations include both practical projects engaging universities, culture, and media industry professionals, but also include supporting and developing educational opportunities (internships, student exchanges, curricula development, or shared curricula opportunities) deemed necessary to the developing field.

Unsurprisingly the network, established at a university, is fundamentally research and education based, but with a core focus on enabling iterative design practice in museums and heritage sites. The network enables collaborations and interdisciplinary support for deepening our collective understanding of designing and curating with strong influences from games research and development. We work, for example, to increase opportunities for funding by sharing experiences with different financial models and agencies, developing educational curricula, assignments and programs (both graduate and undergraduate), to stimulate interdisciplinary publication, and to support knowledge exchange in this emerging postdigital field, which includes museum studies, human computer interaction, game design, and artistic practice, among others. Figure 1 shows the current list of DDHN network participants and affiliations, and Fig. 2 presents selected projects shared through the network.

It is important to note that our network is supported by its foundational context within games education at the University of Skövde, where, since 1997, an international and highly successful framework for interdisciplinary research, development, and design of digital games, gamification models for learning and education, and intersections with cultural stakeholders have been developed. Skövde's games research has then evolved over decades of experience to combine technical humanist expertise with an emphasis on user experience and cultural impact. Since the mid-2000s, mirroring the move toward postdigital practice that Parry claims is evident in museums, the education and research at University of Skövde has transformed from a technical approach to game development to a much deeper commitment to understanding the socio-cultural impacts of digital games and media as they are embedded in cultural networks that take their presence as a given.

In addition, the work of the DDHN is connected to shifting foci within other related and changing disciplinary fields that have similarly tried to connect changing academic interest to digital cultural aims. Digital Humanities scholarship, has for example, in the face of the growing ubiquity of media within culture, tried to re-attune its attention back to the *human* within Humanities, and away from pure techno-centric inquiry. This work clearly follows Parry's claim [5], that technology is recognized as a form of normativity in museum contexts and cannot continue to be developed with a tool-centered approach, or "a discourse of 'technical revolution'" [5, p. 25], at the expense of new theoretical work, focused for example on user experiences, and new conceptions of what constitutes *a visitor*. N. Katherine Hayles [25], alerts us to this epistemological shift and explicitly claims that in Digital Humanities "we think, through, with, and alongside media." From the perspective of the technogenesis

DDHN Network Participants	Affiliations
Lissa Holloway-Attaway, María Guadalupe Alvarez Díaz, Per Backlund, Lars Kristensen, Torbjörn Svensson, Marcus Toftedahl, Lars Vispsjö	**University of Skövde** Sweden
Maria Engberg	**Malmö Högskola** Sweden
Malin Jogmark	**Marinmuseum Karlskrona** Sweden
Astrid Selling, Kristin Borgehed	**Folk Practice Academy** Sweden
Jonathan Sterner	**Mobile Storytelling** Sweden
Anders Sundnes Løvlie	**Copenhagen ITU** Denmark
Dagny Stuedahl	**Norwegian University of Life Sciences** Norway
Indrek Ibrus, Martin Sillaots	**Tallinn University** Estonia
Paul Bennun	**SomethingElse** UK
Jay David Bolter,	**Georgia Institute of Technology** USA
Rebecca Rouse, Benjamin Chang, Silvia Ruzanka,	**Rensselaer Polytechnic Institute** USA

Fig. 1. Current list of DDHN network participants and affiliations.

framework she offers, "humans and technics have co-evolved together" [25, p. 10]. This is critical to our own understanding of postdigital curatorial work that places human and technical concerns on equal, and mutually constitutive, footing. Supported by other current investigations into the Digital Humanities (Burdick et al., Bartscherer and Coover, Gold) [26–28], this scholarship recognizes the fluidity of recursive

Seeing Secrets
University of Skövde

Mobile AR panorama experience connecting users to stories of hidden women's labor in textile making and archiving in the 19th Century.

KLUB
University of Skövde

Transmedia storytelling with physical books, AR application, and location-based experiences to teach children local folklore.

Augmenting Neptun
Swedish National Marine Museum

AR panorama application for experiencing submarine interiors at the Swedish National Marine Museum in Karlskrona, Sweden.

Karlsborg Fortress Adventure
University of Skövde

Pervasive game including live acton, film, and motion sensing for visitors to explore the history of an ancient fortress.

Special Treatment
Applied Interactives; art(n) Laboratory

Virtual Reality installation examining the strength and persistence of memory, set in the Birkenau concentration camp.

Below Stairs
Rensselaer Polytechnic Institute

Mobile AR role-playing game invites visitors to an 1850's house museum in Troy, NY to experience life there as a servant.

Fig. 2. Information on selected projects shared through the DDHN seminar meetings.

digital/human borders (so-called *posthuman* subjects) and calls for expanded disciplinary perspectives and sites of study. Collectively they also provide a strong foundation for future investigations into digital museum and heritage studies, tracing as they do shifts in the academy and in research practice based on the postdigital conditions for technological development. And within this condition, the performative body of the user/visitor is a particularly rich site for investigation and central to the mission of the DDHN where we are committed to active pedagogy and research and scholarship *in practice*.

3 Curating Sustainable Development and Impact for Future Advancement

Currently the DDHN is working to support a number of key initiatives and ongoing research projects bringing games and heritage into alignment. Most significantly, we understand that to develop the connections between games and cultural heritage, we must work to train faculty, students, and heritage specialists to support postdigital design. In short, we understand that the work of *curation* in today's museum or heritage site is distributed beyond the museum walls or site location. Curation has become shared, across many cooperative sectors connecting multiple stakeholders, users, sites, and archives, from education to research to heritage.

Postdigital curators must be understood as multiple and varied; they are not solely specialists operating within, for example, exhibition design at the museum (as may be traditionally understood). Nor are they technical specialists working within IT departments, or in academic disciplines, who administer (curate) tools to support a discrete set of objects or devices for users/visitors in museum contexts. Computer scientists cannot work in isolation from culture specialists nor can we design from sites of difference. Graphic artists, historians, exhibition designers, sound designers, game designers, narrative designers, performance specialists, computer scientists, and media experts of all kinds must come together in networks of exchange.

Further, attention to the multimodal and performative literacies required from the new curator-visitor, is key to developing sustainable research and education intiatives. Leeker, Schipper, and Beyes [29] claim that in fact performativity is key to understanding how digital cultures operate at a fundamental level, because "the ubiquity and pervasiveness of digital media and their networked infrastructures profoundly influence the ways and styles in which performativity appears and is enacted" [29, p. 9]. Their claim is that "digital cultures are performative cultures" [29, p. 9] reinforce the need to understand the nuances and game-like functions of the user-enabled stories currently being *enacted* in museum contexts. We must understand the layered ways in which game-stories are performed, but also how they are read and received within the inter- and intra-active cultural contexts in which they are encountered. Like universities, museums are, at their core pedagogical and educational, and they transmit cultural and historical information, responding to their receivers' expectations and needs. We must then be attentive to these new and emerging forms of postdigital literacy, from development to reception, which requires a complex approach. Burnett, et al., for example, draw on Deleuzian concepts of the "baroque" to articulate literacy as highly flexible and situated—not a skill set to be learned, but a set of actions to be performed [30].

The training of *postdigital curators* must now attend to the blended nature of their mission: to create emergent and transformative user experiences that bring humans/technologies, places/spaces, and historical distance/active presence into union though the information they construct. As acknowledged by Parry in his discussion of the postdigital museum, this requires a deep understanding of critical applied practice supported by interdisciplinarity, layering, and augmentation [5]. As such, the new wave of research and development in digital games beyond entertainment (that is serious games, games for impact, art games), as well as advances in sophisticated technologies currently easily available for non-commercial use (AR, VR, haptic and motion sensing), are well-positioned to align themselves with the postdigital condition of museums, the mediated stories and literacies postdigital curators wish to tell, and the audiences positioned to actively engage them by doing. As discussed above, to support these new needs and aims, the DDHN is focused on education, research in practice, and scholarship. Figure 3 presents a set of ongoing Educational Initiatives of the DDHN, and Fig. 4 describes current DDHN research projects that have received funding.

Educational Initiatives	Partners
Undergraduate **student exchange** program in Games	University of Skövde, Rensselaer Polytechnic Institute
Expansion of 1-year **Master's Program** to 2-years for Digital Narratives	University of Skövde
Development of new 2-year **Master's Program** in Art and Games with a focus in Heritage Games for Digital Culture	University of Skövde
Development of new **MS/PhD Program** in Critical Game Design	Rensselaer Polytechnic Institute
Development of new **undergraduate minor**, "alt.code," bringing together computer science, humanities, and arts. Funded by the National Endowment for the Humanities.	Rensselaer Polytechnic Institute

Fig. 3. Current DDHN educational initiatives.

In addition to working together to develop educational initiatives, the DDHN is also developing opportunities for faculty exchanges and research collaborations. An anthology of interdisciplinary scholarship on the topic is in the development phase, with co-editors from several partner institutions including University of Skövde, Malmö Högskola, the Georgia Institute of Technology, Georgetown University, and Rensselaer Polytechnic Institute. A multi-sited mixed reality project on the topics of

Lead Institution & Funding Source/s	Project Description
University of Skövde; Skaraborg Municipal Association Growth Committee	**KASTiS:** Developing a regional platform for Western Sweden for the use of gaming technology in a variety of museums and cultural heritage sites
University of Skövde; Skaraborg Municipal Association Growth Committee, Vastra Götland's Department of Culture	**KLUB:** Transmedia storytelling with physical books, AR application, and location-based experiences to teach children local folklore in Sweden's Skaraborg region.
University of Skövde; The Swedish Institute, the Nordic Council of Ministers	**The Baltic Sea Region Cultural Gaming Project:** engaging Swedish and Latvian youth in the co-creation of digital games to learn about each others' cultures, communities, and public spaces.
University of Skövde and partners across 9 Baltic countries; Denmark, Estonia, Finland, Germany, Latvia, Lithuania, Poland Norway, Sweden	**Culturability:** gaming and culture as a primary focal point for sustainable development in the Baltic Sea Region
Rensselaer Polytechnic Institute; Rensselaer Alumni Association; Friends of Folsom Library, RPI HASS; Mohawk Hudson Gateway	**Finding Roebling:** Mixed Reality exhibition that tells the story of Washington Roebling, the man who built the Brooklyn Bridge
The City of Cohoes and Rensselaer Polytechnic Institution; New York State Complete Streets Funding Program	**Augmented Mural Series:** development of a set of painted murals with Augmented Reality components about the cultural heritage of the City of Cohoes, New York.

Fig. 4. Selection of currently funded DDHN research projects.

migration and oppression, "Sanctuary Cities," is being developed across partners at Rensselaer Polytechnic Institute, University of Skövde, and HKU Univesity of the Arts Utrecht. And housed at University of Skövde but incorporating collaborations from a variety of DDHN partners, the new X-Lab (Experimental Media Lab) will focus on research production on Mixed Reality and Heritage.

In conclusion, in response to the new context of postdigitality at museums and cultural heritage sites, the Designing Digital Heritage Network has begun the work of connecting researchers, designers, artists, and museum and heritage professionals developing work in this new age. Moving forward the DDHN will continue to offer a series of international seminars on the topic, and develop an online presence that will act as an information hub and archival repository for the emerging community. On the horizon, challenges and opportunities we see for the field include issues related to user accessibility, documentation and archiving of created works, and the iteration and implementation of best practices in postdigital design across research, pedagogy, and design production.

References

1. Parry, R.: Recoding the Museum: Digital Heritage and the Technologies of Change. Routledge, London and New York (2007)
2. Cameron, F., Kenderdine, S. (eds.): Theorizing Digital Cultural Heritage: A Critical Discourse. MIT Press, Cambridge (2007)
3. Din, H., Hecht, P. (eds.): The Digital Museum: A Think Guide. American Association of Museums, Washington, D.C. (2007)
4. Parry, R. (ed.): Museums in a Digital Age. Routledge, London and New York (2010)
5. Parry, R.: The end of the beginning: normativity in the postdigital museum. In: Museum Worlds: Advances in Research, vol. 1, pp. 24–39. Berghahn Books (2013)
6. Flanagan, M.: Critical Play: Radical Game Design. MIT Press, Cambridge (2013)
7. Bogost, I.: Persuasive Games: The Expressive Power of Videogames. MIT Press, Cambridge (2010)
8. Sicart, M.: The Ethics of Computer Games. MIT Press, Cambridge (2011)
9. Anderson, E.F., McLoughlin, L., Liarokapis, F., Peters, C., Petridis, P., de Freitas, S.: Developing serious games for cultural heritage: a state-of-the-art review. Virtual Real. **14**(4), 255–275 (2010)
10. Mortara, M., Catalano, C.E., Bellotti, F., Fiucci, G., Houry-Panchetti, M., Panagiotis, P.: Learning cultural heritage by serious games. J. Cult. Herit. **15**(3), 318–325 (2014)
11. Rouse, R., Engberg, M., JafariNaimi, N., Bolter, J.D.: Special section: understanding mixed reality. Digit. Creat. **26**(3–4), 175–227 (2015)
12. Vosinakis, S., Koutsabasis, P., Makris, D., Sagia, E.: A kinesthetic approach to digital heritage using leap motion: the Cycladic sculpture application. In: Proceedings of the IEEE Games and Virtual Worlds for Serious Applications (VS-Games) Conference (2016)
13. Barba, E., MacIntyre, B., Rouse, R., Bolter, J.: Thinking inside the box: meaning making in a handheld AR experience. In: Proceedings of the IEEE International Symposium on Mixed and Augmented Reality (2010)
14. Rouse, R.: MRx as a performative and theatrical stage. Digit. Creat. **26**(23–4), 193–206 (2015)
15. Tuan, Y.: Space and Place: The Perspective of Experience. University of Minnesota Press, Minneapolis and London (1977)
16. Benedikt, M.L.: To take hold of space: isovists and isovist fields. Environ. Plan. B **6**, 47–65 (1979)
17. Choi, Y.K.: The morphology of exploration and encounter in museum layouts. In: Complex Buildings: The Proceedings of the First International Symposium on Space Syntax, vol. 1, pp. 1–10 (1997)
18. Wineman, J.D., Peponis, J.: Constructing spatial meaning: spatial affordances in museum design. Environ. Behav. (2009). https://doi.org/10.1177/0013916509335534

19. Kozel, S.: Closer: Performance, Technologies, Phenomenology. MIT Press, Cambridge (2008)
20. Grusin, R.: Premediation: Affect and Mediality After 9/11. Palgrave Macmillan, New York (2010)
21. Hansen, M.B.N.: Bodies in Code: Interfaces with Digital Media. Routledge, New York (2006)
22. Bardzell, J., Bardzell, S.: What is "critical" about critical design? In: CHI 2013, Paris, France, 27 April–2 May 2013. ACM (2013)
23. Irani, L., Vertesi, J., Dourish, P., Philip, K., Grinter, R.: Postcolonial computing: a lens on design and development. In: CHI 2010, Atlanta, Georgia, USA, 10–15 April 2010. ACM (2010)
24. Engberg, M.: Augmented and mixed reality design for contested and challenging histories. In: MW17: Museums and the Web (2017)
25. Hayles, K.N.: How We Think: Digital Media and Contemporary Technogenesis. University of Chicago Press, Chicago (2012)
26. Burdick, A., Drucker, J., Lunenfeld, P., Presner, T., Schnapp, J.: Digital_Humanities. MIT Press, Cambridge (2012)
27. Bartscherer, T., Coover, R. (eds.): Switching Codes: Thinking Through Digital Technology in the Humanities and the Arts. University of Chicago Press, Chicago (2011)
28. Gold, M.K.: Debates in the Digital Humanities. University of Minnesota Press, Minneapolis (2012)
29. Leeker, M., Schipper, I., Beyes, T.: Performing the Digital. Transcript-Verlag, Germany (2017)
30. Burnett, C., Merchant, G., Pahl, K., Rowsell, J.: The (im)materiality of literacy. Discourse: Stud. Cult. Polit. Educ. **35**(1), 90–103 (2014)

4D Modelling in Cultural Heritage

Anastasios Doulamis[1]([⊠]), Nikolaos Doulamis[1],
Eftychios Protopapadakis[1], Athanasios Voulodimos[1],
and Marinos Ioannides[2]

[1] National Technical University of Athens, 15773 Zografou, Athens, Greece
{adoulam, ndoulam}@cs.ntua.gr,
{eftprot, thanosv}@mail.ntua.gr
[2] Cyprus University of Technology, 3036 Lemesos, Cyprus
marinos.ioannides@cut.ac.cy

Abstract. This chapter describes the main research outcomes and achievements of 4D modelling in cultural heritage. 4D digital modelling implies the creation of precise time-varying 3D reconstructions of cultural heritage objects to capture temporal geometric variations/distortions, i.e., a spatio-temporal assessment. The key research challenge for 4D modelling, was the data collection over heterogeneous unstructured web resources. Such "in the wild" data include outliers and significant noise, since they have not been created for 3D modelling and reconstruction purposes. In addition, GPS and geo-information is limited or non-existent. However, such data allow for a massive reconstruction of the content even for monuments that have been destroyed due to natural phenomena or humans' interventions. The key outcomes include (i) a Twitter-based 3D modelling of CH objects so as to reconstruct CH monuments and sites from unstructured image content, (ii) the development of a search engine and a (iii) recommendation system for different CH actors (curators, conservators, researchers), (iv) 3D reconstruction of the historic city of Calw in Germany, (v) the creation of a 3D virtual environment in real-time and (vi) launch of a 4D viewer enabling the easy handling of the 3D geometry plus the time. The results show the main innovation of the proposed 4D dimension, i.e., the time in precise modelling of the rich geometric content of the monuments.

Keywords: 4D modelling · Tangible cultural heritage
3D reconstruction, tweets analysis and recommendation systems

1 Introduction

Digitalizing cultural sites and objects and creating 3D digital models is an important task to preserve Cultural Heritage (CH) [1]. Among all CH resources, the outdoor large-scale cultural sites are mostly sensitive to weather conditions, natural phenomena (earthquakes, flooding, etc.), excavation procedures, and restoration protocols [2, 3]. This implies an imminent need for a spatio-temporal monitoring of those sites to identify regions of potential material degradation, unstable structuring conditions, localize spatial modifications and detect environmental damages [4]. A time varying 3D model should be developed to assess the spatial and temporal diversity of CH objects but again under a cost-effective framework able to be applied to large-scale sites [5].

© Springer International Publishing AG, part of Springer Nature 2018
M. Ioannides et al. (Eds.): Digital Cultural Heritage 2017, LNCS 10754, pp. 174–196, 2018.
https://doi.org/10.1007/978-3-319-75789-6_13

On the other hand, several actors are involved in CH community. (i) CH researchers and archaeologists can better document sites and objects (CH resources), relate their operational uses with past social and political structures, economical factors and past advances in science and technology [6]. (ii) Conservators can better assess the effect of different restoration methods on maintaining the structure and the nature of the cultural items, while simultaneously simulate and predict material degradation factors [7]. (iii) Curators can exploit the digital counterparts to design exhibitions and disseminate cultural knowledge to wide public [8]. (iv) Creative industries and Small Medium Enterprises (SME's) can build new services promoting Europe's culture worldwide, forging Europe's cohesion and integration through its diverse cultural legacy and boosting European economy. During the recent severe economic crisis, creative enterprises and tourism industries are some good examples of withstanding economic recession and (though slightly) contribute towards sustainable growth of Europe's economy [9]. (v) Finally, the simple visitors and the public can share unique cultural experiences on handling digital CH objects and navigating through a digital cultural world. Each of the aforementioned players has different needs regarding digital model parameters and scales. Therefore, we need to develop digital models able to respect all diverse requirements of the CH community users [10, 11].

On the other hand, the rapid progress in technology regarding visual capturing accompanying with respective progress in respective software tools has stimulated the generation of millions of image content being nowadays stored onto distributed and heterogeneous internet repositories, like Flickr, Picasa, Photosynth, etc. [12]. This content provides a unique opportunity for cultural heritage documentation, like for 3D reconstruction, through the fact that the overwhelming majority of these images have been captured for personal use and thus they are not suitable for such documentation process [13]. Thus, many of these images contain irrelevant material like views of other objects, or of the city instead of the monument itself [14]. Therefore, content-based filtering algorithms are necessary for an effective and computationally efficient e-documentation process that exploits the "wild Internet image collections".

In this book chapter, we recent achievements in 4D modelling (reconstruction) derived as a results of the four dimensional (4D) Cultural Heritage World Project, (4D-CH-World [15]), which aims at analyzing, designing, researching, developing and validating an innovative system integrating the latest advances in computer vision and learning, as well as, 3D modeling and virtual reality for the rapid and cost-effective 4D maps reconstruction in the wild for personal use, and support the aim of our European Commons and the digital libraries EUROPEANA and UNESCO Memory of the World (MoW) to build a sense of a shared European cultural history and identity.

Currently, 3D digital models are generated under a spatial-temporal independent framework. This means that digitalization information of common parts (surfaces) of an object is not exploited to digitalize similar surfaces of the same or other objects. Furthermore, the digitization process at a current time instance does not exploit results from reconstructions obtained at previous time instances. Last but not least, the scale dimension of each 3D model is generated differently for each users' category (e.g., CH researchers, curators, visitors) leading to the creation of independently scaled 3D models [11]. As an additional drawback, one can also refer to the lack of a semantic enrichment of the digital information to assist CH community users in their research and work. This makes 5D modelling too complex to be validated under real-life large-scale application domains.

Spatio-temporal dependency means that a 3D model at a current time instance is generated taking into account information of the same object from previous reconstructions (temporal dependency) and common surface properties (spatial dependency). Predictive refers to the ability to select regions of interest to be reconstructed differently by fusing/integrating selective 3D capturing methodologies with respect to surface features (material and geometric properties) and users' needs.

This chapter is organized as follows: The overall methodology and a summary of the key achievements is shown in Sect. 2. The techniques used to recognize objects from distributed multimedia repositories of CH objects are presented in Sect. 3. The 4D modelling search engine and recommendation system is discussed in Sect. 4. Section 5 deals with the 3D reconstruction of the historic city of Calw in Germany while the developed 4D viewer is shown in Sect. 6. Finally Sect. 7 draws the conclusions.

2   The Recent Achievements in 4D Modelling for Cultural Heritage

In the following we summarize the overall achievements of the 4D CH World project. The key achievements are organized into five main outcomes:

Groundbreaking photograph recognition and data sampling from data bases and web: A novel search engine has been developed to mine cultural data from distributed multimedia repositories such as Flickr, Picasa, and the web [16]. The search engine has been improved using tweets messages by initially proposing an algorithm which is able to identify key events from a pool of simple tweets messages [17]. The method supports two main phases; event detection from tweets and on the fly 3D reconstruction from the visual content embedded on common tweets clusters with respect to a cultural heritage object (an event) [17, 18]. For the first case, we propose a modification of existing document-based information retrieval metrics such as Term Frequency-Inverse Document Frequency (TF-IDF) criterion by including information regarding retweeting and number of followers. This new metric is then transformed in space and time adopting a Wavelet Transform. In the sequel, multi-assignment graph partitioning is proposed to localize clusters of events processing tweets messages.

Regarding the on-the fly 3D reconstruction, we proceed with outliers' removal, image clustering via a dense based scheme and key images extraction [16, 19]. The latter are selected so that they mostly represent all different orientations of CH monument at spherical coordinate system. The selected images are fed to SfM tool for 3D modelling. The fact that a small but representative number of images is selected severely reduce the time needed for reconstructing the 3D model.

Search and retrieval for further non digital content: We have investigated the combination of the aforementioned event detection approach from the Twitter on cultural heritage photos uploaded on this social medium [20]. In particular, we have analyzed tweet messages based on their textual information. Then, the embedded visual content is extracted to build up 3D CH models that represent high level semantics of the images. These high level semantic information is exploited for searching and retrieving non-digital content. The models are evolved in time and thus the four dimension is added.

In addition, a novel content-based recommendation system of CH objects was developed [21]. The system dynamically models end-users preferences, creating common profiles and then rank and filter media information exploiting both visual similarities and user's profiles. Relevance feedback mechanisms are exploited for the automatic profile estimation [22–24]. Relevance feedback is a method for dynamically updating user's preferences according to a set of relevant/irrelevant data selected from the user based on user's interaction [25–27].

City area and buildings reconstruction using acquired data: Several photogrammetric and computer vision methods are investigated for city modelling and buildings reconstruction [28, 29]. The mediaeval city of Calw in Germany has been selected for demonstration of the proposed 3D modelling methods. We have reconstruct a major part of the city of Calw and embed these reconstructions on the 4D Viewer [30]. The reconstruction faces not only 3D geometry of the buildings but also time evolution.

Development of appropriate simulation model: The 4D viewer [31] supports 4D reconstructions, that is, 3D geometry plus the time. The viewer has been tested at Calw case. It has been supported by Virtual Reality and Augmented Reality functionalities. The users are able to navigate through time for selected CH objects, see semantic information and tags assigned to these objects and relate these assignments with different historic periods, manipulate the CH at different angles and views with respect to their needs and information preferences [32].

Depiction of future urban structures: Adeep learning algorithm has been developed through the exploitation of convolutional neural networks. The algorithm receives big volumes of LiDAR data of an urban region and classify the structures of the buildings and the type of the material used [33]. Urban buildings consist an integral part of cultural heritage. They shape the sense of belonging somewhere, of social traditions, of cultural identity of a history spanning centuries. Therefore, automatic detection and recognition of specific types of urban buildings is extremely important for disseminating cultural heritage to general audience.

3   Recognition and 3D Reconstruction of CH Photos from Distributed Multimedia Repositories

In this section, we deal with the recognition and 3D reconstruction of photos from distributed multimedia repositories. The key concept is to 3D reconstruct CH monuments and buildings based on the huge amount of media information found over the web. The main challenge, however, in this case, is the unstructured nature of the content which have been derived from applications different than for 3D modelling. Such a tool can stimulate a massive 3D reconstruction of CH objects of interest to face (i) looting, (ii) mankind destructions (war, fire) and (iii) environmental defects on the objects (earthquakes) [34]. We consider in the wild (unstructured) 3D reconstruction on two different multimedia repositories; the first refers to tweets messages (see Sect. 3.1) while the second on the web-based unstructured multimedia tools (see Sect. 3.2).

3.1   3D Modelling of Images from Tweets' Messages

3D reconstruction of a CH asset from images located on the Twitter is a research challenging process since Twitter images are collected for purposes different than digitization [17]. Therefore, they are (i) incomplete in the sense that several parts of the CH objects are missing, (ii) presents a lot of noise (e.g., existence of other objects), (iii) have been captured from quite different conditions in the sense of resolution, image calibration and registration [17, 20].

To reconstruct the images from tweets messages, we need first to introduce a novel event detection algorithm. This algorithm analyzes tweets signals and through the use of apt characterization metrics identifies the events. Events detection acts as a medium to refine visual information of tweets messages constrained upon textual properties. Finally, tweets of similar content are organized together to create 3D models by "structuring" image content of the same object/place. 3D models are created by initially filtering the image content through suitable features and finding correspondences between similar images.

For an efficient tweet event detection algorithm, text characterization is required. Text characterization is accomplished through the extraction of textual features that categorize the significance of a word in tweets. The information theoretic metrics used for textually characterizing a document, such as Term Frequency-Inverse Document Frequency (TF-IDF) metric [35] or distributional features [36], are not suitable for the tweets case. Tweets are very short messages (no more than 140 characters), leading to statistical inaccuracies in estimating traditional document metrics over tweet posts. In addition, Twitter is distinguished from similar websites by some key features. Users may subscribe to other users' tweets – this is known as following and subscribers are called followers. Moreover, Twitter has the re-tweet feature that gives users the ability to forward an interesting tweet to their followers. For all these reasons, new metrics are required to model tweet posts.

In our research, we have introduced three information theoretic metrics for measuring the importance of a word on a tweet post. These three metrics are described in details and mathematical formulation in [17]. The first metric, called Conditional Word Tweet Frequency (CWTF), we consider as a document the collection of tweets extracted over the k-th time interval and as a corpus of documents the assembly of tweets over the p previous time intervals. The main difference of CWTF from the classical description of TF is that here we count the number of tweets that contain a specific word within the current examined time interval k instead of counting the number of times that a word appears within a document. That is, all tweets that contain the specific word contribute the same to the calculation of CWTF.

The second metric, called Word Tweet Frequency (WTF), considers the frequency of appearance of the specific word w in the tweets. Finally, the third metric, called Weighted Conditional Word Tweet Frequency (WCWTF) compensates the aforementioned metric with respect to the significance of a tweet as expressed either by the number of followers or by the number of re-tweets it produces. The number of followers indicates the credibility of the author of the tweet, which also implies credibility for the textual information of the respective tweet post. The number of re-tweets is a metric for ranking the importance of the semantic information (textual content) posted by the tweet.

A wavelet transformation is the exploited to localize the signals both in time and in frequency domain. This is important since tweets are not synchronized messages. At the end, a graph-cut approach is exploited to extract the events, exploiting as similarity distance the cross correlation criterion since this can directly express the similarity of two feature vectors being invariant in scale and translation. Then, clustering is modeled as a graph partitioning problem, by adopting an optimal methodology that cuts the graph into clusters so that intra-cluster elements present the maximum coherence, while the inter-cluster elements the minimum one. In this graph partitioning problem, we contribute by allowing for a multi-assignment clustering since, in our context, one word can belong to several clusters (events). This is achieved by introducing a modification of the spectral clustering algorithm that handles multi-assignment clustering problems. Finally, tweets of similar content are organized together to create 3D models by "structuring" image content of the same object/place. 3D models are created by initially filtering the image content through suitable features and finding correspondences between similar images.

Figure 1 shows the performance of the three introduced information theoretic metrics as regards the precision and recall values. The Fig. 1 evaluates the performance when using wavelet transform or not. As we can see, the third information theoretic metric outperforms the other two ones.

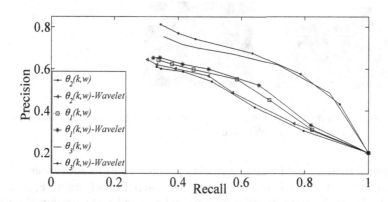

Fig. 1. Precision-recall curve of the three proposed metrics using both wavelet and non-wavelet representation (Figure created by the authors and cited in [17]).

3.2 3D Modelling of Images from Distributed Web-Based Multimedia Repositories

Nowadays, there are available extremely large collections of images and videos, most of them located on distributed and heterogeneous platforms over the web. The proliferation of billions of shared photos has outpaced the current technology for browsing such collections and entails the necessity for developing new efficient image retrieval techniques.

The presented approach takes into account both images metadata description, including geo-location and user generated tags, and visual information. It exploits image metadata to retrieve an initial set of images and then it uses visual information to perform a two-step unsupervised image clustering. Based on the assumption that the initial retrieved set will contain sufficient number of images depicting the same object, this algorithm needs neither a priori knowledge of the retrieved dataset nor a reference image to compute visual similarities and perform clustering [14, 19].

Images' visual information is encoding through the usage of local descriptors such as the ORB [37]. Then, a DBSCAN [38] dense-based clustering scheme is employed to find out compact image points and remove the outliers. Initially a set of images is retrieved by using text query. This initial set contains a lot of outliers that have to be removed. After the computation of local descriptors and the construction of the similarity matrix, DBSCAN algorithm takes care of this step and removes the most prominent outliers. We also introduce a modification of the DBSCAN, called CSP, to better reply on the problem of image clustering in such an unstructured environment. Finally, through spectral clustering, two sets of images that contain the rear and the front view of the monument, are being constructed.

Figure 2 shows the location of the ORB extracted image features and the dense of the outliers. This way, we are able to remove the outliers and improve the 3D reconstruction performance.

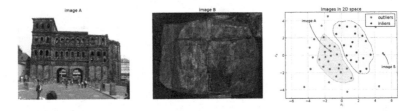

Fig. 2. Representation of images in a 2-dimensional space and depiction of image clusters and outliers (Figure created by the authors and cited in [14]).

Figure 3 presents the F1-score regarding partitioning performance using the two different proposed approaches as for outliers' removal (DBSCAN and CSP) along with the center-based clustering algorithm k-means and density-based algorithm Mean Shift. Both the proposed approaches outperform k-means and Mean-Shift with the CSP behaving better than the conventional DBSCAN, especially for a large number of image outliers. The results have been obtained by averaging F1 scores on cultural heritage objects of our "wild" image dataset.

Finally, Fig. 4 shows the gradual 3D reconstruction performance of a historic monument in Germany, the Porta Nigra. We can see that a rough 3D reconstruction can be achieved even when a very small number of images have been selected.

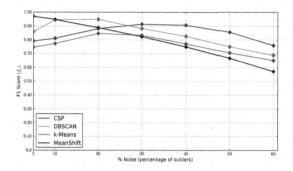

Fig. 3. The effect of a different number of clustering algorithms on outliers' removal performance (Figure created by the authors and cited in [14]).

Fig. 4. 3D reconstruction of rear and front view sides of Porta Nigra. For this reconstruction 30 images were used that contained 20% of outliers (Figure created by the authors and cited in [14]).

4 The 4D Modelling Search Engine

4.1 Searching Unstructured Content

Our approach for cost-effective space and time reconstruction of tangible Cultural Heritage objects, involves an entire workflow of computer vision, photogrammetry, and 3D reconstruction, semantic enrichment, indexing and searching techniques. The 4Ds reconstruction approach presented in the current research work is innovative in the sense that it combines advanced techniques from Computer Vision, Photogrammetry, 3D representation and semantic representation in order to produce feasible and cost-effective 4D views of Digital Cultural Heritage content that exists 'in the wild' [4, 5].

The pipeline of the 4D Reconstruction method proposed in this paper consists of the following processes, which are shown in Fig. 5.

The Search engine. It is the entry point of the 4D Reconstruction workflow and is responsible for acquiring visual and textual content 'in the wild', i.e. from publicly available online sources, as well as for metadata capturing. The results of the search engine form the reconstruction data set that will capture the content of Cultural Heritage through space and time.

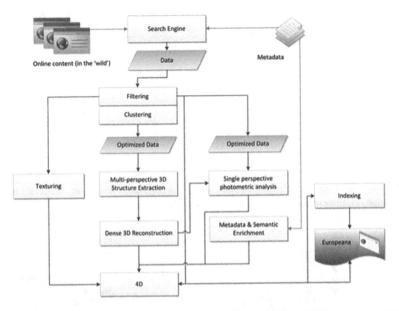

Fig. 5. The 4D reconstruction workflow of Digital Cultural Heritage (Figure created by the authors).

The Filtering and Clustering engines are responsible for analyzing the visual content of 2D images and for applying advanced Computer Vision filtering and clustering algorithms that will optimize the acquired data set. Images found 'in the wild' and especially in web search engines, are not accurate. The optimization goals of those engines are twofold: (a) the acquisition of multiple-perspectives' 2D content and (b) the identification of different lightning conditions of the same cultural object. Filter-optimized and cluster-optimized data are directed towards the 3D Reconstruction and Photometric engines respectively [39, 40].

The 3D Structure Extraction engine employs algorithms for 3D structure extraction from 2D images based on multiple perspectives of the same cultural object. These perspectives have been identified by the clustering engine. The goal of the 3D Structure Extraction Engines is to produce dense clouds of 3D points that will be used in the dense 3D Reconstruction engine.

4.2   The Recommendation Engine

The main purpose of the recommendation engine is to further refine the retrievals obtained using various CBIR techniques as the ones presented in Sect. 4.1. The reason behind the proposed mechanism lies in the need of multiple uses of the same data sets in different applications (e.g. subsets of the same data can be used for 3D reconstruction, touristic promotion, books publication, etc.). An image filtering scheme for images of cultural interest has been developed [21]. The model utilize a semi-supervised approach for the creation of an appropriate distance learning metric, which is used for the filtering. User's feedback is involved only for a minor set of data, defined using optics algorithm and sparse modelling representative selection. Such approach facilitates the refinement of image data sets collected online from depositories, such Flickr, always under the scope of the end user needs.

The meta-filtering approach is based on a total ranking approach, for every available image x_j, described by the following equation:

$$r_j = \sum_{\substack{i=1 \\ i \neq j}}^{|P|} \frac{1}{w_i^p d_A(x_i, x_j)} + \sum_{\substack{i=1 \\ i \neq j}}^{|N|} \frac{1}{w_i^n d_A(x_i, x_j)} \tag{1}$$

where r_j is the overall ranking score for an image j, given its feature vector x_j, $|P|$ and $|N|$ denotes the size of user annotated images as positive and negative to current search respectively, $w_i^p (w_i^n)$ is a weight value for the importance of the i-th annotated positively (negatively) image, and $d_A(x_i, x_j)$ is a distance metric defined both on user's annotated and the non-annotated images of the data set.

For any image points, we need to take the distance of them. Similar to the approach of [41], the distance metric learning (DML) problem is to learn an optimal A from a collection of data points C on a vector space R^m together with a set of similar pairwise constraints S and a set of dissimilar pairwise constraints D. Both sets of constraints should be provided by the user as a relevance feedback in order to guide the problem to an acceptable solution. The problem formulation is stated as [41]:

$$\min_A t + \gamma_s tr(A \cdot S) - \gamma_d tr(A \cdot S)$$
$$s.t. \ tr(XLX^T A) \leq t \tag{2}$$
$$A \in S_+$$

Thus, the DML problem has been approached as a semi-definite problem (SDP), which can be solved efficiently with global optimum using existing convex optimization packages.

The meta-filtering approach is based on three main phases. The first stage of the methodology aims at the detection of representative samples and its annotation as relevant or irrelevant by the user. The second stage involves the distance metric learning according to the user defined relevance sets. The final stage ranks the rest of the images using both similarity and dissimilarity rankings based on the previously stated distance metric.

The proposed methodology was applied in three cultural monuments. These monuments were Knossos, Porta Nigra and Fontana dei Quatro Fummi (see Fig. 6). For every monument, four cases of image filtering are employed. The filtering scenarios can briefly described as: (a) need for exterior images of the monument, (b) special attributes, (c) people around the monument and (d) various images (e.g. animal pictures, night sky, signs, etc.). In every scenario the relevant images are taken from one category and the non-relevant from the rest three in order to construct the

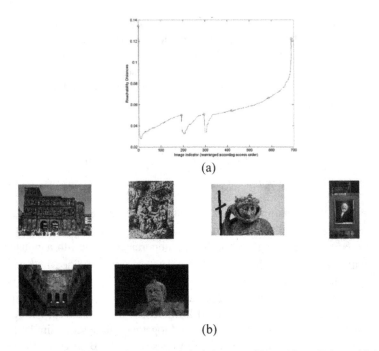

(a)

(b)

Fig. 6. (a) Optics algorithm results on the original data set of Porta Nigra. Points with 'o' mark the separation between sub-clusters. (b) The corresponding images of the marked points (Figure created by the authors and cited in [21]).

pairwise constraints shown in Eq. (2). In every case the ratio was 6 relevant to 18 irrelevant. Leading to user feedback of 24 images in total.

Finally, in Fig. 7, we present the final marking and adaptation after the feedback from the users. The results are obtained using both likes and dislikes of the users on images regarding their preferences and information needs. A predefined number of images with the higher values are retrieved as relevant. Dashed line indicates minimum value among these images.

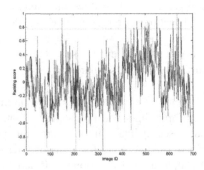

Fig. 7. Final ranking score using both accordance and discordance to the user's selection. A predefined number of images with the higher values are retrieved as relevant. Dashed line indicates minimum value among these images.

5   3D Reconstruction of the History City of Calw in Germany

The testbed area selected is the historical center of the city of Calw, a frequently visited area located 35 km southwest of Stuttgart (Germany), close to the northern part of the Black Forest (see Fig. 8). The old city counts with a broad history and rich cultural heritage. Among the 15th and 17th centuries, Calw was a commercial center of wood dissemination and processing, cloth production and salt trade, becoming an urban pole which was more important than Stuttgart, the real capital of the Federal State Baden-Württemberg, which is the third most extended and populated region (of sixteen) of Germany.

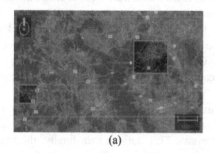
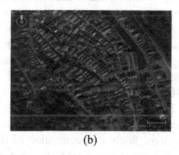

(a)   (b)

Fig. 8. (a) Location of the historical center of Calw relative to Stuttgart and (b) aerial perspective of this area.

The rich cultural heritage of Calw explains the existence of huge amounts of images, sketches, plans, drawings and maps. The Calw City Archive has several collections with high historical value, like the sketches, plans and drawings dating back to the 10th and 11th centuries, and some photos captured in the middle of the 19th century. In total, more than 3,500 photos between the years 1860 and 2014 have been offered in addition to many plans of the old town, sketches and paintings dating back to the early medieval ages (from 1,100 onwards). Furthermore, the city is still continuously visited and photographed by tourists, allowing to meet thousands of images in Open Access Image Repositories (OAIR) accessible online such as on Flickr, Picasa or Panoramio [28–30].

For acquisition of data, Leica ScanStation P20 (TLS system) and a photo camera Nikon D800E, both owned by the Institute für Photogrammetrie (IFP), were used. Additionally, several aerial images supplied by the Landesamt für Geoinformation und Landentwicklung of Baden-Württemberg (LGL-BW) were processed to obtain a complementary photogrammetric point cloud for the roof buildings (see Fig. 3). Regarding to the software was used: (a) Leica Cyclone for managing, registration, and modeling point cloud; (b) Adobe Photoshop for texture preparation, and (c) Trimble SketchUp for texture wrapping onto the 3D models.

This model scans 360° in horizontal and 270 in vertical direction around the fixed scan station. The maximum measuring range is of 120 m, with a frequency up to 1 million points per second. The Leica Scan Station P20 can register large datasets, including maps of intensity values and RGB images. The most representative technical parameters of this TLS model can be found on its product specifications.

For image capturing, the photo camera used was the Ricoh GXR, a digital compact camera of the Japanese Ricoh Company. This model has interchangeable units, each housing a lens, sensor and image processing engine. Each unit has features optimized for different purposes and environments. The lens used was a Carl Zeiss Lens Biogon 2.8/21 ZM. The images were captured with infinite focal length and using the function mode dial A (aperture priority), which leads to adjust the shutter speed for getting an optimal time exposure of the images.

Two types of images were used: (a) close-range, and (b) aerial images. Both imagery data were used for covering some deficiencies shown in the TLS point cloud and for obtaining additional information such as related to textures. Close-range images were captured from different positions at ground level.

Additionally, six aerial images of the historical center of Calw city were used for reconstructing the roof of the church, where TLS data could not be obtained. These images were supplied by the Landesamt fur Geoinformation und Landentwicklung of Baden-Württemberg (LGL-BW) and were captured with a ground sampling distance of 10 cm.

The different data sources (laser and image data) are integrated into a unique coordinate system in a procedure called registration. This procedure is performed into two steps: firstly the registration of the successive TLS stations and, finally, the registration are included with the photogrammetric point clouds. TLS scan stations are merged and registered into a unique point cloud referred into a local coordinate system. However, this point cloud shows some gaps such in the roof areas. Thus, a complete reconstruction of the building is not feasible due to missing data. A detailed description of the point clouds is shown in Fig. 9.

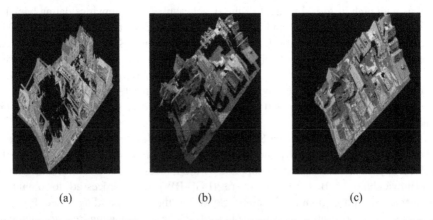

(a)   (b)   (c)

Fig. 9. Point cloud obtained by means of (a) TLS and (b) aerial photogrammetry, and (c) both merged and registered (Figure created by the authors and cited in [29, 30]).

Roof area can be reconstructed using aerial images. For this, a point cloud derived from these aerial images is created. SURE software, developed by the IFP, is used to extract geospatial information from aerial images with a remarkable level of overlap. Software performance is based on the algorithm called Semi Global Matching. Two steps are carried out: (a) determining the image orientation manually or automatically, and followed with a Bundle Block Adjustment and (b) applying Dense Image Matching algorithm to retrieve geospatial information from each single overlapped pixel, based on the first step.

A system of constraints is established by means of equivalent tie-points in the different point clouds, which are partially overlapped. The Iterative Closest Point (ICP) algorithm, implemented in the used software, performs rigid registration for at least two given laser point clouds which already partially aligned to merge. Basically, two steps are carried out: (a) to create a pairing between the same scanned points from different scan stations, and (b) to compute rigid registration for matching these points and minimizing the distances in between (see Fig. 10). Some images of the final 3D model reconstructed are exposed in Figs. 11 and 12. From both figures, we can see the high detailed model and the accuracy achieved. More specifically, Fig. 11 presents the 3D model of the protestant church of St. Peter and Paul and Fig. 12 a block of some characteristic buildings of the town.

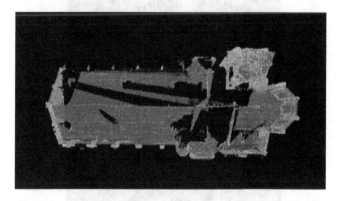

Fig. 10. Top overview of the obtained TLS point cloud. Internal black gaps correspond to missing data (Figures created by the authors and cited in [29, 30]).

6 The 4D Viewer

6.1 Modelling for 3D Realtime and VR Environments Production Pipeline

The results of a computer generated 3D model through SfM and/or dense matching is bound to the quality and quantity of the source images available. It reflects the time epoch for which all images were taken. Missing features of a model as well as anomalies in the resulting 3D model can be substituted through a camera matched, manual modelling approach. This technique also allows the 3D reconstructions using historic photos. However, the results obtained might be subjective and are depending on the operator's personal perception and his skills in 3D modelling. Nevertheless a

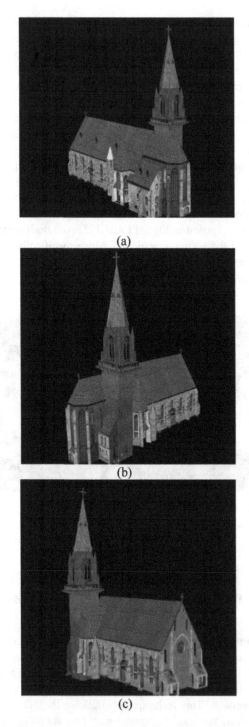

(a)

(b)

(c)

Fig. 11. Different viewpoints on the 3D photorealistic model of the church (Figure created by the authors).

Fig. 12. 3D building model obtained in a certain area surveyed.

comparison between a SfM calculated structure and the para-metrical model can lead to an adequate accuracy level. As once defined by Paul Debevec (1996) [42], an expert of computer vision, his interpretation of photogrammetry is as follows: "A method for interactively recovering 3D models and camera positions from photographs." [42].

The city of Calw in Germany has been chosen as a test site for 3D reconstruction where different approaches were applied to model the central square of the settlement in different time settings (see Sect. 5). According to the project plan not only the central square of the town, but also the somewhat larger historical settlement core was modeled.

The results will be made accessible in an interactive virtual 3D realtime environment, powered by a game engine allowing the user to walk or fly-through the 3D model of the settlement and retrieve additional information on places and buildings on his demand. Further the switch into different time periods of the environment or a building will be possible depending on the accuracy and quantity of the source material which is necessary to model out the complete set of structures [31]. In Fig. 13, we show some of the 3D reconstruction results.

In order to automate the process of image rectification one could also use the calculated camera positions generated by a SfM processing and therefore bypass the manual alignment of the vanishing points as described above, eliminating subjective factors in the rectification process. This however requires more than one view to allow for the simultaneous image data processing in a bundle block adjustment.

Fig. 13. Historical image and the resulting 3D model of the City Hall of Calw (Figure created by the authors and cited in [29]).

To illustrate this process, we set up a test scene consisting a 3D model of the Hermann-Hesse Birthplace building, which was previously constructed through a manual camera match approach, from which several rendered images from different viewpoints were taken to provide a source for the SfM model generation. Any SfM sofware, such as VisualSfM, will deliver the camera positions, orientations and a sparse 3D model, which can be reimported to a 3D modelling program (e.g. Autodesk 3Ds Max). Inside the 3D modelling program one of the reconstructed camera views was chosen to verify the matching of the perspective with the background image, which served as a template for a newly constructed geometry, representing the outlines of the object (house). Since the constructed geometry, matched seamlessly with the vanishing points of the projected background image it can be confirmed that the camera match calculated from the SfM procedure is adequate for this purpose. An example of the camera setup is shown in Fig. 14.

Fig. 14. Set-up with the calculated camera position and the 3D Model of Hermann Hesses Birthplace (Figure created by the authors and cited in [29]).

Within the photogrammetric and GIS community some standard data formats have established. For semantic building and city models the OGC standard CityGML is well-known. However, the computer graphics community deals with completely different data formats, such as Collada or 3Ds max. Suitable data conversion therefore have to be performed to fuse information given by modelling exports with photogrammetric processing steps. Figure 15 exemplarily shows the Hermann Hesse birthplace, which has been selected for testing purposes and has been simplified as input for the reconstruction algorithm. Top left depicts the textured model of the building, top right the corresponding point cloud. The reconstructed façade is shown on the bottom left and the suggested completion of the model in CityGML is depicted on the bottom right.

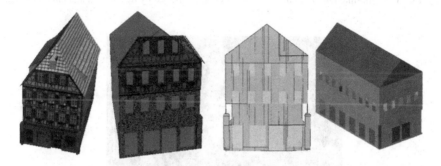

Fig. 15. From Left to Right: Textured model of the Hermann Hesse birthplace, simplified CityGML model with an overlying point cloud, reconstructed primitives, bottom right: grammar based completion (Figure created by the authors).

6.2 The 4D Viewer

The main role of a 4D viewer is to depict not only the 3D geometry of a CH asset but also its evolution in time. For this reason, time parameters have been added in the viewer. The user can also manage different angles of a monument and different cameras views. Such extensibility has a huge impact in the field of cultural heritage especially for city views and city momentums where big data manipulation over the web can be easily controlled by any end user using parameters to scroll through (i) time and (ii) 3D object manipulation [43]. This is also very important in searching CH content taking into account time constraints. For instance, image a monument under different weather conditions or its impact on different climate phenomena and material decay factors.

On the bottom of the screen a slider is provided which allows the user to move through different time periods accompanied with the images of the monument in the current period [44]. Sliding over the images the user can navigate in time and across different parts of the model (Fig. 16). The slice tool enables the user to view intersection of the reconstructed model with the help of a slicing plane (Fig. 17). This provides an insight to the interior construction of the model.

Fig. 16. The time-line feature in the VR viewer (Figure created by the authors and cited in [44]).

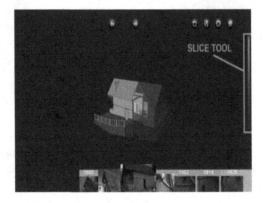

Fig. 17. The slice tool in the VR viewer (Figure created by the authors and cited in [44]).

7   Conclusions

Time dimension is a crucial part of a precise 3D reconstruction. This is especially critical for outdoor CH monuments that undergo natural decay due to environmental phenomena and disasters. 3D modelling a CH object in time independently is a process which is time consuming, tedious and of great effort. This is mainly due to the fact that most of the geometric structures of a monument remains intact through time. To overcome this issues, in this chapter we investigate innovative aspects regarding 4D modelling of cultural heritage items that is, 3D geometrically reconstruction plus the time.

Our research focuses on unstructured visual items collected from distributed multimedia repositories located over the web or from visual content uploaded on the short tweet posts. For the first case, we implement a clustering algorithm enabling the removal of the outliers. For the second case, we develop an event detection scheme from the tweets messages and then we apply an image clustering to find the most representative data to trigger a computationally efficient 3D reconstruction through time. A search engine is developed accompanying with a recommendation system.

3D modelling is evaluated on a historic German city, that is, of Calw. The results derived are of high resolution and reconstruction accuracy. The 3D models are embedded on a 4D viewer the key functionality of which is the time slide. This allows for the users to navigate through time on content of interest.

Acknowledgement. This work is supported by the FP7 project: Four Dimensional Cultural Heritage World (4D CH World) funded by European Union under the grant agreement 324523 and the H0202 project: Transforming Intangible Folkloric Performing Arts into Tangible Choreographic Digital Objects (TERPSICHORE) funded by RISE European Union programme under the grant agreement 691218.

References

1. Pavlidis, G., Koutsoudis, A., Arnaoutoglou, F., Tsioukas, V., Chamzas, C.: Methods for 3D digitization of cultural heritage. J. Cult. Herit. **8**(1), 93–98 (2007)
2. Bond, A., Langstaff, L., Baxter, R., Kofoed, H.G.W.J., Lisitzin, K., Lundström, S.: Dealing with the cultural heritage aspect of environmental impact assessment in Europe. Impact Assess. Project Apprais. **22**(1), 37–45 (2004)
3. Adger, W.N., Barnett, J., Brown, K., Marshall, N., O'Brien, K.: Cultural dimensions of climate change impacts and adaptation. Nat. Climate Chang. **3**(2), 1666 (2012)
4. Kyriakaki, G., Doulamis, A., Doulamis, N., Ioannides, M., Makantasis, K., Protopapadakis, E., Hadjiprocopis, A., Wenzel, K., Fritsch, D., Klein, M., Weinlinger, G.: 4D reconstruction of tangible cultural heritage objects from web-retrieved images. Int. J. Herit. Digit. Era **3**(2), 431–452 (2014)
5. Ioannides, M., Hadjiprocopis, A., Doulamis, N., Doulamis, A., Protopapadakis, E., Makantasis, K., Santos, P., Fellner, D., Stork, A., Balet, O., Julien, M.J., Weinlinger, G., Johnson, P.S., Klein, M., Fritsch, D.: Reconstruction using multi-images available under open access. In: ISPRS Annals of Photogrammetry, Remote Sensing and Spatial Information Sciences, Strasbourg, (1), pp. 169–174, 2–6 September 2013
6. Gomes, L., Pereira Bellon, O.R., Silva, L.: 3D reconstruction methods for digital preservation of cultural heritage: a survey. Pattern Recogn. Lett. **50**, 3–14 (2014)
7. Ene, D., Radvan, R.: Digital model for cultural heritage conservation status evaluation. In: 4th International Conference on Developments in eSystems Engineering, DeSE, pp. 627–631 (2011)
8. Kitamura, K.: Common software for digital exhibition of Japanese cultural heritage in literature. In: International Conference on Culture and Computing, Culture and Computing, 6680347, pp. 137–138 (2013)
9. Bjerke, B., Karlsson, M.: Social Entrepreneurship: To Act as if and Make a Difference. Edward Elgar Publishing, Cheltenham (2013)
10. Doulamis, A., Soile, S., Doulamis, N., Chrisouli, C., Grammalidis, N., Dimitropoulos, K., Manesis, C., Potsiou, C., Ioannidis, C.: Selective 4D modelling framework for spatial-temporal land information management system. In: Proceedings of SPIE - The International Society for Optical Engineering, Paphos, Cyprus, vol. 9535 (2015)
11. Doulamis, A., Doulamis, N., Ioannidis, C., Chrysouli, C., Grammalidis, N., Dimitropoulos, K., Potsiou, C., Stathopouloua, E.K., Ioannides, M.: 5D modelling: an efficient approach for creating spatiotemporal predictive 3D maps of large-scale cultural resources. In: ISPRS Annals of the Photogrammetry, Remote Sensing and Spatial Information Sciences, Taipei, Taiwan, vol. 2(5), p. 61 (2015)

12. Doulamis, N., Doulamis, A., Varvarigou, T.: Adaptive algorithms for interactive multimedia. IEEE Multimedia Mag. **10**(4), 38–47 (2003)
13. Avrithis, Y.S., Doulamis, N.D., Doulamis, A.D., Kollias, S.D.: Efficient content representation in MPEG video databases. In: Proceedings of IEEE International Workshop on Content based Access Interactive Video Libraries in Conjunction with the IEEE Computer Vision and Pattern Recognition Conference (CVPR), Santa Barbara, CA, USA, pp. 91–95, June 1998
14. Makantasis, K., Doulamis, A., Doulamis, N., Ioannides, M.: In the wild image retrieval and clustering for 3D cultural heritage landmarks reconstruction. Multimedia Tools Appl. **75**(7), 3593–3629 (2016)
15. Doulamis, A., Ioannides, M., Doulamis, N., Hadjiprocopis, A., Fritsch, D., Balet, O., Julien, M., Protopapadakis, E., Makantasis, K., Weinlinger, G., Johnsons, P.S., Klein, M., Fellner, D., Stork, A., Santos, P.: 4D reconstruction of the past. In: Proceedings of SPIE - The International Society for Optical Engineering, vol. 8795, p. 87950J (2013)
16. Ntalianis, K., Doulamis, N.: An automatic event-complementing human life summarization scheme based on a social computing method over social media content. Multimedia Tools Appl. **75**(22), 15123–15149 (2016)
17. Doulamis, N.D., Doulamis, A.D., Kokkinos, P., Varvarigos, E.: Event detection in Twitter microblogging. IEEE Trans. Cybern. **46**(12), 2810–2824 (2016)
18. Ntalianis, K., Mastorakis, N., Doulamis, A., Tomaras, P.: Social media video collection summarization based on social graph user interactions. In: Recent Advances In Knowledge Engineering And Systems Science, pp. 162–167 (2013)
19. Makantasis, K., Doulamis, A., Doulamis, N.: A non-parametric unsupervised approach for content based image retrieval and clustering. In: Proceedings of the 4th ACM International Workshop on Analysis and Retrieval of Tracked Events and Motion in Imagery Stream in Conjunction with ACM Multimedia, Barcelona, pp. 33–40, October 2013
20. Doulamis, A., Katsaros, G.: 3D modelling of cultural heritage objects from photos posted over the Twitter. In: IEEE International Conference on Imaging Systems and Techniques (IST), Chania, Crete, October 2016
21. Protopapadakis, E., Doulamis, A., Matsatsinis, N.: Semi-supervised image meta-filtering in cultural heritage applications. In: Ioannides, M., Magnenat-Thalmann, N., Fink, E., Žarnić, R., Yen, A.-Y., Quak, E. (eds.) EuroMed 2014. LNCS, vol. 8740, pp. 102–110. Springer, Cham (2014). https://doi.org/10.1007/978-3-319-13695-0_10
22. Yiakoumettis, C., Doulamis, N., Miaoulis, G., Ghazanfarpour, D.: Active learning of user's preferences estimation towards a personalized 3D navigation of geo-referenced scenes. GeoInformatica **18**(1), 27–62 (2014)
23. Doulamis, N., Yiakoumettis, C., Miaoulis, G., Protopapadakis, E.: A constraint inductive learning-spectral clustering methodology for personalized 3D navigation. In: Bebis, G., et al. (eds.) ISVC 2013. LNCS, vol. 8034, pp. 108–117. Springer, Heidelberg (2013). https://doi.org/10.1007/978-3-642-41939-3_11
24. Doulamis, N., Yiakoumettis, C., Miaoulis, G.: Personalised 3D navigation and understanding of geo-referenced scenes. In: IEEE 14th International Symposium on a World of Wireless, Mobile and Multimedia Networks, WoWMoM 2013, Spain, 4–7 June 2013
25. Rui, Y., Huang, T.S., Ortega, M., Mehrotra, S.: Relevance feedback: a power tool for interactive content-based image retrieval. IEEE Trans. Circuits Syst. Video Technol. **8**(5), 644–655 (1998)
26. Salton, G., Buckley, C.: Improving retrieval performance by relevance feedback. Read. Inf. Retr. **24**(5), 355–363 (1997)

27. Doulamis, N., Doulamis, A.: Evaluation of relevance feedback schemes in content-based in retrieval systems. Sig. Process. Image Commun. **21**(4), 334–357 (2006)

28. Fritsch, D., Klein, M.: 3D preservation of buildings – reconstructing the past. Multimedia Tools Appl. 1–18 (2017). article in press

29. Voulodimos, A., Doulamis, N., Fritsch, D., Makantasis, K., Doulamis, A., Klein, M.: Four-dimensional reconstruction of cultural heritage sites based on photogrammetry and clustering. J. Electron. Imaging **26**(1), 011013 (2017)

30. Balsa-Barreiro, J., Fritsch, D.: Generation of 3D/4D photorealistic building models. The testbed area for *4D Cultural Heritage World* project: the historical center of Calw (Germany). In: Bebis, G., et al. (eds.) ISVC 2015. LNCS, vol. 9474, pp. 361–372. Springer, Cham (2015). https://doi.org/10.1007/978-3-319-27857-5_33

31. Doulamis, A., Doulamis, N., Makantasis, K., Klein, M.: A 4D virtual/augmented reality viewer exploiting unstructured web-based image data. In: 10th International Conference on Computer Vision, Theory and Applications, VISAPP, Berlin, March 2015

32. Doulamis, N., Yiakoumettis, C., Miaoulis, G.: On-line spectral learning in exploring 3D large scale geo-referred scenes. In: Ioannides, M., Fritsch, D., Leissner, J., Davies, R., Remondino, F., Caffo, R. (eds.) EuroMed 2012. LNCS, vol. 7616, pp. 109–118. Springer, Heidelberg (2012). https://doi.org/10.1007/978-3-642-34234-9_11

33. Maltezos, E., Doulamis, A., Ioannidis, C.: Improving the visualisation of 3D textured models via shadow detection and removal. In: 9th IEEE International Conference on Virtual Worlds and Games for Serious Applications (VS-Games), Athens, Greece, September 2017

34. Kyriakaki, G., Doulamis, N.: Metadata framework for long-term preservation of digital cultural experiences: the 'Viopolis' case. In: Proceedings of the 11th International Conference on Applications of Electrical and Computer Engineering, Athens, Greece, May 2013

35. Aizawa, A.: The feature quantity: an information theoretic perspective of TFIDF-like measures. In: ACM SIGIR 2000, pp. 104–111 (2000)

36. Xue, X.B., Zhou, Z.H.: Distributional features for text categorization. IEEE Trans. Knowl. Data Eng. **21**(3), 428–442 (2009)

37. Rublee, E., Rabaud, V., Konolige, K., Bradski, G.: ORB: an efficient alternative to SIFT or SURF. In: IEEE International Conference on Computer Vision (ICCV), pp. 2564–2571 (2011)

38. Ester, M., Kriegel, H.P., Sander, J., Xu, X.: Density-based spatial clustering of applications with noise. In: International Conference on Knowledge Discovery and Data Mining, vol. 240 (1996)

39. Abdel-Wahab, M., Wenzel, K., Fritsch, D.: Automated and accurate orientation of large unordered image datasets for close-range cultural heritage data recording. Photogramm. Fernerkund. Geoinf. **2012**(6), 679–689 (2012)

40. Ntalianis, K., Doulamis, A., Doulamis, N., Tsapatsoulis, N.: Video abstraction in social media: augmenting Facebook's Edgerank algorithm in video content presentation. In: IEEE International Conference in Image Processing (ICIP), Australia (2013)

41. Hoi, S.C., Liu, W., Chang, S.F.: Semi-supervised distance metric learning for collaborative image retrieval and clustering. ACM Trans. Multimedia Comput. Commun. Appl. (TOMM) **6**(3), 18 (2010)

42. Debevec, P.E., Taylor, J.C., Malik, J.: Modeling and rendering architecture from photographs: a hybrid geometry- and image-based approach. In: Proceedings of the 23rd ACM Annual Conference on Computer Graphics and Interactive Techniques. ACM (1996)

43. Sardis, E., Anagnostopoulos, V., Doulamis, N., Varvarigou, T., Kyriakaki, G.: From 2D to 3D and 4D using timelines in mobile cultural experiences. In: Euromed 2014, Limassol, Cyprus (2014)
44. Doulamis, N., Doulamis, A., Ioannidis, C., Klein, M., Ioannides, M.: Modelling of static and moving objects: digitizing tangible and intangible cultural heritage. In: Ioannides, M., Magnenat-Thalmann, N., Papagiannakis, G. (eds.) Mixed Reality and Gamification for Cultural Heritage, pp. 567–589. Springer, Cham (2017). https://doi.org/10.1007/978-3-319-49607-8_23

Dissemination of Intangible Cultural Heritage Using a Multi-agent Virtual World

Spyros Vosinakis[1](✉) ⓘ, Nikos Avradinis[2],
and Panayiotis Koutsabasis[1] ⓘ

[1] Department of Product and Systems Design Engineering,
University of the Aegean, Syros, Greece
{spyrosv,kgp}@aegean.gr
[2] Department of Informatics, University of Piraeus, Piraeus, Greece
avrad@unipi.gr

Abstract. Most virtual heritage applications focus on the high-quality representation of 'tangible' cultural heritage, leaving out other aspects of culture, such as daily life activities, customs and rituals. The use of interactive digital characters that perform actions in the environment and communicate with users can help towards this end. In this paper we present a platform for virtual heritage applications, which is based on virtual worlds and can support multiple autonomous digital characters. Using this platform, we have constructed a recreation of a part of the ancient agora of Athens, and created an interactive scenario in it. We have performed a first qualitative user evaluation of the scenario and environment, which yielded positive results about the user experience and learning as well as areas of further improvement.

Keywords: Virtual worlds · Virtual heritage · NPCs · Virtual agents

1 Introduction

Advances in interactive 3D technology in the last decades led to a variety of new and promising approaches for representing and disseminating cultural heritage, generally termed as 'virtual heritage' [1]. These applications incorporate a number of distinguishing characteristics that include high-quality visualization of digital content, real-time simulation of realistic or imaginary environments, natural and intuitive user interactions, and single- or multi-user embodiment in the 3D space through animated avatars. Applications of this kind not only allow people to closely observe cultural heritage artifacts that may be difficult for them to approach physically, for reasons of distance, cost or accessibility, but they can also serve as motivating means to supplement people's knowledge and increase their interest in culture.

The majority of virtual heritage applications place more emphasis in the detailed presentation of buildings and artifacts, compared to other, intangible aspects of cultural heritage. This is somehow expected, because in the area of cultural heritage there is great interest in the form and architecture of past constructions. Nevertheless, a high-quality 3D visualization is not alone adequate to ensure that the user experience will be as engaging and fruitful as expected. These reconstructions need to be experienced

© Springer International Publishing AG, part of Springer Nature 2018
M. Ioannides et al. (Eds.): Digital Cultural Heritage 2017, LNCS 10754, pp. 197–207, 2018.
https://doi.org/10.1007/978-3-319-75789-6_14

together with a number of other, intangible aspects of the related historic period and culture in order to be immersed in the cultural context [2]. E.g. visitors might be interested in observing aspects of daily life, activities and rituals taking place in the buildings, typical usage of the artifacts being presented, related stories and events, etc.

The demonstration of such features in virtual heritage applications requires the introduction of digital characters that can participate and act in the simulated environment. These characters can be either controlled by humans (human avatars), or controlled by a computer program, with varying levels of adaptability to the environment or human user input [3, 4]. Furthermore, the use of techniques from the field of Artificial Intelligence, such as Intelligent Agents and Natural Language Processing, can enhance computer-controlled characters with features such as planning, personality and emotions, and conversing with users [5]. Virtual heritage applications have recently started to take advantage of the affordances of digital characters, and have incorporated them in the representation environment.

In this paper we present our work towards the use of multi-user 3D environments enhanced with digital characters for the presentation of intangible aspects of cultural heritage. We have developed a generic platform based on the OpenSimulator virtual world, which enables the creation of interactive scenarios and stories using programmable agents and 'smart objects', i.e. 3D objects with interactive behavior. The agents embodied as digital characters can move in the environment and hold conversations with users, whilst both users and agents can interact with the smart objects in the context of a larger story or quest. As a first application example, we have constructed a part of the ancient agora of classical Athens, and prepared an interactive scenario, in which a visitor and his companions want to make an offering to the gods. We present the design and implementation of the platform, the setup of the environment and the interactive scenario, as well as a first qualitative user evaluation of the environment. The evaluation results indicate that users may easily learn about intangible aspects of culture, explore and interact with virtual agents in virtual worlds for virtual heritage.

2 Related Work

Digital characters have been introduced in virtual heritage applications in a variety of ways. The most obvious approach is to have them operate as *'animated props'*. Such characters usually execute pre-scripted animation sequences that are sometimes parameterized for greater diversity, and their operation is independent from any changes in the environment or user activity. Their primary contribution in cultural heritage applications is to demonstrate the appearance and typical activities of indicative people in the place and time of reference.

More interesting and dynamic character behavior can be achieved with the use of *virtual crowds*. In this case, characters move and act collectively imitating the behavior of real human crowds. In most virtual crowd systems, individual agents are automatically generated based on generic rules that define their appearance and properties, and they are assigned a role from a predefined set. E.g., in the work of Maïm et al. [6] a real-time simulation environment presenting a reconstructed district of ancient Pompeii has been populated with a crowd of virtual Romans.

A different utilization of digital characters with more essential contribution to the user experience is to have them operate as *virtual guides*. In that case, the characters have the additional ability to communicate with the users, and their goal is make the experience livelier and pleasant for the visitors by presenting places, objects or related stories to them. There are plenty of virtual guide implementations in virtual museums and reconstructed cultural sites, which vary in terms of the means of communication and the adaptability of the presentation, e.g. [7].

In an attempt to integrate the affordances of the previous approaches, Panjoli et al. [8] have proposed a framework for digital characters in virtual heritage applications that consists of three distinct levels of interaction, depending on their distance from the user. The first level is the living background, where the character operates as part of the virtual crowd and facilitates the user immersion in the environment. Characters that are closer to the user switch to the interaction level; they pay attention to the user and allow for some basic interactions with him. The final level is the dialogue, where the user and character interact in natural language using text or speech. A first implementation of this framework is found in the Roma Nova project.

Finally, *intelligent agent* approaches can be used to offer a long-term, goal-oriented operation of characters in cultural heritage applications. Intelligent agent architectures such as the *BDI (Beliefs – Desires – Intentions)* approach can be used to implement digital characters with the ability to accumulate new knowledge about the environment using the input received by their sensors, to prioritize their next tasks according to their long-term goals, and to plan a sequence of actions to achieve the desired results. This approach leads to a more elaborate behavior that is not as predictive and repeatable as in the case of following pre-scripted orders. Approaches based on intelligent agents may possibly lead to the implementation of the recently proposed concept of *cultural agents* [9], which are digital characters that can select or recognize correct cultural behaviors and transmit cultural knowledge, and are considered more appropriate for virtual heritage applications.

The City of Uruk [10] is a virtual heritage application that uses intelligent agents in a virtual world to present daily life in an ancient city. The characters have been built based on a BDI architecture and follow a daily routine that involves movement, interaction with objects and communication with other characters. The agents' actions are shaped by their beliefs about the environment. They can follow pre-scripted plans in order to perform some standard activities, and they can also update their goals and generate dynamic plans as a result of certain changes in the environment. Finally, they have the ability to communicate with human visitors using natural language. They can talk about their current goal and planned actions, and they can also present information about the surrounding objects and environment. In a study aimed to validate its learning effectiveness [11] the application yielded positive results regarding student performance.

Our work also focuses in the use of intelligent agent approaches for virtual heritage applications, emphasizing in the presentation of intangible aspects of cultural heritage, such as daily life activities and rituals. While the majority of similar applications created so far are single-user, we wanted to explore the suitability of this approach in multi-user environments and for that purpose, we designed and tested a collaborative scenario in which users can work in groups in order to explore and learn about a specific ritual. Additionally, given that there are only a few evaluations of multi-agent virtual heritage applications in the literature, we decided to set up a user evaluation of our environment to gain some useful insights on the suitability of this approach for the dissemination of cultural heritage.

3 A Platform for Multi-agent Virtual Heritage Applications

We have developed a platform for cultural heritage applications in virtual worlds that includes multiple autonomous agents moving and interacting with the users and the environment. The platform provides a set of high-level tools and reusable components that aim to assist developers, and allows the execution of complex virtual heritage scenarios that may include features such as:

- demonstration of activities, habits and rituals of ancient cultures,
- agents communicating with users and presenting locations, elements or activities of interest, and
- scenarios requiring user participation, such as interactive stories and quests.

The architecture of our platform (Fig. 1) follows a three-tier client-server model based on OpenSimulator, an open source alternative to the virtual world of Second Life. Users join the application using a compatible browser that connects to the OpenSimulator server, and they are embodied as avatars in the representation space, which also includes the embodied agents (named NPCs – non-player characters in OpenSimulator terminology). The interactive behavior of the environment is orchestrated by a special object named Interface Unit that mediates between the virtual world and a multi-agent simulation environment. The latter is an external application implemented in Java, which handles the agents' behavior and conversations, using an abstraction of the actual world and its contents. Thus, the agent operation takes place in two parallel layers: the low-level execution layer of the virtual world, in which the NPCs move and interact with the objects and users of the environment, and the high-level layer of the multi-agent simulation, in which the agents update their beliefs, prioritize their goals, and decide about their next actions.

The elements of the virtual world that have an active role in the platform are the Interface Unit, the NPC Controllers, the user HUDs and the smart objects. The functionality of the Interface Unit is twofold: it constantly updates the multi-agent simulation with any changes happening in the 3D environment, and it also triggers actions related to the active objects of the virtual world. For the first function, it makes use of a specially built extension to the OpenSimulator server (Region Module), which monitors the placement of all entities of the environment and identifies any changes. For the second function, it communicates with specific scripted objects in the 3D environment. Specifically, digital characters have an attached object named NPC Controller, which controls their actions, user avatars have an attached Heads-up Display (HUD) object that triggers specific actions and presents information, and smart objects are can also receive messages from the Interface Unit and adapt their behavior accordingly.

The multi-agent simulation environment controls and monitors the behavior of the agents that participate as NPCs in the application. The operation of each agent is driven by a respective Agent Controller, which updates its beliefs, takes any required decisions

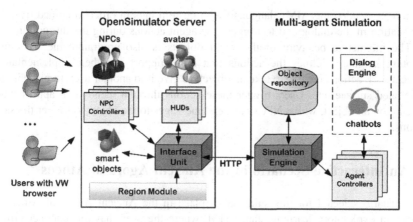

Fig. 1. System architecture of the multi-agent platform.

and executes the current plan. The agents' sensory input is based on an object repository that stores basic geometric information (size, position and rotation) of all elements that actively participate in the simulation, i.e. agents, users and selected objects. The repository is constantly updated by the Interface Object to reflect the active status of the 3D world. The multi-agent environment is equipped with a dialog engine based on AIML (Artificial Intelligence Markup Language [12]) for the agent-user communication.

The agents' behavior in the environment is controlled by pre-scripted plans, which are assigned to them during the lifecycle of the application. Each plan is a composite program that results to the execution of a sequence of actions taking into account the perceived status of the environment. The plans are described using a dedicated high-level scripting language, the *Plan Definition Language (PDL)*. Each plan defined in this language has a unique name and an arbitrary number of argument variables. The plan implementation is encoded in an imperative programming manner that allows sequential, conditional and iterative execution of commands, based on the definition of PDL. The supported commands fall into the following categories:

- actions that are executed by the NPC in the virtual world (locomotion, animation, interaction with smart object),
- "internal" actions that affect the internal values of the agent,
- message passing between agents,
- dialogs with users,
- memory processes (store/retrieve temporary information), and
- perception of specific elements based on criteria.

Finally, the execution of a new plan can be called during the plan implementation, thus leading to more complex plan definitions.

Dialogs between users and agents can start either with agent or with user initiative. The second is possible if the agent is available for discussion and the user clicks on its controller to start a dialog with it. In both cases, the agent part of the dialog is driven by the dialog engine. Designers can create a number of AIML bots, each of which is based on its own collection of AIML files that define how the agent responds to user input.

We have extended the AIML language with custom tags in order to embed dynamic information in the dialog and to trigger new agent actions during the discussion.

The interactive behavior of the smart objects is also programmable. A simple scripting language defines the actions that they support and their implementation. Typical such actions include to take an object, to give it to another user, to place it on a designated surface, etc. Users trigger these actions through menus that appear when clicking on an object, whilst NPCs can send messages to the object to trigger the same actions.

4   An Interactive Scenario in the Ancient Agora of Athens

The scenario selected for this study takes place in the Ancient Agora of Athens. It adopts an exploratory learning stance [13], where the users have to uncover critical information themselves, and collaborate to fulfil the quest. We have created in OpenSimulator a reconstruction of the central part of the agora around the second half of the 5th Century BC, modeled in real-world scale according to measurements from the excavations of the American School of Athens [14] (Fig. 2a). The scenario aims to acquaint users with the multiple functions and locations in the agora and provide knowledge about ancient Greek worship practices. The story revolves around one of the user avatars, in the role of a visitor that arrives for the first time at the agora, accompanied by two friends, wishing to secure the gods' favor to have a rich harvest at the end of the farming season. Being unfamiliar with the place and local customs, the three visitors cooperate in order to identify locations and persons of interest for their cause, as well as gather information about the proper way of worship.

Two roaming citizens (NPCs) serve as guides, providing information about different deities and indicating that the main character needs to secure the blessing of Demeter, the protector goddess of agriculture. For this, the main character needs to visit one of the two temples located in the agora. In order to pay respect to the god and request assistance, the main character has to perform a libation and in particular a 'sponde', that involves offering watered wine to the goddess, to be poured over the altar while reciting a prayer. The main character must now gather the necessary artifacts to perform the ritual, by visiting the vendors' stalls, in particular a pottery seller to buy a proper container and a wine seller to buy the proper kind of wine. This task can be delegated to his friends.

By visiting the wine seller's stall, users can get information on the different kinds of wine and the uses of each kind in everyday life and then choose the correct one for the purpose. At the pottery seller's stall, users can get acquainted with the different kinds of pottery, the features distinguishing one from another as well as the particular functions of each type of pottery, once again choosing the proper one to perform the ritual.

The priest at the temple is the master of ceremony, monitoring the main character's actions and sayings to ensure that the ritual is followed step by step. One of his aides, the 'neokoros', is assigned support tasks but most important he can further break down the ritual into steps that the main character has to follow in order for the ritual to be successfully completed. Another aide is assigned the task to play music using a double flute, while the ritual takes place. The main character is first required to cleanse himself

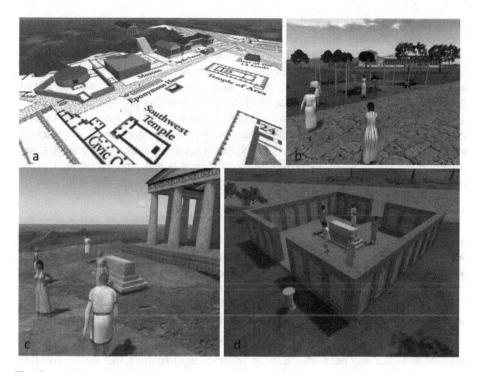

Fig. 2. a. Construction based on the ground plans, b. Users visiting a wine seller, c. Users and priest outside the temple of Hephaestus, d. Performing a ritual in the altar of the 12 Gods

by using the 'perirranterion', a washing basin located outside the altar. Then, the prayer must be recited in the proper order and the offering to the goddess must be given. This is done by slowly pouring wine from the 'oenochoe', the container the wine is brought into, to the 'phiale', a ceremonial cup provided by the priest. Some of the wine from the phiale has to be poured on the altar for the god, while the rest is consumed by the main character and his friends, when the prayer has been recited. This signals the closure of the ritual and the visitors may now depart the temple and the agora.

The scenario uses twelve NPCs and a wide variety of smart objects, including various pottery types, the washing basin, the flute, etc. Besides the musician, all other NPCs are able to hold conversations with the users that are related to their role in the scenario. Screenshots of the development and execution of the scenario are shown in Fig. 2b, c and d.

5   User Evaluation

We performed a qualitative user evaluation of the environment in which 12 users in four groups of three completed the above scenario in the computer lab. The goals of the evaluation were to: (a) identify if it would be possible for users to find out information about the ritual on the basis of exploration of the environment and natural language dialogues with avatars, (b) assess their user experience and identify potential areas of improvement. The only information provided to users was to talk to avatars to find out more about the offering. The tasks to be identified and performed were: to buy a container, to fill it with proper wine, to go outside the temple and cleanse, to learn about the ritual from the 'neokoros', and to properly perform the ritual with the aid of the priest. All participants were students of design engineering (av. age: 21.38, st.dev.: 1.38); six had previous experience with virtual worlds and relevant games. During each group session, an evaluator was observing 'over the shoulder' and took notes of utterances and behaviors. At the end of each group session, a retrospective think-aloud session occurred, in which users went through their acts and reported on their experiences. Furthermore, chat logs were reviewed for clarifications and validation of observations.

Overall, the results of the evaluation were very encouraging:

- All user groups managed to make the offering to the Gods fairly fast.
- All users tended to explore the world and their capabilities with enthusiasm.
- Many users were impressed by the environment and they spontaneously made various positive comments, e.g.: "nice avatar clothes"; "nice buildings; are they exact copies?"; "it feels great that I can talk to an avatar in physical language".
- At the end, all groups orally repeated the process of making a libation to the Gods.

In addition, a total of 43 UX issues (Table 1) were identified during group interactions. Most issues may be characterized as minor or easy to correct, like for example that "some avatars provide incomplete information" (this was a design decision to promote exploratory learning), or that "too much information into avatar utterances, which disappear fast from chat window." Others require further design and testing, like bugs.

Table 1. User experience issues, types and occurrences.

Type of UX issue	UX issue	Occurrences	
Cooperation	Users cooperated later on by assigning tasks to each other	2	6
Cooperation	Users cooperated from the start with task assignments	2	
Cooperation	Users preferred to talk aloud in the lab, than use the chat	1	
Cooperation	Two users cooperated; the third mainly followed	1	
System help and support	Chat window kept open to review procedure for libation	4	15
System help and support	*"We would like a clear starting point"*	2	
System help and support	More help, signs and feedback about the process to be followed	2	
System help and support	We can't find a particular place or avatar	2	
System help and support	Some avatars provide incomplete information	1	

(*continued*)

Table 1. (*continued*)

Type of UX issue	UX issue	Occurrences	
System help and support	Chat is confusing when all users are nearby and talk to others	1	
System help and support	*"We would like private conversations"*	1	
System help and support	*"We would like to see our group mates in specific clothing"*	1	
System help and support	More information about objects (utility, history, etc.)	1	
Task comprehension	*"I did not understand what the avatar wants me to do"*	2	6
Task comprehension	Users explored the virtual world a lot before taking on the task	2	
Task comprehension	*"We did not get the order of the steps at first, but later on"*	2	
Tech. issues	Warning/error messages appear in chat window (bug)	2	3
Tech. issues	System froze for a while	1	
U-A interaction	*"Whenever I tried to talk to the citizens, they walked away"*	3	10
U-A interaction	Avatar interrupted while communicating with other team (bug)	1	
U-A interaction	Too much information into avatar utterances, which disappear fast from chat window	1	
U-A interaction	*"Not sure if the avatar is talking to me"*	1	
U-A interaction	In dialogue with avatars, it would be nice to move the camera to focus on the avatar's face and enlarge font size for text	1	
U-A interaction	*"At first we did not know how to respond to physical language"*	1	
U-A interaction	*"Not sure how to give object to the avatar"*	1	
U-A interaction	Avatar does not understand a simple user response	1	
U-O interaction	Message boxes appear at the upper right not perceived by user	2	3
U-O interaction	Unnatural body posture of washing over the fountain	1	
	Total issues	43	

6 Conclusions

We have presented a multi-agent platform based on virtual worlds for cultural heritage applications, as well as the design and user evaluation of an interactive scenario using this platform. The platform has been designed so as to be able to support a wide variety of environments and scenarios, given that the behavior of the agents and objects can be scripted and the dialogs can be adapted accordingly. Its operation does not have to be restricted to scenarios such as the one presented in this paper, where the users are participating in a pre-scribed story. It could also allow for a free exploration of the environment, where users can observe activities performed by NPCs and discuss with them to learn more about their life and customs. Alternatively, NPCs could assign quests to visitors and reward them with giving them improved clothes or access to extra content.

The preliminary evaluation results of the environment and scenario are encouraging, since that all users managed to timely finish the task, they had a positive experience, and they learned the key points of the ritual. The vast majority of identified UX issues were minor and will be further considered for improvements. We believe that the multi-user and collaborative nature of the tasks also had a positive impact of the experience, and thus it is important that the adoption of multi-user persistent virtual worlds as a platform for the dissemination of cultural heritage is further explored. Finally, digital characters that can interact with users and the environment seems to be an appropriate basis for dissemination of intangible heritage in interactive 3D environments.

References

1. Addison, A.C.: Emerging trends in virtual heritage. IEEE Multimedia 7(2), 22–25 (2000)
2. Pujol, L., Champion, E.: Evaluating presence in cultural heritage projects. Int. J. Herit. Stud. 18(1), 83–102 (2012)
3. Lombardo, V., Damiano, R.: Storytelling on mobile devices for cultural heritage. New Rev. Hypermedia Multimedia 18, 11–35 (2012)
4. Papagiannakis, G., Schertenleib, S., O'Kennedy, B., Arevalo-Poizat, M., Magnenat-Thalmann, N., Stoddart, A., Thalmann, D.: Mixing virtual and real scenes in the site of ancient Pompeii. Comput. Animat. Virtual Worlds 16(1), 11–24 (2005)
5. Luck, M., Aylett, R.: Applying artificial intelligence to virtual reality: intelligent virtual environments. Appl. Artif. Intell. 14(1), 3–32 (2000)
6. Maïm, J., Haegler, S., Yersin, B., Mueller, P., Thalmann, D., Van Gool, L.: Populating ancient Pompeii with crowds of virtual Romans. In: International Symposium on Virtual Reality, Archaeology and Intelligent Cultural Heritage (2007)
7. Oberlander, J., Karakatsiotis, G., Isard, A., Androutsopoulos, I.: Building an adaptive museum gallery in Second Life. In: Museums and the Web, Montreal, Quebec, Canada (2008)
8. Panzoli, D., et al.: A level of interaction framework for exploratory learning with characters in virtual environments. In: Plemenos, D., Miaoulis, G. (eds.) Intelligent Computer Graphics 2010. SCI, vol. 321, pp. 123–143. Springer, Heidelberg (2010). https://doi.org/10.1007/978-3-642-15690-8_7

9. Champion, E.: Defining cultural agents for virtual heritage environments. Presence Teleoperators Virtual Environ. **24**(3), 179–186 (2015)
10. Bogdanovych, A., Rodriguez-Aguilar, J.A., Simoff, S., Cohen, A.: Authentic interactive reenactment of cultural heritage with 3D virtual worlds and artificial intelligence. Appl. Artif. Intell. **24**(6), 617–647 (2010)
11. Bogdanovych, A., Ijaz, K., Simoff, S.: The City of Uruk: teaching ancient history in a virtual world. In: Nakano, Y., Neff, M., Paiva, A., Walker, M. (eds.) IVA 2012. LNCS (LNAI), vol. 7502, pp. 28–35. Springer, Heidelberg (2012). https://doi.org/10.1007/978-3-642-33197-8_3
12. Wallace, R.S.: The anatomy of A.L.I.C.E. In: Epstein, R., Roberts, G., Beber, G. (eds.) Parsing the Turing Test, pp. 181–210. Springer, Dordrecht (2009). https://doi.org/10.1007/978-1-4020-6710-5_13
13. De Freitas, S., Neumann, T.: The use of 'exploratory learning' for supporting immersive learning in virtual environments. Comput. Educ. **52**(2), 343–352 (2009)
14. Thompson, H.A., Wycherley, R.E.: The Athenian Agora: Results of Excavations Conducted by the American School of Classical Studies in Athens, vol. XIV: The Agora of Athens: The History, Shape and Uses of an Ancient City Center. The American School of Classical Studies at Athens, Princeton (1972)

A Tour in the Archaeological Site of Choirokoitia Using Virtual Reality: A Learning Performance and Interest Generation Assessment

Maria Christofi[✉][iD], Christos Kyrlitsias[iD], Despina Michael-Grigoriou[✉][iD], Zoe Anastasiadou, Maria Michaelidou, Ioanna Papamichael, and Katerina Pieri

GET Lab, Department of Multimedia and Graphic Arts,
Cyprus University of Technology, Limassol, Cyprus
{mu.christofi,cm.kyrlitsias}@edu.cut.ac.cy, despina.michael@cut.ac.cy

Abstract. A Virtual Reality (VR) application of the archaeological site of Choirokoitia has been designed and developed. The virtual reconstruction of the site simulates its current structure and is based on real data acquisition. The VR application allows the participants to virtually navigate through the archaeological site and acquire historical information for various important points of it. This study assesses the learning performance of the application's users and their interest for the topic. Findings demonstrated a strong significant improvement in learning performance of the users with the change in their interest following a bell-shaped distribution. This indicates that the developed VR application can be used as a teaching tool for Cultural Heritage purposes.

Keywords: Virtual Reality · Cultural Heritage · Virtual worlds
Virtual heritage · Learning assessment

1 Introduction

Preservation and promotion of Cultural Heritage (CH) sites are nowadays achieved also with the support of modern technologies. Towards this end, digital media are used for the digital reconstruction of archaeological sites and monuments [4] and dedicated terms, such as that of virtual archeology [13] and virtual heritage [3], exist in literature demonstrating the wide interest of the community about these topics. ICT technologies, such 3D visualizations, multi-touch surfaces, interactive multimedia applications have been widely used in the last years with topics related to Cultural Heritage. The most advanced technologies and usually those with a high cost of production are hosted in the place of interest, such as for example within the museums, while applications affordable and accessible to every day users are mostly limited, at least up to now, to standalone desktop, mobile devices and online applications.

M. Ioannides et al. (Eds.): Digital Cultural Heritage 2017, LNCS 10754, pp. 208–217, 2018.
https://doi.org/10.1007/978-3-319-75789-6_15

In a comparative study of interactive systems in a museum by Michael et al. [12], the authors evaluated the experience of young users with six in total (traditional or technologically supported) exhibits; a traditional exhibit, that was a traditional printed map, and five interactive ICT systems; a virtual tour projection, a multi-touch table application and three different augmented reality applications. They quantified high-level interaction qualities such as enjoyment, satisfaction and desire to perform again. They concluded that the experience scores top marks for the interactive ICT systems.

Virtual Reality (VR) is also one of the advanced technologies used towards this end. VR is used to immerse the user into a computer-generated world often resembling the real world, where he can explore and manipulate interactively the 3D environment [10]. The use of VR for entertainment reasons [8] is probably the most well-known amongst the general public and even though the educational use of VR is often overshadowed, interesting applications and studies covering these topics have been already demonstrated. Virtual Reality Learning Environments (VRLEs) simulate the real world through the application of 3D models that initiates interaction, immersion and trigger the imagination of the learner [9].

According to Roussou [14], the key issue of VR in Cultural Heritage is not only to visually represent, in a photo-realistic manner, places, monuments or landscapes that do not exist, never existed, or may not be easily experienced, but to present these in a meaningful and engaging way, to add the extra touch that will render the representation an experience. The suitability of VR for learning about archeology and the past in CH settings was investigated in a study [16], and results confirmed that VR systems allow a different kind of learning but also questioned the common believe about their advantage for children in comparison with other interpretation methods.

Loizides et al. in their 2014 study [11] compared the visit in two virtual museums (an engraving museum and a virtual Byzantine icons museum). In both cases users had the opportunity to visit the museum using either a Head Mounted Display (HMD) or a stereoscopic Powerwall. Overall, both technologies were considered a positive way to present 3 cultural heritage to individuals and the virtual reality has easy portability for remote setups.

A study by Zaharias et al. in 2013 [17], investigated the user experience (UX) and learning effectiveness of the "Walls of Nicosia", a 3D multi-touch table. Two groups of students participated in this empirical study: (a) The traditional group where students took a guided tour throughout the museum and learned about the walls of Nicosia through printed maps exhibited at the museum and (b) the virtual group where students interacted with the multi-touch application. Results showed no statistically significant differences in the learning performance but the virtual group reported user experience at significantly higher levels.

A Greek Cultural Heritage institution, the Foundation of the Hellenic World, has offered a variety of educational VR exhibits in its Cultural Center [6] that are very popular amongst the visitors. In some of these exhibitions, the visitors can conduct virtual experiments, assist an ancient sculptor to create a statue of the god Zeus, and walk through the ancient city of Miletus. In 2009, the Center unveiled "Tholos" [2], a 130-person VR theater [7] in which the first productions have featured interactive tours of ancient Athens' agora (market).

A new era arrived this year for Virtual Reality; the first VR commercial headsets have launched for the public. VR is now accessible for everyone to use, not only for developers and researchers. This opens new doors for the Virtual Reality field, by giving the opportunity for everyone at his own space and pace to exploit the advances of Virtual Reality. Sites of interest that are not easily accessible by visitors, either due to distant location and mobility limitation or due to the structure of the site, are now virtually accessible by anyone who owns a low cost VR headset. Moreover, possible visitors located remotely, have the opportunity to experience the site virtually at first and travel to visit the site at place in case they assess due to their virtual experience that it is worth it.

The first aim of our study was the design and development of a Virtual Reality tour of Choirokoitia due to the fact that is one of the most important prehistoric sites in the eastern Mediterranean. Choirokoitia is a Neolithic settlement [1] located in the district of Larnaca, Cyprus. The excavated site of Choirokoitia is intact and includes all the attributes that express an outstanding universal value. Choirokoitia is included in World Heritage list of Unesco and was given enhanced protection status. It is a popular destination and there are organized school trips from all over Cyprus. The investigations of this study were two fold: (i) evaluate the user's learning performance and (ii) investigate whether their interest for the archaeological site increases due to the use of the VR application developed.

The following paper is organized in three sections: 'Materials and Methods' where adequate information is provided for the design of the study, 'Results' where findings of the data analysis are given and lastly a 'Discussion and Conclusions' section where the significance of the results are explored and ideas for future directions are described.

2   Materials and Methods

2.1   The VR Application of Choirokoitia

Excavations of Choirokoitia have shown that the settlement consisted of circular houses built from stone and mudbrick with flat roofs and that it was protected by successive walls. In order to reconstruct virtually the archaeological site as it stands in nowadays (Fig. 1), a visit to the actual site was made, and photos were taken from the site itself and the archaeological findings. The site has been digitally reconstructed, using 3D modeling, that was used within the interactive application. The user can navigate in the virtual Choirokoitia using a controller. He is allowed to virtually walk towards any direction (using the left joystick) and rotate the looking direction (using the right joystick) among the vertical axis. The developed application has been integrated with a VR Head Mounted Display (HMD) which allows the user to be immersed and observe the virtual site. With the support of HMD's tracking system the looking direction can be

Fig. 1. The archaeological site of Choirokoitia has been virtually reconstructed with accuracy on spatial locations of the houses (top) and with attention in structural details of the site (bottom).

also changed intuitively by the user, around any axis, by physically rotating his head.

In the virtual world there are six information points noted with an information blue sign (Fig. 2), in specific areas. When the user visits one of these points, a stereo audio recording is automatically played by the system. Each audio lasts about half a minute each and includes information about the specific area that is located. The information included in the audio recordings have been acquired by the information plates which exist at the real site.

2.2 Experimental Design

A within group experiment was conducted. Quantitative data were collected using two questionnaires. The first one was a pre-test questionnaire (PreQ) which contained three parts, one part for collecting demographic information (age, gender, education, computer use knowledge, previous VR experience), a second part for evaluating learning performance, which was a knowledge test (KT) regarding the archaeological site of Choirokoitia and a third part for assessing the participants' interest in visiting the real site and learn more about the CH of Cyprus.

The second was a post-test questionnaire (PostQ) containing three parts, one part evaluating learning performance once again, another part assessing the participants' sense of presence in the virtual world and lastly a part evaluating again the participants' interest.

Fig. 2. An information point, noted with the blue sign, near the entrance of the virtual archaeological site. (Color figure online)

The two parts of the test, testing the knowledge and the interest of the participants were identical in both, PreQ and PostQ. All the questions related to the interest and presence were measured with a 5-point Likert style questions. The knowledge test included 10 multiple choice questions with 4 choices each, related with the archaeological site of Choirokoitia. All the information for the correct answers is included in the audio clips played when the information points were visited. The presence questions that were used are based on the Slater-Usoh-Steed (SUS) presence questionnaire [15].

2.3   Materials

The VR system that was used for the experiment included the HMD Oculus Rift DK2 which was coupled with a positional tracker. The desktop computer used was equipped with an NVidia GeForce GTX 770 graphics card. A Speedlink Torid gamepad and stereo headphones were also used. The virtual site was created with the game engine Unity3D. The 3D models were created using the software Autodesk Maya and were textured using the pictures taken during the visit to the site. The audio clips played in the application were recorded and edited in Adobe Audition CS6.

2.4   Procedures

The participants were conducting the experiment one at a time. Upon arriving, participants were briefed about the study without providing any information that disclose its purpose. After that, they were asked to read and sign the consent form of the experiment. Then, they were asked to fill in the PreQ and were specifically instructed to answer all the questions carefully and to the best of their knowledge. After they completed the PreQ, they received written instructions about their task in the virtual place, the navigation controls, the information points and their available time. The Oculus Rift HMD and the headphones were fitted on each participant and the experimenter started the application. The exposure of the participant in the virtual environment lasted up to eight minutes. After the completion of the eight minutes, the HMD and the headphones were taken out and the participant was asked to complete the PostQ.

2.5 Scenario

The participants were put in the VR application of Choirokoitia (Fig. 3). They were free to navigate anywhere they wished for up to eight minutes. They were instructed though that in the virtual world they would have to locate six information points, which were visually represented with blue information signs floating in specific areas of the archaeological site. When participants were close enough to one of these points, the corresponding recorded audio was played automatically and participants listened information about the specific area that they were looking at.

Fig. 3. A participant immersed in the virtual archaeological site of Choirokoitia. (Color figure online)

3 Results

In total 23 participants took part in the study from which 4 of them quited the experiment before its completion. Data collected from the remaining 19 participants were used for the analysis. The 4 participants who did not complete the experiment showed signs of motion sickness. This is an common issue of HMD technologies, which constitutes a subject of research [5]. The 19 participants aged from 18 to 46 years old with a median of 21. 11 of them were male and 9 female. The majority (15 out of 19) of participants were university students with all of the rest of them holding at least a higher education degree. A high percentage (84.2%) of the participants reported that they are using computers in a daily basis, but only 4 stated that they use Virtual Reality technologies one or more times a week. All of the participants apart from 2 had not previously visited the archaeological site of Choirokoitia. It was verified that the participants were hearing clearly the audio clips, with the information about the archaeological site, with a relevant question at the post-questionnaire with a mean 4.11, SD = .809 and a median 4.

3.1   Presence

Participants had a strong illusion of presence within the virtual site. This information was recorded at the PostQ by using four 5-point Likert style questions ($\alpha = .632$). The median for all participants used in the analysis, was 3.5 on a scale of 1 to 5, which indicates that the sense of presence was quite high.

3.2   Learning

The assessment of learning performance of the participants is based on the analysis of the knowledge test (KT). By having a look at the graph plotting PreQ and PostQ scores in KT (Fig. 4), it was obvious that the performance of most of the participants improved after their experience in the virtual world. 15 out of the 19 people who participated demonstrated an improvement in learning performance in the PostQ KT compared to the PreQ KT. The rest of the participants had the same score while no one had a reduced score. The mean score of the participants in the PreQ KT was 4.11 correct answers out of 10, whilst in PostQ KT increased to 6.84 correct answers.

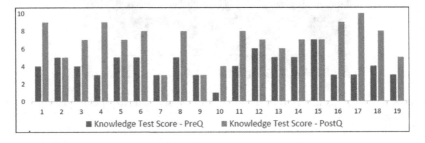

Fig. 4. Participant's scores in the pre- and post- knowledge test demonstrating an improvement in learning assessment.

A paired-samples t-test was conducted to compare the participants' score in pre-questionnaire and post-questionnaire knowledge test. There was a strong significant difference in the score in pre-questionnaire ($M = 4.11$, $SD = 1.370$) and post-questionnaire knowledge tests ($M = 6.84$, $SD = 2.035$); $t(18) = -5.468$, $p = .000$. This result suggests that the use of the VR application of Choirokoitia increased the knowledge of the participants about the archaeological site. However, the change in score of pre- and post- knowledge test has not been found correlated with the illusion of presence ($r = .014$, $n = 19$, $p = .953$).

3.3   Interest

Through the questionnaires we recorded the participants' interest in the Cultural Heritage before and after their virtual visit in Choirokoitia. The change in the overall interest (post- minus pre- interest) of the participants are following a bell shaped distribution (Fig. 5). The interest of six participants was increased while five participants showed a decrease. For the remaining eight participants no change was occurred.

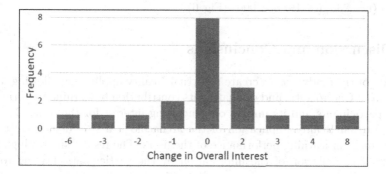

Fig. 5. Participants' change in interest after experiencing the virtual tour forms a bell shaped distribution.

To statistically compare the change in participants' overall interest in the CH of Cyprus, a paired-samples t-test was conducted. The overall interest for each participant was measured using the averages values from four questions; two regarding the interest in visiting and two the interest in learning about the archaeological site. There wasn't a significant difference in the interest assessed in the PreQ ($\alpha = .918$, M = 3.6184, SD = 1.06839) and the PostQ ($\alpha = .936$, M = 3.7237, SD = 1.14229); t(18) = $-.639$, p = .531. This result suggests that the virtual visit did not affect the participants' overall interest in CH.

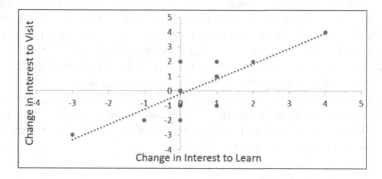

Fig. 6. Participants' change of interest in visiting and change of interest in learning about archaeological sites are linearly correlated.

We further investigated separately the change in interest in visiting archaeological sites and the change in interest in learning more about the CH by grouping the two related questions for each analysis and by conducting paired-samples t-tests. None of these analysis demonstrated significant results. Neither the change of the overall interest has been found significantly correlated with the presence $(r = .342, n = 19, p = 152)$. However the change of interest in learning and the change of interest in visiting archaeological sites have been found strongly correlated $(r = .835, n = 19, p = .000)$ (Fig. 6).

4   Discussion and Conclusions

The aim of the study was to create a Virtual Reality application allowing a virtual tour of Choirokoitia and evaluating its contribution to learning performance of the participants and its impact on generating interest for the topic. The use of the Virtual Reality application of the archaeological site, demonstrated an improvement in learning performance of the users. The results show a high percentage of assimilation of the information by the participants, leading to the conclusion that it can be used as an alternative to traditional teaching method for CH. This can be exploited by educators, to convey information about remote sites to students, for places that are not accessible easily or are located in an isolate place. Moreover the VR application can be used for self education by the participants. However, safer conclusions about the learning performance will result from comparative assessments with traditional teaching methods and with other technologically supported ways of information presentation.

Ways of exploiting VR applications for the promotion of CH sites should be explored. Towards this direction, an aim is to achieve an increase in the interest of the participants in learning and visiting physically the archaeological site. This was not demonstrated through the results of the current study. A possible explanation for this is that all the information about Choirokoitia for which the participants assessed, was provided to the user through the audio clips played when visited an information point. Moreover, more knowledge was also gained through the observation of the visual representation of the site. We speculate that these led the participants to believe that all the knowledge that could be gained through a physical visit to the site, has been gained by their virtual visit, but this is not true. Ways that provide to the participants the feeling that more information could be explored should be further investigated.

In future studies, it will be also interesting to assess the user experience, the enjoyment and desire to use again the VR application. Serious games design principles could be incorporated in the development of the virtual tour contributing in satisfaction of use by the participant.

References

1. Choirokoitia. http://whc.unesco.org/en/list/848. Accessed 22 July 2016
2. Tholos. http://tholos254.gr/en/index.html. Accessed 20 July 2016
3. Addison, A.C.: Emerging trends in virtual heritage. IEEE Multimed. **7**(2), 22–25 (2000)

4. Beraldin, J.A., Picard, M., El-Hakim, S., Godin, G., Borgeat, L., Blais, F., Paquet, E., Rioux, M., Valzano, V., Bandiera, A.: Virtual reconstruction of heritage sites: opportunities and challenges created by 3D technologies. In: Proceedings of the International Workshop on Recording, Modelling and Visualization of Cultural Heritage, pp. 141–156 (2005)

5. Fernandes, A.S., Feiner, S.K.: Combating VR sickness through subtle dynamic field-of-view modification. In: 2016 IEEE Symposium on 3D User Interfaces (3DUI), pp. 201–210. IEEE (2016)

6. Gaitatzes, A., Christopoulos, D., Roussou, M.: Reviving the past: cultural heritage meets virtual reality. In: Proceedings of the 2001 Conference on Virtual Reality, Archeology, and Cultural Heritage, pp. 103–110. ACM (2001)

7. Gaitatzes, A., Papaioannou, G., Christopoulos, D., Zyba, G.: Media productions for a dome display system. In: Proceedings of the ACM Symposium on Virtual Reality Software and Technology, pp. 261–264. ACM (2006)

8. Hsu, K.S., et al.: Application of a virtual reality entertainment system with human-machine haptic sensor device. J. Appl. Sci. **11**(12), 2145–2153 (2011)

9. Huang, H.M., Rauch, U., Liaw, S.S.: Investigating learners' attitudes toward virtual reality learning environments: based on a constructivist approach. Comput. Educ. **55**(3), 1171–1182 (2010)

10. Lee, E.A.-L., Wong, K.W.: A review of using virtual reality for learning. In: Pan, Z., Cheok, A.D., Müller, W., El Rhalibi, A. (eds.) Transactions on Edutainment I. LNCS, vol. 5080, pp. 231–241. Springer, Heidelberg (2008). https://doi.org/10.1007/978-3-540-69744-2_18

11. Loizides, F., El Kater, A., Terlikas, C., Lanitis, A., Michael, D.: Presenting cypriot cultural heritage in virtual reality: a user evaluation. In: Ioannides, M., Magnenat-Thalmann, N., Fink, E., Žarnić, R., Yen, A.-Y., Quak, E. (eds.) EuroMed 2014. LNCS, vol. 8740, pp. 572–579. Springer, Cham (2014). https://doi.org/10.1007/978-3-319-13695-0_57

12. Michael, D., Pelekanos, N., Chrysanthou, I., Zaharias, P., Hadjigavriel, L.L., Chrysanthou, Y.: Comparative study of interactive systems in a museum. In: Ioannides, M., Fellner, D., Georgopoulos, A., Hadjimitsis, D.G. (eds.) EuroMed 2010. LNCS, vol. 6436, pp. 250–261. Springer, Heidelberg (2010). https://doi.org/10.1007/978-3-642-16873-4_19

13. Reilly, P.: Towards a virtual archaeology. In: Computer Applications in Archaeology, pp. 133–139. British Archaeological Reports, Oxford (1990)

14. Roussou, M.: Virtual heritage: from the research lab to the broad public. BAR Int. Ser. **1075**, 93–100 (2002)

15. Slater, M., Usoh, M., Steed, A.: Depth of presence in virtual environments. Presence Teleoperators Virtual Environ. **3**(2), 130–144 (1994)

16. Tost, L.P., Economou, M.: Worth a thousand words? The usefulness of immersive virtual reality for learning in cultural heritage settings. Int. J. Archit. Comput. **7**(1), 157–176 (2009)

17. Zaharias, P., Michael, D., Chrysanthou, Y.: Learning through multi-touch interfaces in museum exhibits: an empirical investigation. Educ. Technol. Soc. **16**(3), 374–384 (2013)

Preparing Student Mobility Through a VR Application for Cultural Education

Giouli Pappa[1], Nikoletta Ioannou[1], Maria Christofi[2(✉)] ⓘ,
and Andreas Lanitis[3] ⓘ

[1] Department of Multimedia and Graphic Arts, Cyprus University of Technology,
Limassol, Cyprus
giouli.pappa@cut.ac.cy, nik.ioan@gmail.com
[2] GET Lab, Department of Multimedia and Graphic Arts,
Cyprus University of Technology, Limassol, Cyprus
mu.christofi@edu.cut.ac.cy
[3] Visual Media Computing Lab, Department of Multimedia and Graphic Arts,
Cyprus University of Technology, Limassol, Cyprus
andreas.lanitis@cut.ac.cy

Abstract. The potential of VR as a basis for developing dedicated applications for Cultural Education is explored through the design and development of a VR application called Celestial Breeze. Celestial Breeze is a dedicated application that aims to provide knowledge about the culture of different European countries. The design of the application is based on multimedia learning theories in an attempt to maximize the learning outcomes of the users. Emphasis is given in examining the effectiveness of Celestial Breeze as a tool of information dissemination in relation to the age and gender of the audience. We evaluated the application through a user study with 20 participants - half of whom were under aged- but all belong to Generation Y. The comparison of pre- and post- test results pinpoints the positive learning outcomes of Celestial Breeze on participants indicating in that way the potential of using immersive applications for cultural education.

Keywords: Virtual reality · Cultural heritage · Intangible heritage
Tangible heritage · Virtual worlds · Culture · Social etiquette
Multimedia design · Learning principles · Generation Y

1 Introduction

Recent advancements in the field of Virtual Reality (VR) provide numerous possibilities of using VR for Cultural Heritage (CH) related applications. This paper describes our ongoing work for foreign language students training in the cultural sector by exploiting an immersive Virtual Reality system especially designed to this end. Following a linear way of representation of information in line with Declarative knowledge strategy of learning [8], Celestial Breeze aims at raising students awareness regarding the cultural heritage of the European Union, prior

© Springer International Publishing AG, part of Springer Nature 2018
M. Ioannides et al. (Eds.): Digital Cultural Heritage 2017, LNCS 10754, pp. 218–227, 2018.
https://doi.org/10.1007/978-3-319-75789-6_16

to their mobility period. Users, immersed in the Celestial Breeze, took a virtual tour of selected European countries by popping up on a roller coaster.

In this paper, we first try to establish Celestial Breeze project within the current research and particularly in the field of virtual cultural learning for students mobility preparation. We will later present our adopted learning strategy as well as describe the system architecture. We shall further examine if such an application contributes to the knowledge and cultural awareness and on a second level if the gender and age of the learner play a role in this. Finally, conclusions and recommendations based on the findings of a pilot test aiming at a preliminary evaluation of the system will be drawn and the importance of cultural awareness in preparation for the period abroad will be discussed.

2   Literature Review

Literature analysis deploys several aspects that are significant to this research such as Virtual Reality and Cultural Heritage, Virtual Mobility and Learning Theories.

2.1   Virtual Reality and Cultural Heritage

Virtual heritage, namely the digitization and projection through virtual environments of the cultural treasures of the world, helps to preserve, research and the transmission of cultural heritage [7] but also to bring together people and different cultures without going there. The original purpose of virtual heritage is "the preservation and interpretation of our cultural and natural history" with "non-destructive public access" to heritage sites [7]. Celestial Breeze, could be seen as a vector of the virtual heritage, as it exhibits to the user authentic objects of different European cities which fall within the tangible and intangible heritage, facilitating the user to become familiar with the specific culture, before deciding to go there.

As the European Commission refers "Cultural heritage enrich individual citizens' lives, is the driving force for the cultural and creative sectors, and plays a role in creating and strengthening Europe's social capital. It is also an important resources for growth, jobs and social cohesion, providing the opportunity for the regeneration of urban and rural areas and promote sustainable tourism" [7].

The potential of combining education with entertainment [9] has been exploited through the development and evaluation of dedicated VR applications that aim to promote cultural heritage knowledge. In a comparative study of interactive systems in Leventis Municipal Museum in Nicosia, children between the ages 9 and 11 were asked to use and choose between six different types of museum exhibits, one traditional and five interactive ICT exhibits (VR tour, touch table, three augmented reality exhibits). The VR tour scored high on the question if they would like to do it again, which according to the researchers might be due to its enjoyable entertainment [15].

Another study compared the visit in two virtual museums (an engraving museum and a virtual Byzantine icons museum). In both cases users had the opportunity to visit the museum using either a Head Mounted Display (HMD) or a stereoscopic Powerwall. Twelve participants were selected (7 female and 5 male) to take part in the study ranged in age between 20 and 40 years old and were from diverse vocational backgrounds and of different technological literacy levels. Overall, both technologies were considered a positive way to present cultural heritage to individuals and the virtual reality has easy portability for remote setups [13].

Virtual Reality applications have been touted as an effective source for teaching culture as the Y generation (persons born in 1980 and following that) [10] is more likely to engage in technologically advanced instruction than to merely interact with students or the instructor when in face-to face learning environments [5]. These assertions suggest that a virtual reality application could facilitate students learning of a foreign culture.

2.2   Erasmus Students and Virtual Mobility

Since 2014, around to 500,000 people participated in Erasmus+. Erasmus+, is a people exchange program, to which the key priority is the physical mobility activities, concerning education and training of the participants. The program enhances skills like language, occupation and inter cultural awareness and thereby the less privileged students are able to study abroad. While strengthening the participating organizations to increase their capacity for innovation, quality teaching and the ability to work with young people and modernizing curricula [2]. Virtual Mobility can be a supplement to physical mobility, but can also be an alternative to this. While physical mobility is increased to the Universities, the cost and the necessary facilities, difficult some students who wish to make the actual journey, so they can not have access, causing a kind of social exclusion can be avoided by means of virtual mobility (Kenyon, Lyon and Rafferty, 2002) [6].

According to the elearningeuropa.info, Virtual Mobility means: The use of information and communication technologies (ICT) to obtain the same benefits as you would have with physical mobility but without the need to travel [6]. Having that in mind, Celestial Breeze falls on the philosophy of virtual mobility, which offers the opportunity for students to take a course in another country through the use of ICT. In this way students acquire in addition to all the above positives offered by the Erasmus+ program and additional technical skills [6]. In this way Celestial Breeze could be used as part of Erasmus+ as a preparatory stage, since it can prepare virtual participants and thus facilitate the conduct of a smooth transition from one country to another [2].

There are four types of Virtual Mobility: (1) a seminar or virtual course as a supplement or section Higher education; (2) A virtual curriculum in higher education; (3) Virtual work placement; and (4) education and supplement the activities for an experience of physical mobility. The first three types of VM can be understood as a complement or substitute to physical mobility, while the latter could only work as an educational complement activity or to experience true mobility [6]. At present, Celestial Breeze falls in the first category, but the main goal in the future is to fulfill and the four types.

2.3   Mayer's Cognitive Theory of Multimedia Learning and Declarative Knowledge

The principle known as "Multimedia Principle" states that "people learn more deeply from words and pictures than from words alone" [8,14]. However, simply adding words to pictures is not an effective way to achieve multimedia learning. The goal is to instructional media in the light of how human mind works. This is the basis for Mayer's cognitive theory of multimedia learning.

Gagne and Briggs (1979) identified 3 subtypes of this major category of learning, each of which slightly involves different cognitive processes: labels and names, facts and lists, and organized discourse. Our main interest and instructional design of our Celestial Breeze is on labels and names. Actually, this type of learning involves pairing of information. Indeed, learners make a connecting link between two elements either propositional or image-based. Learning of labels becomes more difficult when the number of labels to be learned increases, or when connections between the idea pairs is less meaningful [8,11].

The learning of labels and names is often referred to as paired associate learning. Examples of learning labels and names are foreign language vocabulary learning, learning the names of the countries and their flags etc. In each case, a pair is linked together but its worth noting that linking labels does not necessarily require learning the meaning of the two linked ideas but rather learning that one thing links to another [8].

3   Design and Development

The methodology used for designing and developing this study was adapted from Alessis and Trollips theory based on multimedia learning [17]. Planning, designing and developing are the three main stages in this model. Based on the chosen model, the methodology proposes a set of standards that guides the design and development tasks. It also suggests other ways of being creative and brings onto the surface techniques that can be used for designing, developing and integrating numerous components of a multimedia application [17].

3.1   Analyzing the Learners

This project is addressed to intermediate level English learners who have basic computer knowledge. None of them had ever experienced VR instruction before. In general, members of this audience that reach this advanced level of education, have already developed their study skills yet with unfamiliar content, they tend to profit from concrete referents to ease their reasoning. The learners possess certain general world knowledge that will be helpful in learning through an immersive environment. The learners age generally ranges from 14 to 35. Half of them are children (i.e. ages up to 18 years) while the remaining are adults. Most of them are about equally divided between females and males. No color blindness or other severely limited visual problems were detected. None of them indicated that he/she had fear of heights.

3.2   Design Implications

To be easily learned, recalled, and used, new declarative knowledge must be tied to the Learners existing (i.e. prior) knowledge. As a matter of fact, in order to be stored in long-term memory, incoming information must be meaningful. Thus, it must be linked to some prior knowledge of it. In cases of little prior knowledge to form links with, learners have to employ artificial links that tend to focus on surface similarities. Similar sounds, shapes, sensory impressions, or motor procedures (as in our case) are such cases in point. When even these "tricks" cannot be made, one has to resort to sheer rote repetition to have the information be stored in long-term memory [16].

3.3   Celestial Breeze

In this study, we examined the cognitive consequences of learning in a Virtual Reality Environment designed to promote an understanding of cultural differences among selected European countries. Having that in mind, a Virtual Reality Learning Environment (VRLE) was designed and used: The Celestial Breeze[1] roller coaster in which the learner is called upon to discover different European cities while traveling on it.

The Celestial Breeze is based on experiential learning philosophy. Viljo Kohonen's "Learning is the process of creating new knowledge and understanding through the transformation of experience", to be more precise. In this case, experience is considered the use of a Virtual Reality Environment and the familiarity one has with European culture. Using something familiar, like European cities and their culture, helps the brain to fill in the gaps for the unfamiliar which is the new knowledge provided by the roller coaster experience [17].

3.4   Developing

Devices and Equipment. The application was developed using the game engine Unity 4.6.1 in which the programming, level design and implementation of animations and text was done. The VR setup included the Oculus Rift DK2 and a desktop computer which was equipped with an NVidia GeForce GTX 770 graphics card. The modeling of the featured items was made using Autodesk Maya 2014 and for their texturing Adobe Photoshop CS6 was used. For the editing of the music, Audacity 2.0.6 was used. To achieve easy interaction, conventional input devices such as keyboard and mouse were used. The optical output from Oculus Rift DK2 was combined with audio using headphones in order to enhance the immersion experience.

---

[1] A video showing the VR application Celestial Breeze is available at https://www.youtube.com/watch?v=y2SzIMX6xfw.

The Virtual Ride and the Featured Objects. The roller coaster is a simple ride with the same beginning and end. The learner is placed in a round cart which then transports them slowly along the ride. While the user moves along, he will be able to see on the left and right hand side, various 3D objects which belong to a specific country, along with a description of that object (Fig. 1). Additionally, the flag of each country also appears on the side of the railway track in the beginning of each country, indicating to the learner the country he is passing by. These signs contain information for each object and pop up whenever the learner is in a close distance. The countries are presented sequentially, accompanied by four or five representative objects and their relevant information in close distance following Mayers Multimedia principle. Although it is a roller coaster, the learner has the ability to adjust the speed, allowing him to stop whenever he wants to and thus observe the object and read the information provided. The information for each country is be a variety of interesting facts that relate to culture, pop culture, history, geography, cuisine, traditions, social etiquette, phrases and transportation to name but a few. The information shown for each image does not exceed the size of a post-it note as having too much text on screen would bore the learner and discourage them from continuing the ride. Our sources of information were primarily received by Wikipedia [4] and the justlanded.com site [3]. The information is related to tangible and intangible CH of the aforementioned countries. These countries were chosen as they are the most popular receiving countries throughout Europe for Erasmus+ students [1]. The majority of the relevant studies were primarily focused on museums and their exhibits or tourism of a particular country as those represent a knowledge that is mostly common to people (related to Viljo Kohonen's experiential learning philosophy [12]).

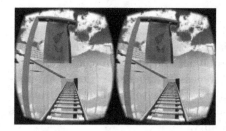

Fig. 1. Two screenshots from "Celestial Breeze". On the left the Cypriot flag indicates the country the learner is passing by. On the right two 3D objects from Germany along with their description.

A formative and a summative evaluation report for Celestial Breeze was conducted. The formative evaluation included design reviews confirmed with a survey given to tutors of English in FL classrooms with years of experience. The survey included questions about the following: existing curricula, instructional facilities as well as community organization and mores. The task analysis and test specifications were reviewed by instructional designers and revised upon their input. These data lead to a further revision of the task analysis. Once Celestial Breeze was produced and questionnaires were printed, they were reviewed by two experts in multimedia design and their suggestions were incorporated in further revisions of the virtual reality application.

4   Experimental Evaluation

4.1   Methodology

Participants. The experiment involved 20 individuals (9 men and 11 women). People were divided into 2 focus groups based on their age. In group A, there were 10 adults aged between 19 and 35, while in Group B, there were 10 children aged 14–18. The majority of the participants did not have a previous experience with VR. Note that for children, parental consent form was primarily requested.

Fig. 2. A participant immersed in "Celestial Breeze", reading an information sign.

Evaluation. The overall goals of the evaluation include the following questions: I. How much information does the Celestial Breeze communicate? II. Is it fun to join in? III. Is the design of the 3D environment considered a convincing one? A common approach to analyze the effectiveness of immersive education applications is the comparison of pre and post-test results to highlight the learning effect. These were embedded in questionnaires that were used to detect strengths and weaknesses in the design and the usability.

A within group experiment was conducted in which quantitative data were collected using pre- post- questionnaire. For Group A that consisted of adults, there was no previous reference to the topic, while they were granted by a pre-test questionnaire. The pre-test consisted of factual questions about participants including age, sex and job title as well as value questions including attitudes, opinions and expectations, closed-ended questions with Yes or No answers, Like or Dislike and rank ordering responses. To check any prior knowledge, the third Section of the pre-test involved 9 multiple choice questions evaluating information about the European countries mentioned in the VR application. The post-questionnaire test, which included the same 9 questions, examined the retention of knowledge (if any) gained from the virtual experience and was used to determine the overall satisfaction. The main difference was that the questions of the pre- test did not follow the same order and 8 more multiple choice questions were added to the post- test. These latter questions examined if any further knowledge was gained and thus if Celestial Breeze can be considered as a convincing way to learn. All these multiple choice questions in Section B of the second questionnaire evaluated the load of information the Celestial Breeze can communicate. This methodology was followed for both groups. On average, the whole procedure lasted 25 min.

Experiment. The participants (Fig. 2) were firstly given the pre-questionnaire to fill. Then they were fitted with the Oculus Rift and the headphones and the next stage was the virtual experience through Celestial Breeze (Fig. 2). The learners spent around 15–20 min tuned in. After the virtual experience, the Oculus and the headphones were removed from the participants and they were asked to fill in the post-questionnaire.

Results. Following the procedure mentioned above, the preliminary usability results prove that the Celestial Breeze virtual reality application has the potential to be used as a succor of learning the differences in European cultures and etiquettes and to further serve as a valuable educational tool. Specifically, from the user interface part, experts agree that the application is clearly designed and system information provided is consistent and related to the task; hence intuitive interaction is offered. The fact that the participants are free to move into their ride at their own pace. In terms of learning, there was a comparison of the knowledge questions in pre- and post- questionnaire. The overall percentage of correct answers at pre-test questionnaire for children of both genders, was 48.8%, while after the VR experience the answers increased to an overall of 63%. In particular, the boys mentioned an enormous increase to the proportion of their correct answers, from 44.4% to 70%; while girls showed a relatively lower increase: from 50.7% to 58.8% of correct answers was observed. Yet, adults who in the pre-test questionnaire had scored an overall of 61.4%, in the post-questionnaire test the percentage decreased to 60% (Fig. 3). The decrease in the performance for adults was mainly attributed to male adults whose negative performance was linked to the 'lack of fun element', indicating the importance of user satisfaction in the learning process.

Regarding the element of visual ride fun, in the pre-test questionnaire 8 out of the 20 participants answered that they liked it, while the 80% mentioned that the former reason to join in such an experience would be out of entertainment and curiosity while infotainment (a combination of information and entertainment) comes after. It should be also noted that none of the participants had previously a virtual reality experience. The importance of fun was also confirmed in the evaluation of Celestial Breeze post-questionnaire. Indeed, in the Yes/No question, 17 out of 20 people answered that they did enjoy their ride

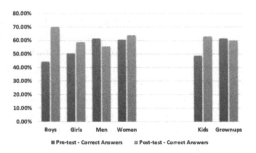

Fig. 3. The percent of correct answers in the pre- and post- questionnaires based on the gender and age of the participants

but in the following open-ended suggestion box, most of them stated that they missed the fun element related to a real world roller coaster.

5   Conclusion - Future Work

Virtual reality, multimedia design principles and learning strategy are of great significance for learners' acquisition of knowledge. The study examined the effect of a virtual reality environment combined with the aspects of learning and fun within two different age groups; children and adults. The preliminary results of the study show that the Celestial Breeze application can have an important impact on knowledge acquisition by younger people and women.

Since the results showcased that the ride could have been more entertaining a game-style motivational element shall be applied in the future to keep the learners focused. Instead of being just viewers in the roller coaster, the learners could become directly involved with the process by allowing more freedom and interactivity within the application. For instance, when arriving at the point where Napolon Bonaparte is located, the mood could suddenly change and the 3D model could come to life. The user could then enter a QTE (Quick Time Event) by pressing various prompts appearing on screen, to interact with the 3D model so that the user is directly implicated in the actions.

As far as the style of the information provided, the captions would be probably a better choice for a participant wishing to learn rather than sentences and iconography would be better fitting for something as interactive and virtual as this experience. Iconography, if done well, can offer more information that text. Smaller details such as different weather conditions, traditional music from each country and a lessening of the experience time length (approximately 10 min) would facilitate both the learning experience and its outcomes. Additionally, the countries could be reduced and instead of having a quiz after visiting all of them, we could create a smaller interactive application of a quiz with leader-boards, which would make it more entertaining to interact with as it will be less passive and more competitive.

Concluding, Celestial Breeze can be used as an educational tool of cultural awareness for English intermediate level learners as proved by the results. The Y generation learners can effectively and actively engage in such a learning method developing cultural awareness. Of course, the primary goals were achieved successfully by a small sample of participants. To pertain concrete results, further tests applied to a larger sample need to be staged.

References

1. Erasmus. http://ec.europa.eu/education/library/statistics/ay-12-13/facts-figures_en.pdf. Accessed 24 July 2016
2. Erasmus annual report. http://ec.europa.eu/education/library/statistics/erasmus-plus-annual-report_en.pdf. Accessed 25 July 2016
3. Just landed. https://www.justlanded.com/. Accessed 22 May 2015
4. Wikipedia. https://www.wikipedia.org/. Accessed 22 May 2015
5. Annetta, L.A., Murray, M.R., Laird, S.G., Bohr, S.C., Park, J.C.: Serious games: Incorporating video games in the classroom. Educause Q. **29**(3), 16 (2006)
6. Caldirola, E., Fuente, A.A.J., Aquilina, M., Gutiérrez, F., Ferreira, R.M.: Smart mobility and smart learning for a new citizenship. Profesinis rengimas: tyrimai ir realijos **2**(5), 202 (2014)
7. Chng, E.: Special issue on virtual heritage: Cultural agents, environments, and objects guest editor introduction. Presence Teleoperators Virtual Environ. **24**(3), iii–vii (2015)
8. Christopher, A.: Model resource, New York. Disponível em: http://aesthetech.weebly.com/uploads/8/3/2/4/832462/model_resourceassignment.pdf. Acesso em 17(02) (2013)
9. Economou, M., Pujol, L.: Educational tool or expensive toy? evaluating VR evaluation and its relevance for virtual heritage. In: New Heritage: New Media and Cultural Heritage. Oxon, Routledge (2006)
10. Feiertag, J., Berge, Z.L.: Training generation N: how educators should approach the net generation. Education + Training **50**(6), 457–464 (2008)
11. Judd, C.H.: Types of learning. Elementary Sch. J. **25**(3), 173–183 (1924)
12. Kohonen, V.: Experiential language learning: second language learning as cooperative learner education. In: Collaborative Language Learning and Teaching, vol. 1439 (1992)
13. Loizides, F., El Kater, A., Terlikas, C., Lanitis, A., Michael, D.: Presenting cypriot cultural heritage in virtual reality: a user evaluation. In: Ioannides, M., Magnenat-Thalmann, N., Fink, E., Žarnić, R., Yen, A.-Y., Quak, E. (eds.) EuroMed 2014. LNCS, vol. 8740, pp. 572–579. Springer, Cham (2014). https://doi.org/10.1007/978-3-319-13695-0_57
14. Mayer, R.E.: Research-based principles for designing multimedia instruction. Acknowledgments and Dedication 59 (2014)
15. Michael, D., Pelekanos, N., Chrysanthou, I., Zaharias, P., Hadjigavriel, L.L., Chrysanthou, Y.: Comparative study of interactive systems in a museum. In: Ioannides, M., Fellner, D., Georgopoulos, A., Hadjimitsis, D.G. (eds.) EuroMed 2010. LNCS, vol. 6436, pp. 250–261. Springer, Heidelberg (2010). https://doi.org/10.1007/978-3-642-16873-4_19
16. Smith, P.L., Ragan, T.J.: Instructional Design. Wiley, New York (1999)
17. Trollip, S.R., Alessi, S.M.: Multimedia for Learning: Methods and Development. Allyn & Bacon, Massachusetts (2001)

Author Index

Printed in the United States
By Bookmasters